LOOKING AFTER
YOUR AUTISTIC SELF

LOOKING AFTER YOUR AUTISTIC SELF

*A Personalised Self-Care Approach
to Managing Your Sensory and
Emotional Well-Being*

Niamh Garvey

Jessica Kingsley Publishers
London and Philadelphia

First published in Great Britain in 2023 by Jessica Kingsley Publishers
An imprint of Hodder & Stoughton Ltd
An Hachette Company

I

A CIP catalogue record for this title is available from the
British Library and the Library of Congress

ISBN 978 1 83997 560 8
eISBN 978 1 83997 561 5

Printed and bound in Great Britain by Clays Ltd

Jessica Kingsley Publishers' policy is to use papers that are natural,
renewable and recyclable products and made from wood grown in
sustainable forests. The logging and manufacturing processes are expected
to conform to the environmental regulations of the country of origin.

Jessica Kingsley Publishers
Carmelite House
50 Victoria Embankment
London EC4Y 0DZ

www.jkp.com

*This book is dedicated to my
husband Cathal, mo mhuirnín.*

Contents

Acknowledgements

I'd like to thank Lisa Clark, Abbie Howard, Carys Homer, and everyone at Jessica Kingsley Publishers. Your encouragement and friendly work attitude made writing this book a pleasure.

Thank you to all the staff and lecturers in the Autism Studies Diploma in University College Cork. I'd like to extend a particular thank you to Claire Droney, who suggested I write a book of strategies, which is how this book began. A big thank you to the inspiring classmates who did the Diploma with me.

Thank you to Davida Hartman of the Adult Autism Assessment Clinic, who has been remarkably encouraging, and gave me confidence in this book. To Trish Barrett thank you for your help with the emotional regulation chapters, and for your continuous support and kindness. Thank you to all the people who have taught me about autism, sensory processing, or emotional regulation, with particular thanks to Micaela Connolly, Eithne Drinan, and Tony Hennessy.

Thank you to all the lovely staff at the Sunflower Clinic, Cork, who have taught me so much about autism over the years. In particular, thank you to Julie O'Sullivan for teaching me about sensory processing, for helping me with the sensory section of this book, and for allowing me to use your 'How full is your cup?' analogy.

Thank you to my family, Trish, Nasser, Anne, Eoghan, Gavin, and Rachel, for your support and encouragement in my writing. Thank you to my in-laws Phil, Charles, Alanna, Brendan, Roisin, and Nigel, for the many ways in which you all helped me write this book. With particular thanks to Charles and Phil for going the extra mile with detailed editing help.

Thank you to all my lovely friends who help me to survive and thrive as an adult, a person, and a parent. To my writer friends, who travel alongside me in my writing journey. And of course to the autistic community, who I have met both online and offline, and from whom I have learnt so much.

A huge thank you to Claire Hennessy, who has been extremely encouraging since my first attempt at writing. Also to Vanessa Fox O'Loughlin, who always points me in the right direction when it comes to the world of writing. And to my fellow writer friends in the Big Smoke Writing Factory for your continuous encouragement and support, with a particular thanks to Eve McDonnell, who has gone above and beyond in cheerleading my writing.

And last, but far from least, thank you to my wonderful husband Cathal, and my three daughters Clara, Amelie, and Iris. To you Cathal, for always being willing to listen to me talk with you (and at you) about autism and writing. Thank you for your endless editing and technical support, and for generally being an amazing partner in life. Thank you to my children, for looking after each other when I'm lost in my writing, and for bringing so much joy, love, and laughter to my every day.

Chapter 1

Introduction

CHAPTER BREAKDOWN

CHAPTER AIMS

› To discuss why autistic adults have unique challenges, and why we need strategies.
› To give the reader a bit of background information about myself, and how getting diagnosed as autistic has helped me.
› To explain how this book is structured.

Being an Autistic Adult

Being an adult is hard. I don't know any adults that don't occasionally wish someone else would solve all their adult challenges and responsibilities. It's hard to be organised, to earn money, to manage a house, to manage relationships, and so on. Add autism into the mix, and the challenges become a lot more than just a juggle of responsibilities. Autism adds many layers of challenges, from social interaction differences to organisation difficulties, from communication misinterpretations to sensory overwhelm.

In my experience, *there is a misconception that autistic children grow into 'less autistic' adults*. I believe this stems from our ability, as autistic adults, to adapt our behaviour to 'stand out' less, and to 'fit in' more. We learn how to hide our differences and hide our overwhelm. But this takes its toll on us, and can actually increase our levels of stress.

In many ways, being autistic affects me more now than it did when I was a child. As a child I was often quiet, happier sitting in the corner reading than joining in with my peers, unless it was a very close friend (I was the opposite of quiet with my best friend; instead I was bossy, giddy, and often hyper). As an adult, it's rarely appropriate to sit quietly in a corner reading. There are so many social situations that demand my presence and social involvement, especially as a parent, and so the amount of social demands on me has increased.

Tasks I used to find easy have now become harder, and my sensory difficulties have become much more challenging. I can no longer tolerate certain fabrics or noises that I used to tolerate. I can no longer socialise as much as I did in my teenage years. It takes a lot more conscious effort to look after my autistic self.

I know I am not alone in this, as I have read many accounts of other autistic adults feeling more overwhelmed as they age. This why we need strategies and creative solutions to help us navigate being an autistic adult. Not just to survive adulthood, but to thrive in it.

Developing Strategies

Throughout my life, I have always fought back when presented with problems or challenges. I do this gently, by slowly accepting I have the problem, and then building up my plans to tackle it. This part of my personality has helped me care for my autistic self, and I think it's a big reason that I masked (masking means acting or appearing non-autistic) my autism for so long. My strategies were so successful in helping me 'pass' as a 'functioning' adult, that I didn't recognise that I was autistic until I began studying for a Diploma in Autism. But even with all of my pre-diagnosis strategies, I was finding being an adult very difficult; learning that I am autistic made me suddenly understand why. Since then, I have adapted my strategies. *I no longer try to mask my autism; I now work to support my autism.*

I regularly ask for help when I am developing my supportive strategies, and I feel no shame in this. I am aware that some autistic adults feel ashamed when they don't naturally know how to do things that adults are expected to know how to do. And I know that it can be scary to admit that something considered 'easy' by society is hugely difficult for you. But I don't agree with being ashamed because I'm autistic. *I don't feel that by exposing my challenges I am admitting my weakness. I think that by asking for help, I am being strong, not weak.*

I have always been a questioner – I was that annoying student in school who never stopped asking questions, as I wanted details and facts in order to process information, and thus caused other students to eye-roll and sigh. Over the years I have asked friends, family, lecturers, colleagues, therapists, and the online community what they do to manage tasks in their adult life. I ask about everything, from how to prepare for a job interview, to how to change my house insurance, to how to manage the endless laundry piles in a family of five. I became known, in my job as a nurse, for asking questions, so much so that other people often came to me to ask questions for them, because they knew that I was confident enough to ask anything.

My tendency to question, along with my passion for the subject of autism, has led me to write this book. I want to share what I have learned in the hope that other autistic adults may find some helpful tips and strategies that improve their adult life.

Who Am I?
I absolutely love to get a fuller picture of writers when I am reading their book, as I like to create a visual image of who they are and where they come from. I have a minimal online presence as I find that going online distracts me from my life (I can get very obsessed) and I also don't like the idea of all my personal data being online. For that reason, I'm including this little introduction to myself, for those of you who would like to know a bit more about the writer.

I was born in Cork, Ireland, in 1986. I still live in Cork, in a house surrounded by trees and wildlife, with my husband and my three daughters. We are a neurodiverse family living in a quirky home full of hammocks, swings, and all sorts of peculiar oddities that bring calm and joy to our daily life.

I worked for many years as a nurse, mostly in cardiac and intensive care, but I stopped working in acute hospitals when my second child was two years old. Although I continued to do some part-time work at weekends in a nursing home, I had to fully stop nursing when I began to experience physical disability from the joint conditions hypermobile Ehlers Danlos syndrome and autoimmune spondylarthritis.

I have many passions and interests, including creative writing, non-fiction writing, reading books, Jane Austen, Charles Dickens, and other classic literature. I love poetry, listening to audiobooks, sewing, being in nature, television, gardening, art, baking, and board games (especially Scrabble and Boggle). I also love reading and learning about human psychology and the mind, and pretty much all things to do with health, well-being, and autism.

Getting Diagnosed as Autistic

My autism awareness journey began with my children, as is so often the case for autistic adults. I knew relatively little about autism until one of my daughters was diagnosed as autistic. I have a tendency to need to know everything I can about a new subject that interests me, especially when it affects my daily life. So I enrolled in a two-year Autism Studies Diploma in University College Cork. As I sat through these fascinating lectures, it slowly dawned on me that I was autistic myself, so I sought out a professional assessment.

After my diagnosis, I was relieved to realise that I could now dissect many of my past experiences and understand how they were shaped by my autism. I began to understand why I lost friends, why I could never eat lunch in the canteen in school, why I often got on more easily with boys, why I only felt calm in university when I was alone in the library, why I couldn't go out partying every night like the other girls in nursing college, and why I found the transition to motherhood so hard. Most importantly, it allowed me to understand and get on top of the anxiety that had followed me through my life like a constant shadow.

I had often felt like a failure of an adult, wondering why I struggle with things that other adults seem to find simple. Even the thought of picking up the phone to renew my car insurance can make my gut clench and I can experience severe nausea. I have occasionally put off these kinds of tasks for so long that I end up paying top prices because I've left it too late to negotiate a better price.

But once I got my diagnosis, this feeling of failure disappeared. I now see that being an autistic adult is not the same as being a non-autistic adult, and I just needed to learn a different approach to being an adult. I needed knowledge. Knowledge is power, and thankfully knowledge can be learnt.

Language around 'Autism'

The language around autism is changing. Autism used to be categorised into many different diagnoses including Asperger's syndrome, classic autism, PDD-NOS (pervasive developmental disorder not otherwise specified) etc. In 2013, the different diagnoses were all grouped together under 'ASD' (autism spectrum disorder) in the updated American handbook for diagnosing mental or psychiatric disorders, which is called the DSM-5 (*Diagnostic and Statistical Manual of Mental Disorders*, 5th edition).

Many autistic people will feel offended if you say they 'have ASD' or are 'on the spectrum'. This is called person-first language, and has been criticised for suggesting that one's autism is an external thing, or an appendage, rather than an integral part of one's identity. Most, but not all, within the autistic community agree that it is desirable to use identity-first language when discussing an autistic person. To use identity-first language, one says that the person 'is autistic', and is called an 'autistic person' rather than a 'person with autism'.

I have chosen to use identity-first language in this book as it feels right to me, since my autism makes up so much of my identity. I am autistic, just as I am Irish, and I am female, and I am tall. I don't have autism, I don't have Irishness, I don't have femaleness, and I don't have tallness. Saying 'I have autism' suggests that my autism is a detachable element, rather than an intrinsic part of me.

How to Use This Book

This book is broken into three parts, and each part is divided into chapters. Each chapter will give a brief explanation of the chapter topic and how it affects autistic adults, followed by strategies and support systems that can be used to help. There is a Glossary at the end of the book so you can easily find the meaning of words, phrases, and abbreviations used in the book.

Along with including research studies, I also provide many anecdotes and examples from my own life, as I believe more can be learnt when facts are mixed with real-life experiences. I hope that in reading these anecdotes, readers will be able to identify (or realise that you do not identify) with some of my own experiences.

PART 1

LOOKING AFTER YOUR AUTISTIC SELF

Chapter 2

Taking Control of Your Triggers

CHAPTER BREAKDOWN

CHAPTER AIMS

› To briefly explain the stress response in autism.
› To explain what a trigger is.
› To guide you towards identifying what triggers your own stress response.
› To encourage you to identify your own needs and strengths.
› To show you how to develop coping strategies to manage and reduce your triggers, using five steps.

The Stress Response

When we are faced with a stress or a danger, our bodies react in a number of ways. Stress hormones, including adrenaline and cortisol, are released. This causes various physical changes, such as a faster heartbeat, and glucose (sugar) rushing to our muscles to get them ready for action. These physical changes are there to prepare our bodies to respond to the immediate stress, through the 'fight or flight response' or the 'freeze response'.

The 'fight or flight' response means our body gets ready either to fight off the danger, or to run away from the danger. The 'fight or flight' response is a self-protective measure, designed to help us to stay safe. For example, if we encounter a hungry lion, it would not be in our interests to continue about our business happily – we need to either fight it or flee from it (flight) to stay alive.

The 'freeze response' means our body shuts down and freezes in response to stress or danger. This is a response that is often shown in movies, for example if a person sees a boulder falling off a cliff towards them, and all they can do is freeze and watch in horror as the boulder builds speed towards them. This response is often associated with panic and high anxiety, and can lead to sudden physical immobility. In the freeze response, you may have thoughts of fleeing to safety, but your body refuses to work.

When we experience a stress response for a few minutes or a few hours, it's called acute stress. When our body continues to respond to stress for a number of hours, days, weeks, or months, it's called chronic stress.

The Stress Response and Autism

Autistic people can react differently to stress than non-autistic people. Research has found that autistic children release higher amounts of the stress hormone cortisol than non-autistic children. Additionally, the levels of cortisol last longer in their bodies, even after the thing that caused the stress has gone (Spratt et al. 2012).

Autistic people can perceive danger from many everyday parts of life, even when there's no real danger present. We can hold onto our stress long after the stressor is gone. We may feel the urge to run out of a supermarket (flight) when the intercom blares out and bright lights glare. We may feel like shouting out loud (fight) when we can't get our heads around a piece of paperwork. We may feel like hiding under blankets (flight) when we have too many demands on us. We may shut down (freeze) and be unable to think, or talk, after a social situation that required so much effort that we feel drained, exhausted, and unsafe.

A study published in 2015 (Bishop-Fitzpatrick et al. 2015) found that autistic adults without intellectual disability experienced substantially higher levels of stress than non-autistic adults. Not only that, but when stress levels increased, autistic adults' social functioning went down significantly.

This research mirrors my own experience, as when I become stressed, my ability to socially function (i.e. my ability to talk to people, feel comfortable, and make choices in a social environment etc.) gets worse fast.

What Is a Trigger?

A trigger is something that sets off your stress response. There are endless types of things that may trigger your stress response. For autistic people, a trigger could be a type of environment (e.g. a busy crowded room), a social difficulty, a sensory experience (e.g. a loud noise), a communication challenge, a demand on your organisation skills, a change in routine etc.

There might be no real danger, but our brains and bodies acts like there is. When we are stressed, our bodies experience changes that may include dizziness, a racing heartbeat, high blood pressure, breathing fast, and sweating (World Health Organization 2008).

Triggers can cause you to feel anxious or overwhelmed, angry or frightened, unsafe or under attack. Sometimes individual triggers may not cause an immediate stress response, but a build-up of triggers, or too many triggers at once, can lead to fight, flight, or freeze mode, and you might experience anxiety, overwhelm, shutdown, or meltdown (see Chapter 11 for information on meltdowns and shutdowns).

Why Autistic Adults Need to Know Their Triggers

One of the greatest gifts of learning that I am autistic has been recognising why I am the way I am. Before getting diagnosed as autistic, I didn't know why I reacted the way I did to certain things. I couldn't understand why I had such enormous surges of emotion and overwhelm, which led me to believe I had an irrational panic disorder.

I now know that I never panic for no reason; there's always a trigger that can either be explained by my autism, or by something in my past emotional development. Psychotherapy helped me begin to understand and identify my feelings. Learning I'm autistic helped me to understand why I had many of those feelings in the first place.

Since getting diagnosed, I have been learning how to identify what triggers my stress response. Until I could identify my triggers, I didn't know that I needed coping strategies for dealing with them. *Learning what triggers you to feel overwhelmed is vital to learn how to look after yourself.* It allows you to get comfortable with why you react the way you do, and allows you to put plans in place to support yourself.

Learning what triggers your stress response is not just important to reduce the psychological impact of stress, but it also improves the physical health of your body. Putting strategies in place to deal with your triggers will help reduce the damaging effect of chronic stress on your body. Over-exposure to the stress hormone cortisol from chronic stress can increase the risk of anxiety, depression, headaches, muscle pain, problems with digestion, heart disease, sleep disturbance, difficulty maintaining a healthy weight, and impaired memory and concentration (Mayo Clinic 2021).

Executive Function, and How It Is Affected by Stress

Executive function is the ability to get things done. It is the ability to organise yourself, and carry tasks through from beginning to end. Our daily lives are full of tasks, and thus we rely on our executive function skills to do everything from getting dressed to leaving the house on time, from working to preparing meals etc.

Autistic people can experience huge challenges in their executive function, even when we feel calm and content. These challenges can range from very mild to severe, and they can significantly impair our ability to get things done.

What Skills Are Involved in Executive Function?

- *Planning*: Recognising that a task needs to be done, and planning how to do it.

- *Organising*: Getting ready for a task: Recognising what tools or skills you will need.

- *Initiation*: Starting a task.

- *Flexible thinking*: Seeing a task through and not giving up when faced with problems.

- *Time management*: Being able to divide your time appropriately to complete all the steps of a task.

- *Finishing a task*: Not giving up on a task, keeping focused and motivated until the end.

- *Evaluation*: Looking back at how you did a task, evaluating how you did it, and learning from it.

- *Emotional regulation*: Managing emotions throughout a task so that the task can be completed.

Research has found that autistic adults have significantly more challenges with executive function skills than non-autistic adults, with one study finding that 20–30% of autistic adults had difficulty with planning, while 20% had difficulty with flexible thinking (Johnston et al. 2019). This study also found that having a higher IQ did not equate to having better executive function skills. Only 35% of autistic adults were found to have no impairment in executive function skills.

Stress can have a direct and immediate impact on any one of the skills we use for executive function. If we are stressed, it can shut down our ability to plan, make us unable to initiate a task, reduce our flexible thinking, decrease our time management skills, make finishing a task impossible, and can make it difficult to manage our emotional regulation through a task.

The biggest executive function challenge that I have under stress is that I lose my flexible thinking. This can cause serious challenges in my daily life. When faced with a problem, I might be able to identify what needs to be done, but have absolutely no idea how to do it.

Example: I remember driving somewhere and I was running slightly late. Being late always increases my level of stress, so this was the first stress trigger. I knew the route I wanted to take, but along the way I met a road block. The route I had planned to take was closed. This unexpected change to my plan was the second trigger. I immediately felt a stress response in my body; my heart rate sped up, and my breathing felt slightly restricted.

> Although I knew the roads around the area extremely well, and there were many alternative routes I could have taken, my ability to think flexibly had completely shut down. So I just sat there staring out of the car not knowing what to do. Being unable to come up with a new plan meant that the journey had become unpredictable, and this unpredictability was the third trigger. To make matters worse, the cars behind me started to beep because I was blocking up the road, which increased my stress levels and added in a sensory challenge, which was the fourth trigger.

This example shows that the more stressed I became, the more my executive function skills deteriorated. It began with my inability to think flexibly, but progressed to an inability to plan, the inability to manage my time, and the inability to complete the task. I also became more and more emotionally dysregulated, and this lasted for hours after the event.

Five Steps to Managing Your Triggers

In order to manage my stress response, I first needed to learn to manage the things that trigger my stress response. I use five steps to manage my triggers, which I will explain throughout this chapter.

The Five Steps to Managing Triggers

1. *The Detective Habit*: Identifying your triggers.

2. *Coping Strategies*: Learn to manage your triggers.

3. *Rationing*: Spread out your triggers.

4. *Recovery*: Plan your recovery time between triggers, and after triggers.

5. *Quick Calm Strategies*: These are strategies to help you calm down quickly. As developing immediate calming strategies is a huge topic, this will be dealt with in the next chapter.

The Detective Habit

In order to start identifying what my triggers are, I began to develop my 'detective habit'. *This is a habit of reflecting on how I felt and behaved in a scenario, so I could learn to identify my triggers.*

I do not consider my triggers to be my faults or flaws. They are simply things that stress me, and it is not my fault that they stress me. If I were to spend time scolding myself about how I behaved or felt in a past scenario, I would merely be wasting my time and making myself feel bad. *It makes much more sense to build strategies based on my strengths rather than on my weaknesses.*

The detective habit is about looking back at a scenario that I found hard, analysing it with non-judgemental eyes, and giving thought and consideration to what could have caused the stress. *Once I identify the triggers, I then make plans to support myself when exposed to the identified triggers.*

How to Use the Detective Habit

To use the detective habit, I look back at a scenario and ask myself these questions:

- *What happened?*

- *What did I feel?* Did I feel stressed, scared, out of control, angry etc.?

- *Was there anything in the environment that could have been a trigger?* Was there a sensory stressor? (See Part 2 to get to know your sensory triggers.) Did the environment mean there was too much information to take in at once? Did the environment create challenges for any of my executive function skills?

- *At what point did I start to feel a stress response?* Was it when someone started talking to me? Was it when someone tried to get eye contact? Was it when I walked into a shop? Was it when the environment changed? Was it at the point of transitioning from one task to another?

- *Were my basic needs met before I encountered the trigger?* By basic needs, I mean hunger, thirst, sleep, body temperature, and physical comfort. I become stressed much more quickly if I am tired, hungry, thirsty, too cold or too hot, or in pain. As I often don't recognise when my basic needs are not met (see Chapter 8 for information on the interoception sense), I have to consciously question if I have forgotten to meet one of these basic needs.

- *What were my strengths in the situation,* i.e. what did I manage well? Which of my strengths could I use in similar scenarios in future?

- *What would have helped me* to feel more comfortable, or avoid becoming stressed and/or overwhelmed?

- *What coping strategies could I use if that situation happens again*, or if I'm exposed to the same trigger or triggers?

When I began using the detective habit, I couldn't always answer each question, but the more I practised, the better I became at it. I began to spot patterns. For example, I often couldn't remember if there was anything in the environment that triggered me, but I did spot the pattern that many scenarios happened in or at supermarkets. I therefore began to ask was there something in the supermarket environment that triggered me. I went back to the supermarket with the intention of identifying my triggers and considered how I felt and what was causing it. I listened to my body, and noticed that my heart sped up when the music got louder. My jaw clenched, and I felt unsafe when I looked at the glaring lights. I began to shake when I walked past the freezer section and continued to shake all the way home.

This was really surprising to me, as I thought I was an autistic person who didn't have light and sound sensory aversions, but now I know that I do; I simply didn't know to equate the uncomfortable feelings in my body with those sensory stimuli.

Using the Detective Habit to Find Your Strengths

Autistic people have wonderful strengths, despite what many people, including some professionals, might think. And I don't just mean the stereotypical autistic strengths like 'attention to detail' and 'heightened sensory skill'.

The DSM-5 (*Diagnostic and Statistical Manual*, 5th edition) is the American Psychiatric Association's guide to mental illness and disorders, including diagnosing autistic people. It suggests that autistic people have rigid thinking, insist on sameness, are inflexible, and are overly ritualised. When I first read these symptoms, I thought I couldn't be autistic, because when I am calm, I can be very flexible. I also enjoy going on holidays and taking a break from my rituals and routines. What the DSM-5 doesn't explain properly, in my opinion, is that many of these diagnostic traits come out when we are stressed, but may improve when we are calm and happy. When we are engaged in these 'repetitive interests' we can have amazing imaginations, and can have creative and flexible thought patterns. However, because autistic people may perceive danger in many everyday activities, and therefore we go through life in a heightened state of stress, our ability to use our strengths is reduced. But that doesn't mean we don't have them.

As an autistic person, I know that it's easy to believe what we read about ourselves, and to put ourselves in a diagnostic box, believing that we are always rigid and repetitive. But no two autistic people are the same, just like no two non-autistic people are the same. *We all have different strengths in different situations, and it's up to us to figure them out.*

I believe it is so important to start acknowledging your own strengths, and figure out when you can use those strengths. The detective habit really helped me with this. *Every time I came up with a coping strategy, I asked myself what strength I was using to develop that strategy.* For this reason, I will now show how I develop my coping strategies using my strengths, in the following scenarios.

Using the Detective Habit on Past Scenarios
Here are examples of how I used the detective habit on past scenarios.

SCENARIO 1
What Happened?
I walked into a new restaurant, in which I had a table booked. The waiter led me to a small table in the middle of the room. After about two minutes I had to get up and walk straight back out of the restaurant and couldn't go back inside.

How Did I Feel?
I remember my heart racing and a feeling of unease, a feeling of not being safe. I remember an intense desire to close my eyes and block my ears.

What in the Environment May Have Triggered Me?
- The music was loud, fast, intrusive, and not calm.

- The tables were much too close together.

- I could hear other people's conversations and I was unable to stop myself hearing them and focus on my own thoughts.

- The decor was very eclectic, with tiles of completely contrasting designs all over the floor. There were too many different patterns everywhere, which caused me visual sensory stress. The layout of furniture was higgledy-piggledy and asymmetrical in a way that didn't make spatial sense to me, and stole my focus.

Were My Basic Needs Met?

No, I arrived hungry knowing I'd be eating a big meal.

At What Point Did I Start to Feel Uncomfortable?

I was already nervous arriving as it was a new place. I looked at the menu outside on the wall and was surprised by the type of food it was; it wasn't what I expected, or desired. Inside the restaurant the feeling of discomfort increased hugely, and on sitting down at the table it became overwhelming.

What Were my Strengths in the Situation?

I was able to tell my husband that I couldn't stay there, despite not knowing why, and asked him to tell the staff that we were leaving. This may seem like a flaw rather than a strength, but actually I was delighted to be able to communicate my need to leave. This ensured I didn't appear rude by just leaving without the staff knowing whether they needed to keep the table for me.

What Would Have Helped Me Enjoy the Evening?

- If I had sat looking out the window, I would not have been bombarded by visual sensory stressors.

- If the music were quieter or different, I would have been less overwhelmed.

- If I had known the menu in advance, I would not have been disappointed by it, and I would have known what to expect.

- I would have preferred a table spaced further apart from other tables.

- If I had not been so hungry, I would have tolerated sensory stress better.

Using my Strengths to Build a Coping Strategy for Going to Restaurants

Planning Strength

As I am good at planning when calm, I can plan ahead the next time I go to a new restaurant. I can look online to see images of the restaurant to see if it will suit me. This will take the unexpected element out of it when I do see it. I can look up the menu and decide in advance if there is a meal that I will enjoy.

I can also plan what phrases I may need, as when I'm anxious I can find it hard to make sentences that sound polite or to the point. I can write these out and bring them in my pocket and glance at them if I need to. Examples include 'This table won't suit me, can I please sit looking out the window' or 'Apologies, but would you mind turning the music down?' or 'Is there a quieter table available?'

Interestingly, an autistic friend of mine lately told me about her strategy for getting the staff to turn down the music in restaurants. She taps her ear and says to the staff, 'My hearing aid is buzzing from the music being so loud, could you please turn it down?' It works every time. I expressed my discomfort with this as it's a blatant lie (she has no hearing aid), and she said, 'No, it's not a lie, my ear is a hearing aid, in a way, and my ear hears the loud music as a horrible buzzing'.

Communication Strength

When I'm not in a state of high anxiety, I am good at communicating my needs. I can phone ahead, when calm, and speak to a member of staff and ask for a suitable table. I can book a table very early in the evening so the restaurant will have fewer people. I can ask for a table by a window so I can look out the window rather than at the multitude of patterns.

Flexible Thinking Strength

I can have a plan B restaurant in mind when I go out, provided I don't need a booking. I will be less likely to need a booking for the plan B restaurant if I go for dinner early in the evening before it gets busy. *As I know my flexible thinking diminishes under stress, it's important I use flexible thinking in advance of going out.*

Sensory Awareness Strength

If I have to go to a restaurant that I know will trigger me, I can prepare myself beforehand by familiarising myself with the venue and having a quiet rest before the meal so that my sensory system feels refuelled. I can eat before I go so that I'm not hungry on arrival, and can simply order a smaller meal. I can bring ear plugs or noise reducers (thanks to technology, there are many tools on the market that reduce how much you hear in your surroundings) to reduce the noise I hear. I can ask the staff to turn the volume down on the music. I can tell my dinner companion/s that I will only be staying for a starter, or for a designated time. Or, I can arrive late, if I tell my dinner companions well in advance, and just join in for dessert to reduce the time I have to stay. I can then plan a sensory rest after the event.

SCENARIO 2

What Happened?

In my early twenties, I used to go shopping in a large supermarket. On a number of occasions I would reach the shampoo aisle and suddenly get what I thought was an anxiety attack, and I would abandon my trolley and leave the shop.

What Did I Feel?

I would feel a sudden intense anxiety. My heart pounded and my breath felt restricted. I felt like I was under attack and something terrible was about to happen.

At What Point Did I Feel Uncomfortable?

The minute I turned out of the clothes aisle and entered the shampoo aisle.

What in the Environment Might Have Triggered Me?

At first, I thought that the anxiety I felt was all down to association; I had had an anxiety attack in that aisle before, and therefore I associated that aisle with anxiety, and so I had an anxiety attack when I went there. But learning that I don't have anxiety attacks for no reason made me revisit this idea. It also didn't make sense that it only happened sometimes, especially in the evenings, and was less likely to happen if I went shopping in the morning.

To figure this out, I went back to that same supermarket (which I had eventually stopped going to) with the sole purpose of finding out what the problem with the environment was. I carried out the same routine as I used to do, which was to get a trolley and first walk through the books and clothes section. I noticed how calm I felt in these sections. I love looking at books, and the book aisle was quiet and calm. I then moved to the clothes aisle, which is also an aisle I enjoy as I love to run my hands over clothes on racks, and I like the smell of the clothes section, and the neatness. I moved from these aisles to the shampoo aisle. I could now immediately understand why this aisle was a problem.

The atmosphere contrasted completely with the calm clothes aisle. Here, there were extremely bright lights which reflected off hundreds of shiny bottles – this caused an intense glare. The sheer amount of choice of shampoos was overwhelming. The floor was squeaky under the trolley, and the light bounced off it. It was the first aisle that had a checkout counter at the end of it, and thus there was high-pitched beeping and a red flashing light coming from the end of the aisle. It was a complete sensory bombardment. Realising that the lights were the main trigger made sense of why I was more likely to be affected in the evening, as lights are more intense and impactful when it's dark outside.

Were My Basic Needs Met?

As this scenario happened on multiple occasions, I cannot answer this. However, I know that if I enter a food shop when I'm hungry, I am much more likely to feel sensory stress as my tolerance is lowered. So it's possible that when I was hungry, I was more likely to experience this need to run away (flight).

Another basic need I've become more aware of in the last few years is my body temperature; I often don't recognise that I'm cold or hot until my husband points it out to me. I tend to get cold in the evenings, and might not notice I'm cooling down until I get goosebumps and start shivering. It's possible that the temperature shift from the warmer clothing aisles to the cooler food and household aisles brought down my temperature and made me feel uncomfortable without realising it.

My Strengths in the Situation

I can't identify my strengths in that situation, other than that I kept on trying, and didn't give up shopping there after the first bad incident. *I don't believe it would have been good for me to just avoid the shop forever more; it's much more empowering to teach myself to manage my triggers.*

What Would Have Helped Me in the Situation?

- The most important thing that would have helped me was to understand why I experienced anxiety in that aisle. If I had the knowledge I have now, if I had known I was autistic, I could have felt self-compassion rather than the feeling of failure and self-chastisement.

- It would have helped if I had tried to be flexible and just avoid that aisle and buy my shampoo in a different shop.

- It would have helped if I had sensory tools to reduce the overwhelm I felt from the sensory bombardment.

Using My Strengths to Develop a Coping Strategy for Supermarkets
Flexible Thinking Strength

- I have good flexible thinking when I plan ahead, so I can make a plan to support myself in the supermarket. This may include making a sensory plan to help me manage the sensory stimuli, and to avoid the aisle if I'm just too overwhelmed by it.

Sensory Plan (Using My Sensory Awareness Strength)

- I can bring sunglasses to reduce glare.

- I can wear headphones and listen to music or a podcast to block out the bothersome sounds.

- I can walk up the aisle from the other direction, so I'm not looking at the checkout flashing lights.

- I can rearrange my routine, so that I walk up the shampoo aisle first, so I know I can calm down afterwards, by walking through the book or clothes aisles.

- If I know my tolerance is low on a given day, I can just avoid that aisle completely.

- I can eat a crunchy snack while shopping to reduce hunger, and to activate my vestibular sense (this will be explained further in Chapter 7), and also to avoid hunger reducing my tolerance to unpleasant sensory stimuli.

Making Choices Strength

I acknowledge that I find too much choice really hard when I have to make a choice suddenly. But if I take my time, then I am good at it. One of my strengths is that I do not get stuck in refusing to try new things, just to avoid the risk of making the wrong choice. I can therefore decide what shampoo I want in advance, perhaps by looking at the choice online. If I need to smell the shampoo, I can bring it to a calmer aisle before I smell it to see if I like it.

SCENARIO 3
What Happened?

When I was 19 years old, a street charity collector came into my space unexpectedly, and stared into my eyes with the most intense eye contact and asked me to support the charity. She explained that the charity helped alcoholics. She looked like a deeply traumatised and unhealthy person, with a skeletal appearance. I was terrified of her and had recurrent nightmares about her for years. I have had a deep discomfort ever since when I pass street charity workers.

What Did I Feel?

Because of her intense eye contact, I felt as though she was looking deep into my soul. The thought crossed my mind that she was going to steal my thoughts, despite me knowing that was an irrational thought. I remember feeling light-headed, weak, and extremely vulnerable. When I would see other charity workers after that experience, I would feel my heart race and I would feel unsafe, and I would cross the road to avoid them.

At What Point Did I Start to Feel Uncomfortable?

As soon as I saw her veering towards me, alarm bells began ringing and my pulse went up.

What in the Environment Might Have Triggered Me?

I was on a busy street in town, and there was lots of noise from people and traffic around me. The woman came right into my personal space (too close for comfort) and smelt strongly of patchouli perfume (I still shudder if I smell this now, many years later).

Were My Basic Needs Met?

I can't remember.

What Were My Strengths in the Situation?

I was socially polite by staying to listen to the person. However, sometimes our social strengths aren't always good for us, and this is an example of that. I would have been better off walking away immediately.

What Would Have Helped Me in the Situation?

- A strategy to enable me to walk away, and not have to talk to her.

- The ability to understand why the encounter was so stressful to me, i.e. if I had known I was autistic at the time.

- Social skills to avoid eye contact.

- If I had a strong smell with me, I could have washed out the smell of her perfume by smelling a smell I liked. Interestingly, when I did walk away from her at last, I headed straight for the Body Shop, which was a shop I adored the smell of. At the time, I had no idea why I felt the urge to go there, but I distinctly remember going in and smelling my favourite soap while I waited for my anxiety to pass.

Using My Strengths to Build a Coping Strategy for Unexpected Encounters with Strangers
Creative Social Skills Strength

I can get creative with my social skills and choose not to look people in the eye. Instead, I can look at their forehead or nose. If I can still feel their piercing gaze, I can look at the ground, put on a listening facial expression, and turn my head to look as though I'm turning my ear towards them to hear them better. Alternatively, I could wear sunglasses – sunglasses make me feel safer, like there's a protective barrier between me and other people.

Facial Expression Strength

I am quite good at using the correct facial expressions, probably due to years of drama, as my mum (I call her my mum, but she is actually my step-mum and the woman who raised me) was a drama teacher. Despite this, I've been told my facial expressions are quite exaggerated, and thus I'm not good at hiding my feelings. I can therefore use my facial expression to suggest I am listening, without having to make eye contact.

Flexible Thinking in Advance Strength

I can come up with strategies to avoid speaking with strangers on the street, such as crossing the road if I see someone who might stop me, using headphones, and pretending to be unaware of other people around me. I could use body language such as tapping my wrist where one wears a watch, to suggest I'm running late. I could prepare phrases such as 'I can't stop, I'm in a hurry' or 'I'll look the charity up online when I have time' etc.

Emotional Regulation Strength

I have become increasingly good, through psychotherapy, at identifying what I'm feeling, and coming up with plans to let go of uncomfortable feelings. For example, putting on certain songs after a stressful encounter can help calm me down. Writing about a stressful situation and how it made me feel can take the thoughts out of my head to make sense of them, and allow me to leave them behind on the paper.

Sensory Awareness Strength

I could bring some sensory tools around with me in my handbag, such as a soap I love to smell, sunglasses, a scarf made of soft material to wrap around myself, and a visually calming image such as a postcard or notebook. After an unexpected stressful encounter, I can use these tools to help myself get calm (see Chapter 5 for sensory tool ideas).

SCENARIO 4
What Happened?

When my eldest daughter was a small baby, I drove to a supermarket that had special baby seats in the trolleys. When I arrived, I realised that I didn't have the correct coin to release the trolley. My lack of flexible thinking meant I could not think up a solution when I did not have the correct coin. It didn't dawn on me that I could go into the shop and get the correct coin. I was afraid to ask someone else who was getting a trolley if they could swap the right coin for my loose change, for two reasons: firstly, I lived in fear of my first daughter crying in public, and of people looking at me disapprovingly if I calmed her through breast-feeding. Secondly, I was afraid to approach a stranger to ask for help.

I eventually could no longer think properly, and felt I needed to escape. I drove home without any shopping.

What Did I Feel?

I felt completely overwhelmed, as if the feelings of confusion and not knowing what to do would burst inside me. I was anxious. I started thinking of the worst-case scenarios, for example that the baby would start screaming if I asked one of the people standing by the trolleys if I could swap my small change for the correct coin. I felt a deep sense of shame that this small obstacle made the task impossible. My feeling like a failure increased my feelings of overwhelm, and made my flexible thinking struggle even more. Being hard on myself is a huge cause of making a situation worse for me, as it makes me even more inflexible and pushes solutions further away.

What in the Environment May Have Triggered Me?

I was in the car at the time, which is a place I usually find very calming. I do not find the car overwhelming to my sensory system. However, I do find supermarkets stressful sensory environments, and the knowledge that I needed to go inside a sensory stressful environment seemed to carry forward the stress that I knew I would experience inside. I remember covering my ears, despite there being no noise, because I was predicting the loud noises (the incessant beeping of the cash registers in particular).

My knowledge that the supermarket was not a suitable environment for attending to a baby's needs was also stressful – I knew there were no seats to breastfeed, no nappy changing facilities etc. I was therefore under time pressure to get the shopping done as quickly as possible before my baby needed any of those things, and this knowledge further decreased my flexible thinking. When things are unpredictable, I get stressed.

Were My Basic Needs Met?

I was constantly exhausted when my babies were small, so no, my basic need of good sleep was not met.

At What Point Did I Start to Feel Uncomfortable?

As soon as I knew I was going shopping with a baby, I began to feel anxious. The anxiety built as I got closer to the shop. When I realised that I had no coin, my tolerance shut down and an enormous wave of anxiety took over.

What Were My Strengths in the Situation?

Looking back, my strength was that I kept trying to go shopping with the baby, despite many many situations where small things like having the wrong coin completely threw me. It would have been easy to ask my husband to take over the shopping, but I recognised that if I hid from the problem, I would only make it worse. It is like the 'if you fall off your bike, get straight back on it again' analogy: the longer you go without retrying the thing that was hard or scary, the harder it will become.

What Would Have Helped Me in the Situation?

- To be alone. It took me a long time to realise that I need to feel in control in shops. When you have a baby with you, you are never fully in control, as babies are unpredictable, and their needs come first. Thus, it is much easier to shop alone.

- If I had the correct coin!

- If I planned what to do if I arrived without a coin.

- If I had shopped online while my baby was young.

- If I had stayed calm and thought about what to do, rather than jumping to worst-case scenario thoughts.

Using My Strengths to Build a Coping Strategy for Avoiding Feeling Stressed When I Don't Have the Right Coin for a Trolley

Planning Strength

I could keep the correct trolley coins in the car at all times.

I could plan to shop without a small baby.

Flexible Thinking When Calm Strength

I wrote out options to deal with the situation, such as 'ask someone to swap coins' or 'go into the shop and ask for change'. I recently heard two people discussing how they both go into the shop and just ask the cashier to lend them the coin and they give it back at the end of the shopping – this had never occurred to me as I would presume the cashier would think I was trying to steal the coin, but apparently this tactic works for them most of the time, but not all of the time.

Emotional Regulation Strength

I can use tools to help myself feel calm, such as having a song on my phone that I associate with feeling calm. Deep, slow breathing while listening to a favourite song is very calming to me. By the time the song ends it may be easier to think flexibly.

I also considered temporary avoidance of the supermarket. I am glad now that I didn't go down this route, as it would have allowed my anxiety about going back to the supermarket to build up and intensify. *Instead of avoiding triggers, I feel it is healthier to stop, think, and plan your coping strategies and try again.*

My Common Autism Triggers

Looking back at these scenarios, plus many more, allowed me to recognise my main triggers. Every autistic person has different triggers, so it's important to get to know your own individual triggers.

My main triggers are:

- *Sensory stressors* (see Chapter 5 for a breakdown of sensory triggers and coping strategies).

- *Sudden demands* that require flexible thinking skills.

- *Unexpected things* happening.

- *Being hungry, thirsty, cold, hot, or tired.*

- *Spontaneity*. Even being with people that I know are prone to spontaneity can be stressful to me.

- *New places, new people, or new things* – because they are unpredictable.

- *Phone calls or situations where I have to try and achieve a certain outcome* (e.g. negotiating a price on a bill) through talking to someone I don't know, or someone I'm uncomfortable with.

- *Confrontation*, the possibility of confrontation, or anxiety-driven thoughts about confrontation.

- *Language processing confusion*, which basically means it can take me longer to make sense of other people's words, especially when I'm stressed. I often find it easier to process written language.

- *Being literal.* This has led me to be socially confused, or miss a joke, or misinterpret the mood of a social situation. I have also misinterpreted signs and instructions by taking a different and more literal meaning from it than other people do.

- *Social faux pas.* I usually realise if I've made a social mistake, but don't always know what I did wrong, or how to fix it, and thus it triggers me.

- *Change of plan.* I find plan changes extremely difficult. I tend to plan every step of not just an activity, but of my day, so if part of the plan changes, it means every step I had planned no longer works in the sequence I had expected. I find it very hard to think flexibly to reshape the new steps of the plan.

- *Anxiety.* I can go through phases where I have a constant level of anxiety, and this level can be quite high. When I have a high baseline anxiety, I am much more easily triggered.

- *Being away from home for too long.*

- *Going too long without solitude.*

- *Having no time to be creative.*

- *Not enough time engaged in my special interests.*

- *Feeling out of my depth.* For example, being in a situation where I don't understand the topic being discussed and feeling inferior as a result.

- *Feeling under pressure.* If I feel under pressure, including time pressure, I can find simple tasks much harder, and my brain feels as though it just shuts down and refuses to find solutions. Strangely, this affects me more in my personal life than in my professional life.

I actually thrived under pressure in work (mostly as an intensive care nurse) and was often praised for staying unusually calm in a crisis. However, when I would finish my shift, I would feel the side-effects of the pressure in a delayed reaction, and needed a huge amount of rest to cope with this. Finding time to relax between work shifts was much more difficult after I had children.

- *Technology*. There is a stereotype that autistic people are naturally excellent at all things technological. Alas, that stereotype doesn't include me. When things go wrong with technology, I really struggle, and tend to get rage surges. I have on occasion had to walk away from computers and phones as I felt such a strong desire to smash them!

- *Transitions*. I find transitioning from one environment to another, or one task to another, can be a big trigger for me, especially if I didn't achieve all I wanted to achieve before the transition.

- *Changes at home*. I find it really difficult when there are changes in my home environment, particularly in the process of transition. I recently had to move to a different bedroom in order to renovate a bathroom, and I found the whole process extremely stressful, as I felt my home was in a state of flux and was no longer a stable and constant environment.

Involving Others in Identifying Your Triggers

Sometimes I'm not aware of my own triggers, or autistic differences, until someone else points them out to me. My husband is particularly adept at recognising what will trigger me to feel overwhelmed and can often predict my reaction. He reminds me to take a moment to take control before a rush of emotion overwhelms me. He might suggest I go to my room for a few minutes or go outside for a break. He might put his arms around me and give me a tight hug, and the deep pressure of this soothes me instantly, which makes me aware that I needed soothing. Sometimes he simply gives me a look which lets me know that he sees the trigger, which is hugely validating, and may even be enough for me to take control and not let the trigger spark my anxiety. *Validating the feelings of an autistic person is one of the best things someone else can do to support that autistic person, especially in times of stress.*

I started asking other people, mostly family members, to tell me what autistic traits they noticed in me, in the hope it would help identify some of my triggers. I was very interested to hear their responses. The main ones were:

- I get cross or anxious when plans change.

- I often lack spontaneity.

- I often ask people to rephrase what they are saying so I can understand, and I ask questions to make sure I have understood.

- I need time to process an invitation or suggestion – I will rarely agree to an invitation immediately.

- My mood can deteriorate in loud, busy places.

- I often ask people to explain things visually to me, rather than verbally.

- I often arrive at events very early, and I leave early.

I enjoyed hearing these responses as I love gaining more self-insight, but some of them did surprise me, and sometimes it wasn't easy to hear things that I didn't know about myself. A word of warning: *if you plan to ask others about your own triggers and traits, be prepared for some surprises, and be aware that you may find some observations upsetting.* I would advise you to only ask people you trust with your feelings, and preferably only people who actually understand and respect autism, or else their comments may be unhelpful. Some of the things that made me a little uncomfortable were:

- I can appear rude and cold, like someone who 'doesn't like people'. This came as a shock to me as I consider myself very friendly. But on reflecting on the comment, I can see how I could come across like that, especially when I meet someone new in a busy social situation where I am working hard to cope with the sensory environment and social overwhelm.

- I can be very black and white, and stubborn about changing my opinion on something.

- I rarely do things spontaneously, and people who know me say they would never suggest a spur of the moment activity to me, as I get visibly stressed. This can lead me to being excluded from invitations.

However, I know myself that if I plan to be spontaneous, then I can be spontaneous. For example, if I'm visiting someone and I have no plan of what we will be doing, I'm fine with spontaneity. It's only if I already have a plan that spontaneity is a problem for me.

- I am bluntly honest. Interestingly, this was a trait people admired in me.

- I am not good at hiding my feelings, and if I disapprove of or disagree with someone, I don't hide it well.

- Sometimes I display the facial expression of an emotion that I'm not feeling – I can look cross or bored but if I'm questioned on how I feel, my feelings don't match my body language.

- I can appear judgemental in my facial expression or my reaction, even when I don't have a negative opinion of what someone is telling me.

These new insights helped me to learn new social skills. For example, I began coming up with phrases to use in situations when I might feel uncomfortable, so I would not appear rude. I also began practising my facial expressions and social reactions, and asked my family if I was expressing the correct response. I learnt a lot from this, and it was a bit of fun too; asking my children to tell me what facial expression I was showing led to lots of laughter.

Don't Hide from Your Triggers

When I first began to identify my triggers, my first thought was 'Now I know what to avoid'. But I soon realised that I would become agoraphobic if I tried to live a life avoiding all my triggers. I also wouldn't be able to experience so many things that bring me joy.

If I never made myself try new social situations, I would not have opportunities to meet new and interesting people. If I avoided all loud noise, I'd never experience the joy of live music. If I avoided shopping centres, I couldn't teach my children about financial management, and I would not know about new products that would be of interest to me. I would be cutting so much potential pleasure out of my life because of fear. Not only that, but by hiding from life, I would be wasting my mind and my very being.

I therefore realised that I cannot shut all triggers out of my life; instead

I need to learn to deal with them. *Taking control of my triggers means taking care of myself while still living a full life. This involves planning and preparing myself to cope with triggers.*

Ration Out Your Triggers

One of the ways I take control of my triggers is by rationing them out. This means being careful that I don't plan too many triggering events or activities close together. By spreading triggers out, I give myself time to recover after each one, and time to prepare and plan for the next one.

- *Spread out socialising*: This is particularly important for me at very social times like Christmas and birthdays. If I see too many people in a short time, I get exhausted and my tolerance goes down, making it more likely that I will experience anxiety over small problems. I therefore spread things out over days and weeks, and plan for recovery time after each event.

- *Ration out socialising in triggering environments*: I alternate socialising at home and in other venues, as I feel very calm and safe in my own home environment. If I meet someone in a café, I avoid meeting another person in a café for a day or two. This helps avoid a build-up of triggers and thus reduces my chances of getting overwhelmed.

- *Ration out sensory triggers*: Rationing things out carefully across a day or week gives me opportunities to plan for rest and solitude between events. This helps me cope with triggers in the activities or events. The more triggers I experience, the more likely I am to become overwhelmed. I think of it like the game Jenga: *I can keep taking the risk of exposure to sensory triggers, but at a certain point the whole things topples.*

  If I had a big event like a wedding, I would plan to stay at home and avoid socialising the day after. I would have an easy meal ready so I wouldn't need to go to the shop, or get stressed about cooking etc.

- *Get creative about taking sensory breaks.* When I worked long nursing shifts, I had to get creative to make sure I got quiet breaks in my day. We typically got a 20-minute break in the morning, a 30-minute break for lunch, and a 20-minute break in the evening, as part of the 12–13-hour shift. I used to divide my break-times between time alone and time socialising with colleagues. I would spend the first 15 minutes socialising and eating, and then go somewhere quiet such as the hospital chapel, or outside to the empty bike shed, or a bench. Here, I would close my eyes and focus on my breathing so that my stressed state could calm down. This really refuelled me for the next part of my shift.

I noticed that staff who spent their lunch-breaks alone and didn't give an excuse or state a reason were often spoken about negatively. I heard a range of comments said about people who didn't socialise at all at break-time, such as 'she never joins in' or 'he thinks he's too good to sit with us'. For fear of these comments being made about me, I would always make an excuse to leave my colleagues at lunch, so I would say things like 'I'm just going to phone home' or 'I've a headache and just need some quiet, I'll see you back in the ward' (it was usually true as I always had a headache at work), or 'I'm going for fresh air, see you back in the ward'. I have often noticed that people are much more accepting of different needs or wants, once the reason has been stated. I didn't know I was autistic at the time, but I knew I needed solitude and silence to help me cope with my workload.

- *Prioritise and plan for your triggers*: If I need to do a number of triggering activities in a row, or go to a number of triggering places, I take a moment to plan how I will manage best. I might plan to do the hardest thing first, while my energy is highest and my tolerance of triggers is at its best. Or I might make a priority list of the activities, so I can make sure I do the most important one first. I often leave the nicest thing until last, as it acts as a motivator.

- *Keep some time off to yourself*: I used to pack our weekends with activities that I thought my children needed, as it's what everyone else did. When the Covid-19 lockdowns began in 2020, I quickly realised how much the family benefitted from doing nothing, or very little over a weekend. I now try to plan no more than one social activity at a weekend, and instead just do what we feel like in the moment. Having one day a week when I truly rest from the world outside is very restorative.

- I also know that I find it hard to have too many things on in evenings. So if I plan something for an evening, I make sure I keep the next evening free for relaxing at home.

Plan Your Recovery Time

The world is full of triggers, and dealing with them takes energy, mental planning, and work. I don't have infinite energy to cope with triggers; *I need time to rest and refuel my energy levels.* I therefore pre-emptively plan time for myself to rest or decompress during and after social situations, or any situation that I know will require a lot of my coping strategies.

Examples of recovery strategies:

- During an event such as a conference, *go outside alone at the coffee break* for some peace and fresh air.

- *Listen to a song that calms you.* Listening to music can help calm the mind. I have one or two songs that I use as my 'recovery songs'. I find that when I dedicate the time to listen to the whole song, and do nothing else while listening to it other than focusing on breathing slowly, it can reset my stress level to zero (or at least lower it).

- *Put an eye mask on in a bathroom or private place for a few moments.* When I get stressed, I become more sensitive to light, and so blocking out light has a lovely calming effect on me.

- See Part 2 for developing *sensory self-care tools and skills.*

- *If you're at home, lie down in bed with the curtains closed.* I often listen to an audiobook while doing this.

- *Engage in your special interest or hobbies.* I am very lucky to love books and audiobooks, and I can easily bring them with me everywhere I go. I also find that thinking about something that really stimulates me can be helpful; using my brain to learn about something interesting can be really restorative to me.

- *Take a small walk alone after social events.* Before I go home to a busy household, a small walk really helps me to process the event I've just left. It also calms down my sensory system. When I worked as a nurse, I loved walking home after the long shift. It was a lovely opportunity to process what had happened that day, and to leave it behind me before I reached home. This was important as intensive care nursing takes a large emotional toll.

- *Go to a quiet place alone.* There is little else as restorative to me as silent solitude.

- If travelling somewhere new, *research (before you go) where you can rest and recover*. If I go to a new town or city, I look up where the libraries, galleries, and churches are, as they are usually quiet, peaceful places. They tend to be free of charge, so I don't feel obliged to buy something to enter; this is important as when I'm stressed I don't want to have to interact with other people, or to have to think about money, which is a trigger in itself.

- *Use a Quick Calm Plan*. This is a plan of which strategies you can use to help yourself calm down quickly when you are overwhelmed, and will be discussed in the next chapter.

KEY POINTS

◊ Triggers are things that set off a stress response in our brains, and make our body feel the need to fight, flight, or freeze.
◊ Autistic people can get overwhelmed or stressed from exposure to their triggers.
◊ Every autistic person has different triggers, so it's important to get to know your own.
◊ The detective habit is a method of reflection that can help identify one's triggers, and then create strength-based coping strategies.
◊ Other people can be helpful in identifying your triggers, but take caution that the person you ask is sensitive and uncritical.
◊ Autistic people can react differently to triggers at different times. If your basic needs are not met, or if you are stressed, you are more likely to react strongly to a trigger.
◊ Rationing out your triggers helps avoid triggers building up and becoming overwhelming.
◊ Planning time to rest after a build-up of triggers is really important, as is having a few techniques to calm yourself when out and about.

References

Bishop-Fitzpatrick, L., Mazefsky, C.A, Minshew, N.J., and Eack, S.M. (2015) 'The Relationship between Stress and Social Functioning in Adults with Autism Spectrum Disorder and without Intellectual Disability'. *Autism Research* 8 (2), 164–173. https://dx.doi.org/10.1002/aur.1433
Johnston, K., Murray, K., Spain, D., Walker, I., and Russel, A. (2019) 'Executive Function: Cognition and Behavior in Adults with Autism Spectrum Disorders (ASD)'. *Journal*

of Autism and Developmental Disorders 49, 4181–4192. https://dx.doi.org/10.1007/Fs10803-019-04133-7

Mayo Clinic (2021) 'Chronic Stress Puts Your Health at Risk'. Accessed 4 October 2021 at: www.mayoclinic.org/healthy-lifestyle/stress-management/in-depth/stress/art-20046037

Spratt, E.G., Nicholas, J.S., Brady, K.T., Carpenter, L.A., Hatcher, C.R., et al. (2012) 'Enhanced Cortisol Response to Stress in Children with Autism'. *Journal of Autism and Developmental Disorders* 42 (1), 75–81. https://dx.doi.org/10.1007%2Fs10803-011-1214-0

World Health Organization (2008) 'Managing Stress'. Accessed 4 October 2021 at: www.who.int/hac/techguidance/tools/manuals/who_field_handbook/g5.pdf

Chapter 3

Quick Calm Plans

CHAPTER BREAKDOWN

CHAPTER AIMS

› To explain why I use Quick Calm Plans when I am stressed.
› To discuss why it's important to try and make your Quick Calm Plan when you are calm rather than when you are stressed or anxious.
› To guide you through creating Quick Calm Plans.
› To explain, with the aid of research, why it's beneficial to have a visual version of your Quick Calm Plan.
› To discuss stimming as a calming strategy.
› To explain my own experience of stimming.

What Is a Quick Calm Plan?

When I have been so strongly triggered that I simply can no longer function properly, I need a Quick Calm Plan. This is when I am totally overloaded and I have to prioritise myself, *now*.

A Quick Calm Plan is a series of strategies or tools that you can use to calm down, refuel your energy, and to reduce the feeling of being overwhelmed.

When I am overwhelmed and have either shut down (see Chapter 11 for more on shutdown) or am about to shut down, I cannot think flexibly, and therefore it's very important to have a Quick Calm Plan made *before* I become overwhelmed.

The strategies or tools I use in my Quick Calm Plan completely depend on where I am and what I'm doing. If I'm at home, I can use the strategy of going to bed in a dark room. If I am not at home, then I cannot use the strategy of lying in bed, but I can use an eye mask in a quiet private place. If I am out with the children, I need to stay switched on to mind the children; I need to push out my shutdown until I am home, and so need strategies to help me get through the overwhelm such as breathing techniques, reducing the noise I hear, and taking a drink of water.

While I am aware that not all autistic adults are able to postpone having a shutdown or meltdown, I do think that autistic adults are often able to hide their overwhelm, and continue to function to a degree, until they have a chance to shut down somewhere they feel safe to do so. Autistic children learn that public meltdowns and shutdowns attract negative attention, and I think this can lead older autistic children and autistic adults to learn to postpone their shutdowns and meltdowns as part of masking (see Chapter 16 for more on masking). I'm not suggesting that it's a good idea to postpone shutting down or melting down just to mask your autism, but I do find that shutting down publicly can actually intensify my overwhelm. For that reason, I prefer to postpone shutting down until I am somewhere I feel emotionally safe to do so. Being responsible for my children has been one of the biggest causes of me having to postpone shutting down, as I need to make sure they are safe and cared for before I can allow myself to shut down. I therefore use Quick Calm Plans both to postpone shutting down and to manage shutdowns and meltdowns.

Clues That Tell Me When I Need a Quick Calm Plan

When I am overwhelmed, or close to becoming overwhelmed, I tend to notice physical signs and symptoms in my body and in my thoughts. I don't experience all these signs at once; I might experience one, or two, or many of these signs. I have started to recognise these signs as my body's way of giving me clues that I need some urgent self-care.

Clues I need to use a Quick Calm Plan include:

- Body shaking.

- Realising I'm doing repetitive body movements such as rubbing my index finger against my thumb, or twitching my eye or head very slightly.

- Headache.

- Jaw clenching.

- Nausea.

- Racing thoughts or a jumble of indecipherable thoughts.

- Heightened anxiety.

- Feeling as though my limbs are disconnected from my body; feeling ungrounded.

- A strong desire not to talk to anyone.

- Speaking in broken sentences, or only being able to say one word at a time. For example, I might be unable to say 'I need to go to bed now' but I can say 'Bed'.

- Stuttering.

- Sometimes I can open my mouth as if to speak but I can't seem to get the word from my brain to my mouth, and thus I know what I want to say but I can't say it. This happens to me extremely rarely, but when it does happen, it's very distressing.

- An intense or overwhelming craving for something I associate with safety, such as a favourite TV show or a special interest.

- Exhaustion.

- Craving sugar.

- Wanting to hide under the blankets in my bed.

- Feeling like I will scream if one more demand is put on me.

- Feeling like I might burst into uncontrollable crying.

- Hopelessness.

- Feeling like everything is just too much and I cannot cope.

- Breathing fast.

Ideas for Quick Calm Plans

Everyone will have different strategies that help them relax or deal with overwhelm. It is worth brainstorming what works for you, and making a list of ideas that you can use each time you make your Quick Calm Plan. Every time you discover a new strategy or a new tool, it's worth recording this and adding it to your list of ideas.

Ideas of strategies and tools to use:

- *Remove yourself from the stressful situation, if possible.* Even a quick break away from a stressful situation can help me calm down, as it allows my brain to feel as if it has the space to work again. My most common way to escape is to pretend I need to use the bathroom.

- *Ask yourself are your basic needs met?* If your basic needs are not met, you need to meet them as fast as you can.

  - Are you thirsty or hungry? If hungry or thirsty, you need to get food and water. It can help to always bring an energy bar or snack and a drink with you. Avoid coffee and caffeine as they may speed up your heart rate and increase anxiety and the feeling of being stressed.

  - Are you cold or too hot? If you are too hot, can you take a layer of clothing off? (I always wear layers of clothes so I can easily change my body temperature.)

  - Are you exhausted? Tiredness makes coping so much harder. Can you have a rest or a nap?

- *Controlled breathing.* There are many breathing techniques available for calming the mind and body. One technique I use includes putting my hands on my belly and breathing into my belly so that my hands rise up, and then breathing out through pursed lips. Another technique I use is breathing slowly while mentally repeating the words 'Breathe in, breathe out, pause. Breathe in, breathe out, pause.' This really helps me to feel calmer fast, and helps me to avoid panicking. When I panic, I tend to start breathing too fast, or I instinctively try to calm myself by taking giant deep breaths. Both these breathing techniques can cause hyperventilation, which means you breathe out too much carbon dioxide.

MANAGING HYPERVENTILATION

Hyperventilation is caused by over-breathing. It can happen from breathing too fast, or breathing too deeply. Hyperventilation leads to you not having enough carbon dioxide in your body. Carbon dioxide is the main gas we breathe back out during an exhale, but our body needs some carbon dioxide to keep the right balance of gases within it. Having too little carbon dioxide can make you feel dizzy, breathless, have muscle tingles, and basically feel awful.

When you feel stressed or anxious, you may feel an urge to breathe faster or deeper, as if you are hungry for more oxygen. But when you are hyperventilating, you actually need to breathe less, not more. This is because you need to bring up the amount of carbon dioxide in your body (i.e. stop blowing out so much air). You can do this by taking smaller breaths and holding your breath after you inhale for the count of four, and again holding your breath after you exhale for the count of four (NHS Borders 2005).

I highly recommend learning proper breathing techniques with your medical professional if you are prone to hyperventilation. Breathing can be used as a calming tool when you are stressed, but take care to use slow, controlled breaths with pauses between them, to prevent blowing out too much carbon dioxide.

- *Take a drink.* This brings focus and feeling into your throat and mouth, and re-awakens the digestive system, which can get sluggish when you are stressed.

- *Find somewhere you can be alone.* Solitude is my number one goal when I am overwhelmed. This might be as simple as walking into the utility room away from my children, or it might be lying down in bed, or going into a bathroom and closing the door. Even a few seconds can be enough to calm things down, but nothing compares to an hour in bed alone.

- *Go home and go to bed for a while*, if your responsibilities allow you to.

- *Hold a hot water bottle, heated pad, or warm mug just under your chest bone.* I tend to feel like there's a knot in my stomach when I am overwhelmed, and the heat really helps this feeling to go away.

- *Lie under a weighted blanket.* Weight and deep pressure is very grounding to the body. This increases your proprioceptive sensory feedback, to help you feel grounded (see Chapter 7 for more proprioceptive strategies).

- *Put something heavy on your lap.* This can be a weighted lap blanket, a heavy box, a bag, a pile of books etc.

- *Smell something lovely* like soap or a preferred herb (lemon verbena, lavender, and mint are my favourites).

- *Splash cold water on your face, the back of your neck, and on your palms and inner wrists.* This has a remarkable calming and alerting effect on me, which helps me regain my focus.

- *Get fresh air.*

- *Watch a favourite TV show.* I avoid watching anything new when I'm overwhelmed, as I need the predictability of a show that I know.

- *Avoid people putting demands on you if possible.* This might mean leaving your environment, or creating a signal that you don't want to be disturbed, such as using headphones or going somewhere secluded, or turning off your phone.

- *Listen to music or an audiobook.*

- *Stimming* helps a lot of autistic people calm down (see below for more on stimming).

- *Darken the room.* Darkness helps block out visual sensory stimuli. Using an eye mask can help if you can't close the curtains.

- *Reduce visual stimulation.* If you find looking at the environment stressful (e.g. if it's cluttered, messy, or arranged in a way that stresses you through asymmetry etc.), then using an eye mask can give your visual sense a rest and encourage you to close your eyes.

- *Take a shower or bath.* I need to stop thinking when I'm overwhelmed, and so showers work better for me, as I find baths make me think more.

- *Singing* is a lovely way to control your breathing and expand your chest, which are very calming activities. I also find singing extremely uplifting.

- *Go into nature*, whether that's a garden or a park, or maybe it's just looking at nature on your phone.

- *Have a warm drink*. This acts in a similar way to the heat on my chest, and eases the feeling of there being a knot in my gut.

- *Turn off the internet on your phone, or turn off the phone* so you can disconnect from people, if the overwhelm is caused by social stress.

- *Say how you feel*. I often find that even just saying how I feel out loud to someone helps ease the feelings.

- *Ask for help*. As a parent, I need to ask for someone (usually my husband) to mind the children before I shut myself away in my dark bedroom, under my weighted blanket.

- *Exercise*. I used to go for a jog when I felt shaky with stress or anxiety, which is an activity that combines fresh air, time alone, and deep pressure into the joints, which is calming to the proprioceptive sensory system (see Chapter 7). But now that I have two interacting joint conditions I can no longer jog. I am starting to find weight lifting to be very calming, as are exercises like yoga or anything that gets the body moving in a safe and organised way. It needs to be predictable for me when I'm overwhelmed, and something I'm familiar with, as I need to be able to switch off my need to think about what I'm doing.

The Benefit of a Visual Version of Your Quick Calm Plan

When distressed, many autistic people can process or understand information much better when it is in a visual format, rather than relying on thinking, memory, or listening skills.

Having a visual version of your Quick Calm Plan will help you to carry out the strategies and remember to use your calming tools, even when you are overwhelmed or stressed.

When we experience high levels of stress, a part of our brain called the pre-frontal cortex stops working properly. This is the part of our brain that regulates (i.e. manages) our thoughts and behaviour. *This means that when we feel intense stress, our memory and ability to think shuts down* (Arnsten et al. 2015). Research suggests that *autistic people continue to be able to process and understand visual information, even when we are very stressed and cannot process information from non-visual sources (e.g. someone talking to us).* For this reason, I think it's really important to make a visual version of your Quick Calm Plan.

There is evidence that autistic children and adults have an 'autistic advantage', i.e. we are better than non-autistic people at visual tasks and visual searches (Kaldy et al. 2016). *In short, our vision is our strength.* This is possibly because it is common for autistic people to think visually, or to 'think in pictures', a phrase first used by the well-known autistic adult Temple Grandin. The theory that autistic people are visual thinkers, and have visual strengths at doing tasks, has been backed up by research such as that of Kunda and Goel (2011).

How to Make a Visual Version of Your Quick Calm Plan

There are many different ways to make a visual version of your Quick Calm Plan. Some people will prefer to store it on their phone, others will prefer to make a detailed spreadsheet, some (like me) prefer writing it out on paper. Whatever works for you, is right for you. Here are some suggestions to try:

- *Write a list on your phone.* I often send myself a text message of my Quick Calm Plan before an event.

- *Carry a handwritten list* with you.

- *Store photos of strategies and tools on your phone.* You can make a folder with images of tools you find helpful, for example noise cancelling headphones, eye mask, weighted blanket, something to do with a special interest. When stressed, just scroll through the photos in the folder to give yourself ideas about what tools to use. It's likely that as soon as you see the tool that will work for you, you will know it. You can make different folders for different activities, such as 'Quick Calm Plan for Home', 'Quick Calm Plan for Work' etc. If you scroll through the images before you go out, it will help you not to forget any tools you want to bring with you.

- *Use an app, such as a note-taking or to-do-list app,* that helps you store your Quick Calm Plan on your phone. This will allow you to access a version of your plan quickly whenever you need it.

- *Draw a diagram* of your Quick Calm Plan.

- *Make a video* of your Quick Calm Plan before you go to an event.

- *Draw stick man drawings* of your Quick Calm Plan.

- *Keep a small notebook with photos of your Quick Calm Strategies* and then you can flick through it and decide which one appeals to you in the moment.

- *I keep a box under my bed with some calming tools,* so I just have to open the box and there are my tools visually in front me – this includes a nice soap to smell, postcards of art I love to look at, an eye mask if I crave darkness, and earphones and a phone charger to ensure I can listen to audiobooks or music.

- *Physically put out the tools you plan to use before you go out.* If I'm going out to a socially demanding event, I lay out my hot water bottle, comfortable clothes, eye mask, bottle of water, and a snack, and leave them on my bed with a weighted blanket and my box of calming tools. When I get home, I can visually see everything I need, so I can start relaxing without having to think about how to do it.

- *Make a mind-map of what strategies you can use.* A mind-map is a simple diagram you draw to visually organise information. Here are some examples:

Quick Calm Plan for Home

- Dim lights
- Eye mask
- Lie in bed
- Listen to audiobook
- Snack and drink water
- Weighted blanket
- Hug hot water bottle

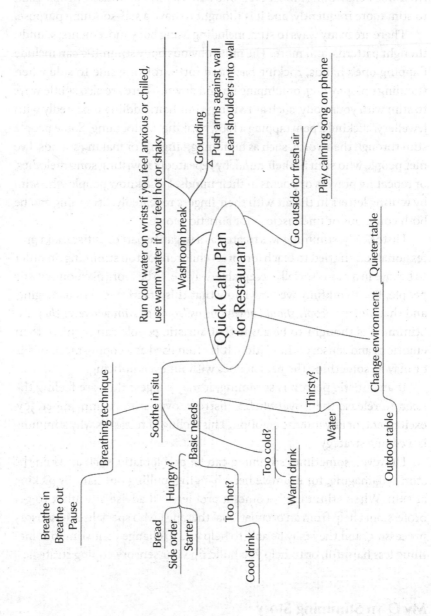

Quick Calm Plan
for Restaurant

Grounding
- Push arms against wall
- Lean shoulders into wall
- Go outside for fresh air
- Play calming song on phone

Washroom break
- Run cold water on wrists if you feel anxious or chilled,
use warm water if you feel hot or shaky

Change environment
- Quieter table
- Outdoor table

Basic needs
- Thirsty?
  - Water
- Too cold?
  - Warm drink
- Too hot?
  - Cool drink
- Hungry?
  - Bread
  - Side order
  - Starter

Soothe in situ

Breathing technique
- Breathe in
- Breathe out
- Pause

Stimming

Stimming, also known as self-stimulatory behaviour, is a repetitive, often rhythmic behaviour. Almost everyone stims a bit, but autistic people tend to stim more frequently, and it is thought to have a self-soothing purpose.

There are many ways to stim, including using body movements, sounds, thought patterns, and more. The more obvious body stimming can include flapping one's hands, rocking back and forth, rocking side to side when standing up, spinning, or jumping up and down. There are also subtle ways to stim with your body, such as twirling your hair, fiddling repeatedly with jewellery, clicking a pen, tapping a foot, blinking, or doodling. Some people stim through their voice, such as humming, singing, or making sounds. I've met people who stim in their mind, by repeatedly rewriting song melodies, or repeating prayers or poems in their minds. I also know people who stim by writing letters in the air with their fingers repeatedly. Stimming can be both conscious or unconscious for autistic people.

Historically, stimming was treated as a negative part of autism, and professionals often tried to teach (or force) children to stop stimming, in order to behave in a more 'socially acceptable' way, i.e. to be more like non-autistic people. But thankfully we now know that this practice is very damaging, and that *autistic people should always be welcome to stim wherever they are.* Stimming is thought to be a way that autistic people can regulate their emotions and sensory stimulation. It is often used as a coping mechanism, or may be something the person does without even noticing.

If an autistic person is stimming, it may suggest they are feeling the need to release their overwhelm, distress, over-stimulation, anger, joy, excitement, or any intense emotion. This feeling of release is why stimming is a coping strategy.

However, sometimes stimming can be problematic, such as when the stim is damaging, for example head banging, pulling out hair, or picking at skin. When stimming becomes a problem, I'd advise any adult to get professional help from an occupational therapist who specialises in sensory processing, and they may be able to help you to change your stim to something less harmful, or to help you build up your sensory coping strategies.

My Own Stimming Story

I have a strange relationship with my own stimming, and it's not something I'm yet fully comfortable with in myself.

As a child, I remember doing a lot of stimming, especially after my father died when I was aged nine. I had a number of ways to stim. I remember doing a lot of spinning around looking up at the sky, which I loved, and I would then collapse in a dizzy, happy heap on the ground.

The stim I didn't love was that I would twitch my shoulder and make a strange sound in my throat. Doing this stim in private felt wonderful, as though all uncomfortable emotions were being expelled from my body through the movement and sound. But in public, this stim attracted a lot of negative attention, and I was called nasty names when I stimmed. I quickly learnt to feel embarrassed about it. I remember forcing the stim to stop when people were around, and sometimes I would go into the bathroom in school just to 'let it out'. I would lock myself in the toilet cubicle and allow my body to release the pent-up tension. I would then feel a lot calmer in my body, but I also felt a lot of shame that I had to do this.

As I got older, I began to be able to transfer the stim to a different part of my body. For example, if I felt my shoulder wanting to twitch, or I noticed I was rocking back and forth on my chair, I would look down at my desk, cup my hands on either side of my face to hide my eyes, and I would blink my eyes fast and furiously to release that feeling of pent-up energy. Hiding and managing my stimming took up a lot of my school day.

As a teenager, I became a master of stim disguise. I consciously developed more 'socially acceptable' stims, such as twirling or plaiting my hair, chewing pens (in a rhythmic repetitive motion), shaking my foot, twisting my necklace. But when I lay down in bed at night, and I relaxed to go to sleep, my whole body would jerk, and my shoulder would twitch, as if to say 'You can suppress me in school but you can't suppress me now'. That was not a pleasant feeling. It would start involuntarily, without warning, usually right before I drifted off to sleep. If I chose to do it voluntarily, it sped up the process and it passed quicker. But if I fought it, it went on longer. If I had a sleepover with a friend, I would wait and listen for my friend to fall asleep before I could release that feeling. I'm not sure if this is common in autism, or if it's just me. I'm not even sure if that's considered stimming, as it certainly didn't feel soothing; it felt more like an explosion of suppressed movement.

Probably because of the negative attention I got from stimming, I still carry negative associations with a lot of my own stimming, and thus it's rarely something I use to soothe myself voluntarily. The stims I regularly do consciously include rubbing a smooth stone between my fingers or rubbing my index finger against my thumb. Besides these conscious stims, my body also tries to get in as many little repetitive movements as it can.

I have three types of unconscious stimming, by which I mean I do them without choosing to do them:

1. *Calm stimming:* This is when I'm at ease, sitting chatting, or concentrating. For example, my mother-in-law has asked me a few times to stop 'tapping a beat' on the car accelerator. This is an extremely subtle movement, and not something that affects my driving safety, but I do tend to shift my foot ever so softly, repetitively, without noticing that I'm doing it. I also often notice myself clenching my jaw rhythmically. When I'm alone and distracted I often nod my head gently, a bit like one of those nodding porcelain statues. I often shake my foot when my legs are crossed, and I click or twirl pens. When I become aware that I'm doing these stims, I recognise that they feel regulating; as though they are organising my body and brain.

2. *Excited stimming:* When I'm very excited or immensely happy, I clench and shake my fists like an excited toddler and make an 'eeee' sound. This happens without planning, it just pops out of me, and feels good. I quite like this stim, even if it does make me look childish.

3. *Distressed stimming:* When I get very distressed, my stimming can be an extra source of distress. Sometimes I nod my head so fast and strong that it hurts my neck – it tends to start unconsciously if I'm alone or at home. If I'm with people, I can suppress it before it begins, but it costs mental energy and causes my jaw to clench and I get a headache. I really dislike this stim as it causes me physical pain, despite the fact that it does feel like it is releasing emotion or stress.

Interestingly, I've recently discovered that I can give my body the feedback it craves from a stim I don't like by doing other physical actions. These include:

- If I make the stimming sound in my throat that I used to make as a child, this stops my head nodding. I wonder if I developed the head nodding stim because I suppressed the sound in my throat stim for years. The sound stim feels embarrassing to me, and so it's not something I would do in public as I know I would get negative attention.

- I can apply weight to my body. This provides intense soothing feedback to my body and my head instantly relaxes. I use a weighted blanket to achieve this or get someone (usually my husband) to wrap their arms around me and squeeze/hug me tightly. My shoulders are the main area that needs the weight or deep pressure.

- I can lean my hands on a wall and, keeping my arms straight, push hard into the wall. This creates deep pressure up my arm and into my shoulders.

- I can circle an exercise elastic band around my shoulders and push my arms forwards so I have to use my shoulder muscles to force the band forwards.

- Singing has a very calming effect on me, and I love the feelings of vibration it creates in my throat. Humming often doesn't work for me, as I can find the throat vibration too intense, and I feel like I'm trapping sound and emotion in, rather than letting it out through my mouth.

The fact that stimming often begins involuntarily for me is a source of stress. I don't like to feel not in control, particularly of my body. It surprises me to read so many accounts of autistic people who find stimming so calming, as it really is a mixed bag for me. By this I mean that I would rather not feel the need to stim, as it requires so much management to fit in socially (I have not yet reached a point where I am comfortable with the odd glances of people if I were to stim in an obvious manner in public). But yes, the feeling of release when I do stim is a positive thing.

A Look at Some Research on Stimming

A study by Kapp et al. (2019) interviewed 32 autistic adults to understand their experiences and thoughts on stimming.

Although most of the study participants did not dislike stimming, many of them experienced feeling marginalised and got negative attention for stimming in public, and therefore many suppressed their stimming when out and about.

The majority of participants said their stims begin involuntarily. Most people interviewed said that stimming was a positive thing, that it creates 'a feedback loop that regulates excess emotion', and thus acts as a soothing comfort.

KEY POINTS

◊ 'Quick Calm Plans' are plans of what strategies you will use to help you calm down from being overwhelmed.

◊ Our body gives us clues that we are getting overwhelmed, and the earlier you listen to these clues and implement a Quick Calm Plan, the easier it will be to feel calm again.

◊ It's important to make your Quick Calm Plan when you are calm, so it's ready to use when you hit overwhelm.

◊ Making a visual image or version of your Quick Calm Plan will allow you to use the strategies when you are overwhelmed.

◊ Stimming, when it feels soothing and good, can be part of your Quick Calm Plan.

◊ When stimming doesn't feel good or is causing harm, you can try and give your body the feedback it craves in a different way. If this doesn't work, an occupational therapist who specialises in sensory processing might be able to help you to manage the problematic stim.

References

Arnsten, A.F.T., Raskind, M.A., Taylor, F.B., and Connor, D.F. (2015) 'The Effects of Stress on Prefrontal Cortex: Translating Basic Research into Successful Treatment for Post-Traumatic Stress Disorder'. *Neurobiology of Stress* 1, 89–99. https://doi.org/10.1016/j.ynstr.2014.10.002

Kaldy, Z., Giserman, I., Carter, A.S., and Blaser, E. (2016) 'The Mechanisms Underlying ASD Advantage in Visual Research'. *Journal of Autism and Developmental Disorders* 46 (5), 1513–1527. https://dx.doi.org/10.1007%2Fs10803-013-1957-x

Kapp, S.K., Steward, R., Crane, L., Elliot, D., Elphick, C., Pellicano, E., and Russel, G. (2019) 'People Should Be Allowed to Do What They Like: Autistic Adults' Views on Stimming'. *Autism* 23 (7), 1782–1792. https://doi.org/10.1177%2F1362361319829628

Kunda, M. and Goel, A.K. (2011) 'Thinking in Pictures as a Cognitive Account of Autism' *Journal of Autism and Developmental Disorders* 41 (9), 1157–1177. https://doi.org/10.1007/s10803-010-1137-1

NHS Borders (2005) 'Hyperventilation'. Accessed 9 July 2022 at: www.nhsborders.scot.nhs.uk/media/213548/Hyperventilation.pdf

Chapter 4

Well-Being and Special Interests

CHAPTER BREAKDOWN

CHAPTER AIMS

> To introduce the concept of well-being.
> To introduce the PERMA model of well-being.
> To discuss why I think the PERMA model of well-being is an excellent match for autistic adults to improve their well-being.
> To explain how creating a routine can make sure you have all the elements of PERMA in your daily life.
> To explain and celebrate autistic special interests, and repetitive interests and passions.
> To caution on how to prevent special interests becoming a problem.

Why I Needed to Improve My Well-Being

Good well-being is not about feeling extreme happiness all of the time. It's also not about never feeling uncomfortable feelings. For me, it's about getting comfortable with who I am, recognising and meeting my needs, and adding meaning to my everyday life.

For years I felt a deep sense of something meaningful missing from my life. This is partially because I had an image in my head that adulthood would be all sunshine and rainbows. I thought I would automatically become confident and calm and have control over everything I did.

When I became an adult, I couldn't understand how I could feel this lack of meaning and this lack of control. On paper, my life ticked all the boxes: I had my chosen career, a wonderful husband, children I adored, a comfortable home. But even the most positive experiences in my life were being overshadowed by emotional and sensory overwhelm.

I couldn't understand why I was finding everyday life so full of anxiety. Having a constantly high level of anxiety affected everything in life, and prevented me from finding a sense of meaning, thus reducing my well-being.

Learning that I was autistic allowed me to analyse my triggers and develop strategies to support my autistic needs. I have now worked on my emotional regulation and anxiety through psychotherapy. This was invaluable to me as it taught me to understand and get comfortable with all my emotions (see Part 3 on emotional regulation). Similarly, learning to manage and understand my sensory system helped me to feel calmer throughout my daily life (see Part 2 on sensory self-care).

I have realised that life will never be fully sunshine and rainbows, but there will be moments of sunshine, and occasional rainbows, if I take the time and effort to notice them. I will never have control over everything, but there are many things I do have control over. I do have control over improving my well-being, and increasing the sense of meaning in my daily life. One of the ways I began to improve my well-being was by applying the PERMA model of well-being to my life.

I began to use the PERMA model of well-being to help me identify the things I enjoy doing, which things are important to me, and what brings me a sense of achievement. This has made me a much more contented person, and allowed me to see that I do, in fact, have a meaningful life.

The PERMA Model of Well-Being

The PERMA model was developed by Dr Martin Seligman, an American Psychologist (who was the President of the American Psychological Association in 1998). The goal of PERMA is to help you identify what things increase your well-being. Once you identify the things that can improve your well-being, it is up to you to make sure you incorporate them into your life.

The model states that there are five main elements that we need in our lives to achieve a state of well-being, and uses the mnemonic PERMA to describe them:

- P – Positive emotion.

- E – Engagement.

- R – Relationships.

- M – Meaning.

- A – Accomplishments.

I heard about the PERMA model while I was in college studying Autism Studies, and although it was only briefly mentioned, it jumped out at me as an excellent model for achieving well-being. I did further research into it, but I have not trained in it and have not worked on it with a professional. I am therefore only able to share my own experience of working with it.

I will briefly explain each element of PERMA.

Positive Emotion

This element is about doing things that increase the positive emotion we feel. Seligman states that there are tricks to increase happiness, such as smiling, and naming three gratitudes about your day every evening (Seligman 2012).

Engagement

To access positive emotion, it's important to engage in things that allow us to get into a 'state of flow'. This includes engaging in activities in which you lose track of time, and doing things that fully engage your mind.

Engagement also means identifying the things we are good at, and intentionally using those strengths when doing our daily tasks. Even mundane tasks can become full of positive emotion if you intentionally use your strengths in order to do them. For example, if you have the strength of being kind, you can think about how you can bring your kindness into your daily activity. Using our strengths helps us feel positive emotions about ourselves.

Relationships

Good relationships are important to our sense of self. Feeling valued by other people, and connecting with other people, whether at work, with friends, or with family, can be hugely beneficial to our self-esteem and well-being.

Meaning

Having a meaning in your life means belonging to something bigger than yourself (Seligman 2012). This is similar to having a purpose in life, and may include being part of a community, a profession, a charity, a creative endeavour shared with others, a political movement etc.

Achievement

To feel achievement, we don't have to be winning awards or getting recognition from others for our work. Achievement is about setting realistic goals and accomplishing them. When others recognise our achievements and praise us or acknowledge us, it feels good, but unless we acknowledge it ourselves, it's useless to us.

PERMA and Autism

Some elements of the PERMA model can be challenging to autistic people, but that doesn't mean they are not important. *It means we have to make extra effort to make sure we include the difficult elements in our lives to improve our well-being.* For example, some autistic people may find making friends challenging, and thus the PERMA element Relationships may need more attention. I will discuss how I used the model to help myself with the harder elements in the next section.

Other elements of PERMA are very natural to autistic people, such as Engagement. The majority of autistic adults have special interests (Grove et al. 2018). Engaging in special interests is a wonderful way to get into a state of flow and thus increase your well-being. *However, caution needs to be taken with autistic Engagement, that it doesn't come at the cost of attention paid to other areas of PERMA.* Too much time spent in activities of Engagement could mean that areas of PERMA such as Relationships are not given enough time and effort. Similarly, putting Engagement ahead of Achievements may lead to the neglect of tasks and chores that maintain a dignified life.

Finding the right balance between the elements that are difficult to you as an individual and the elements that are easy is the key to achieving well-being with the PERMA model.

PERMA and Me

When I first looked at the PERMA model and questioned whether I had all the elements of well-being in my daily life, I felt that I lacked many:

P: I often experienced depressed and anxious moods and thus didn't feel as much positive emotion as I would have liked. I was experiencing increasing health problems when I first began using PERMA, and I tended to focus on my problems rather than on what I was grateful for.

E: When it came to engagement, I could go days without knowing how to find the time to engage in my special interests, and the longer I went, the crankier I would become. I often put off my special interests as I felt guilty about engaging in them, as if I was wasting time when I should be focusing on running a household.

R: I could easily go days without connecting with people outside my immediate family because it was easier in a way to avoid socialising and relationships. Socialising can be tiring, and complicated, and I can hit moods when I just want to avoid it. But I feel down when I don't see other people, and I tend to forget that the world exists outside my bubble. Connecting with other people helps me put myself and my life into perspective. Although my friends and extended family are really important to me, I often let too much time pass between meet-ups. I need to remind myself to make an effort to see them, as arranging meet-ups doesn't just happen by itself (something that took me a long time to learn!).

M: When I asked myself about the meaning in my life, I couldn't think of anything that made me feel part of something greater than myself.

A: I rarely acknowledged my achievements. Instead, I tended to compare myself against others and I believed that I had achieved very little. As I had big career goals when I qualified as a nurse, I felt embarrassed that I was no longer working. I felt a real lack of achievement because I wasn't achieving the 'wonder woman' image that we see in the media, of women who master the parenting and work–life balance, and never appear to need time to themselves to calm their overwhelm.

As a fun experiment, I decided to try to follow the PERMA model, and to see if I could get all the elements of PERMA into my daily life. I had fantastic results.

> To incorporate PERMA into my life, I brainstormed ideas to achieve each element, and then I made a routine for myself to ensure I have all elements in my week. By simple shifts in mindset and behaviour, I was able to hugely increase my overall well-being.

BRAINSTORMING MY PERMA PLAN

(Note: Special interests are in bold text, as I noticed that special interests appeared in every element of PERMA for me.)

Positive Emotion

What can I do to increase my positive emotions?

- Start a gratitude journal.

- Share three gratitudes a day with someone.

- Spend time in nature.

- Physical activity.

- Gardening.

- Warm drinks.

- Uplifting or calm music.

- Painting.

- **Writing.**

- Drawing.

- Rest.

- Reading.

- Sewing.

- Audiobooks.

- Television shows that make me feel calm.

- **Learning about autism.**

- Having fun with my children.

- Time alone with my husband.

- **Jane Austen and Charles Dickens period dramas and books.**

- Time with people who are important to me.

Engagement

What can I do to get into a sense of flow?

- **Creative writing.**

- **Non-fiction writing.**

- Poetry.

- **Learning and reading about autism.**

- Gardening.

- **Read Jane Austen and Charles Dickens books.**

- Singing.

- Exercise.

Relationships

How can I increase and improve my connections?

- Date-night at home with husband.

- Dinner with extended family.

- Call family for chat.

- Friend meet-ups.

- Write letters.

- Send cards.

- Walks with a friend.

- Art project with a friend.

- Hobby classes like painting class; meet people with a shared interest/focus.
- **Socialise by attending events to do with writing/reading.**
- **Socialise by attending events about autism.**

Meaning

What do I enjoy belonging to or want to belong to?

- **The writing community:** when I write, I feel part of the writing community.
- **A book community.**
- **The autism community.**
- Feeling part of the mothering or parenting community.
- Feeling part of nature, or gardening.

Achievement

How can I reach more goals and increase my sense of achievement?

- Make visual goal plans and tick things off as I achieve them, even for small things like chores.
- **Set deadlines for my writing projects and acknowledge when I achieve them.**
- Get physically fitter.
- Set creative art project goals for myself.
- Have a comfortable, clean, and safe home, but not so immaculate that it doesn't feel lived in, and don't let cleaning it take up all my time.
- Be an engaged and present mother, and acknowledge myself when I am doing a good mothering job. Set small goals and projects with the children and have little celebrations when we achieve them.
- Work towards getting a big crop harvest from the garden this year.

- **Attend training on autism and/or gain qualifications.**

- **Write book on autism.**

- Read a classic novel by an author that is new to me.

- **Aim to read all the Jane Austen and Charles Dickens books that I have not read yet.**

Making PERMA Part of Everyday Life

My PERMA brainstorm helped me to identify what is important to me, and what things I would like more of in my life. It also allowed me to see how I can be creative about ways to increase all elements of PERMA, especially by using my special interests and passions to create opportunities for myself. Once I identified what I could do to increase the factors of well-being in my life, I made a routine to figure out how to fit these factors into my weekly schedule.

Once I had a strong routine up and running, I soon found myself enjoying doing daily tasks much more. Doing daily activities with the new mindset of intentionally doing things to increase well-being made me feel much more satisfied with my every day, and made me feel happy and proud of even the basic things I do on a daily basis, no matter how mundane the task is.

I keep my daily routine up on the noticeboard in the kitchen. My routine is not set in stone. It is simply my own recommended guide to my day. Using my ideas from my PERMA brainstorm, I made sure to factor something of each PERMA element into my daily routine.

I also include my basic needs in this routine. The more my basic needs are met, the more things I can do for my well-being. I therefore include meals, drinks, and my sleep routine. As I sometimes experience physical mobility difficulties, it's vital that I also factor in daily exercise and rest, to give my body its best chance of functioning well.

A positive side-effect of having the routine up on the wall is that if I'm very tired or stressed, I can just look at my routine and it reduces the mental thinking I have to do to get through the day. This ensures I remember to prioritise the things that are important to me. This is important, as it's when we are under par that we need to increase our well-being the most.

EXAMPLE OF A DAILY ROUTINE (ON A SCHOOL DAY)

Morning:

- 07:00–07:30: Breakfast (basic need).

- 07:30: Get children ready for school (achievement, meaning, relationships).

- 08:45: Chores (achievement).

- 09:30: Drink water (basic need).

  Do physical exercise (basic need, achievement).

- 10:00: Write (engagement, achievement, meaning) with warm drink.

- 12:00: Options:

  - Meet a friend (relationships).

  - Go out into nature, e.g. gardening or walk (positive feeling, meaning).

  - Do things I need to do, e.g. go to the shop (achievement).

Afternoon:

- 13:00–14:00: Lunch and a drink (basic needs).

- 14:30: School run.

  Prioritise parenting (relationships, achievements).

- 16:00: Physical rest with audiobook (basic need).

- 16:45: Cook dinner (achievement).

- 17:30: Eat dinner as family (basic need, relationships).

- 18:00: Chores – tidy up after dinner (achievement).

Evening:

- 18:30: Connect with someone: make a phone call; write a letter; write cards (relationships).

- 19:00: Prioritise parenting: children's bedtime routine, story time etc. (achievement, meaning).

- 20:00–20:30: Rest/read/telly. Creative time if I'm not too tired, e.g. sewing (engagement, meaning, achievement).

  Text my daily three gratitudes to my gratitude group (positive emotion).

- 21:00–21:30: Start my bedtime routine: get into pyjamas, wash teeth, hot water bottle in bed (basic needs).

  Telly/reading special interest (meaning).

- 22:00–22:30: Go to bed, read, and sleep (basic needs).

Additions to routine:

- Twice a week: Try to socialise with people outside my immediate family (relationships).

- Every second Monday morning: Physical trainer session (basic needs and achievement).

- Every fortnight: Psychotherapy session (basic needs).

- Tuesday night: Singing class (positive emotion, engagement).

- Friday night: Home date with husband, e.g. a candlelit meal and board game (relationship, positive emotion).

- Weekends: Try to see family every weekend (relationships).

- Every season: Try to attend conference, webinar, training session, or event about either writing, books, or autism (meaning, achievement).

What Are Special Interests?

There is a stereotyped image that autistic special interests tend to be something complicated and highly intellectual, like maths or astrophysics, and that autistic people go on to win Nobel prizes because of their special interest. There's another stereotype that autistic people are antisocial people with non-talking interests like fixing clocks.

I think many people think that autistic people have only one special interest, and it's such a hyper-fixation that it drowns out other interests and social skills. I believe these stereotypes have come from mainstream media, and that the incorrect stereotyping of what constitutes a special interest has contributed to many autistic people not receiving a diagnosis or recognition that they are autistic.

In actual fact, a special interest can be anything at all. Examples of special interests include fashion, dogs, knitting, carpentry, computer coding, history, gardening, nature, painting, animals, poetry, religion, physics, specific topics, or political ideas. A special interest is something you feel deeply about that preoccupies your mind; something you want to spend a lot of time (possibly excessive amounts) thinking about or doing. Many autistic people make their careers out of their special interests for this reason.

To me, a special interest is something that brings me joy as it fills me with passion or gives me a sense of meaning. It's something I can fixate on and forget about my anxieties or troubles. Special interests make the world feel right, almost as though they soothe my soul.

Intense and Repetitive Interests

Alongside special interests, a lot of autistic people have intense interests, or interests they engage in very regularly.

I repeatedly watch certain television shows (I'm talking watching full series from beginning to end, again and again). This isn't exactly a special interest, as I don't get fixated on the TV show, and I can potter about and do other things with the show on in the background. I do however crave these shows and get an intense sense of calm when I watch them. Those who devised the DSM-5 (the American Psychiatry Association's handbook for diagnosis, including diagnosing autism) may call this a 'repetitive behaviour', but I call it a 'long-lasting love'. I feel lucky to be able to love things so intensely, and to have things that bring me a high level of calm or joy when I need it.

I think non-autistic people can think that repetitive behaviours are a cause of stress or anxiety for autistic people, but actually the opposite is often true. *It is not the cause of anxiety, it is my cure for anxiety.* Yes I watch things repeatedly when I am more anxious, and thus I 'engage in repetitive behaviour' more when I am stressed, but this is a coping strategy to self-soothe.

In his book *The Complete Guide to Asperger's Syndrome*, Tony Attwood

(2015) states that the three main tools to decrease agitation in autistic children are:

1. physical release of energy

2. solitude

3. engaging in their special interest.

I believe this can also be applied to adults. *Engaging in our special interests or passions is one of the most powerful things we can do to regulate and calm ourselves.* If you don't know what your special interests or passions are, it's a priority to find one by testing out different activities and interests until something feels really good. Special interests don't always find you – sometimes you have to go and find one yourself.

Special Interests and the PERMA Model

Special interests and passions are not only an important tool to help us calm our agitation or anxiety, they are also a wonderful way of getting all the elements of PERMA into your life. When I was filling in my PERMA list, I realised that my special interests found their way into each of the different areas. They were therefore a priority in my routine planning, and I needed to make sure I had plenty of opportunity to engage in these interests.

When Special Interests or Passions Feel Like a Problem

As important as special interests and passions are, there is a tipping point at which they can become a problem. If you realise you are spending too much time on a special interest, to the detriment of other responsibilities or relationships, it's really important to question why this is happening. *Don't presume that the problem is that you have hyper-fixated on the special interest just because you are autistic, because it's more likely that you're over-obsessing about the special interest to prevent yourself feeling uncomfortable emotions (e.g. loneliness or anxiety), or because you are stressed.* Look for the cause, not the symptom.

When one of my special interests is taking over, it's a sign that something is wrong with my mental health, or I'm suffering too much stress. For example, I recently realised that I had become compulsively obsessed with Jane Austen novels. I could read nothing but Jane Austen novels (repeatedly), and when I couldn't read one, I listened to them on audiobook. I kept watching TV adaptations of her books, and was scrolling online non-stop through images of Jane Austen-style houses and clothes. I found myself getting frustrated if I wasn't engaged at any moment with something to do with Jane Austen.

It took a while for me to realise this was happening, and it was actually my daughter who pointed it out to me, when she said '*Pride and Prejudice* again?' My first reaction was to blame my autistic self for letting myself become too obsessed. But when I examined it, I realised that I was really struggling with changes happening in the house, including having workmen around. The special interest was therefore a soothing strategy, but I was over-dependent on that one strategy, when actually I needed a multi-strategy approach.

I made myself take a step back from this special interest, so that I could think about what other strategies I could use. Using only one self-soothing strategy clearly wasn't working, as it was creating its own stress – i.e. feeling stressed when I wasn't engaged in the interest – and it wasn't tackling my sensory stress.

Taking a small break from all things Jane Austen allowed me to think up a fuller plan. The new plan needed to tackle my sensory stress, executive function stress (caused by the increase in demands upon me, such as buying equipment for the workmen, and making sure the kids were ready for school a bit earlier), and the social stress (from having people in the house and thus always having to think about how I behaved and what I said and how I said it). The new plan included: using ear defenders to block out the workmen's noise, taking regular breaks from the house, drawing up a visual plan of what the new home layout would look like so the changes would become predictable, and listening to a Jane Austen audiobook once a day for an hour only. I also reduced all other demands on my executive function by cancelling non-essential appointments or social engagements. By doing all these things, my daily life became easier, and my obsessive compulsive need to engage with Jane Austen novels shrank naturally, thus reducing the stress I felt when I wasn't able to engage in this interest.

Signs that my special interest has become too intense:

- When I cannot feel calm unless I'm engaged in the interest.
- When I feel excessively frustrated with the everyday demands on me outside my special interest, such as meeting my children's needs.

- When I want to spend all my time engaged in my interest rather than connecting with people and the world around me.

- When my special interest stops me meeting my basic needs, for example if it repeatedly keeps me awake at night or if it makes me repeatedly forget to eat.

- When my mind is constantly preoccupied with my special interest to the point that I get exhausted from my own obsession, and I can start to dislike my own obsessive compulsive need to be engaged in my special interest.

Another problem I've had with special interests is making the mistake of tying too much of my identity up with one special interest. A few years ago, I went through a time when I only felt 'good' when I was writing fiction novels. I felt dissatisfied if I didn't write 1000 words a day. I didn't realise that I had post-natal depression (and probably a large dollop of autistic burnout, see Chapter 16) at the time, and I was overly relying on my special interest to make me feel like I was not just a mum, but that I was someone in my own right too. I felt like I had lost a lot of my identity since I became a mum, and this created a huge emptiness inside me. But instead of my writing helping me, it was taking over, and making me more detached from connecting with people.

I remember feeling angry at my children's needs demanding my time, as it meant I lost my writing time. I wanted to spend hours each day writing, and because I couldn't do this, I started continuously thinking about writing instead, figuring out my plots and developing my characters in my head. My thoughts were only on my stories, instead of engaging fully with my babies. I didn't want to socialise with people because it took time away from writing, or thinking about my books. I was spending my evenings writing. If my daughter had a nightmare, I resented the time it took from my writing. If my baby was unable to sleep, I lost my temper (not at the baby, thankfully) because I felt my 'mum job' was done for the day and now it should be my 'writer job' time. When this happened, I knew that to be the best mother that I could be, I needed to stop this obsession with writing. *I believe it is important to prioritise significant relationships over special interests, particularly if you have dependents.*

At first I tried to reduce the time I spent writing, but I found it continued to preoccupy my mind and my lack of time writing actually caused me more stress. Alas, I realised that I had to take a complete break from it. I did not know I was autistic at the time, and thus did not know that I was simply over-relying on one soothing strategy. I believe now that if I had tackled the depression and identity problems, I could have found a balance in which to write and be a great mum at the same time.

So I gave up the thing that brought me the most passion, so that I could re-find my passion and joy for the rest of my life. It worked, and I was able to get back into writing after a few months, once I had established a better life balance with the help of psychotherapy and my family.

It's important to say here that *I don't think it's possible to just cut a special interest out of your life without replacing it with something else.* I see it like one of those old fashioned see-saw-type weighing scales. If I take my writing away, I will feel unbalanced, and so I need to add other things in, to re-balance the scales. When I say I will feel unbalanced, I mean I will feel down, despair, anxiety, or maybe even depression.

When I made myself stop writing, I realised that I needed to add something else creative in. I discovered that I love all sorts of creative activities, including drawing, sewing, and painting. There is no other art form that fulfils me as much as writing, but I still love other forms of creativity, and they all act as soothing strategies for me.

Unhealthy Special Interests

Caution needs to be taken around what your special interest is, to make sure it is not harming you or other people. Sometimes special interests can develop out of hobbies, new activities, or skills, so I always believe *it's important to ask yourself 'Is this a healthy activity if I become a bit (or a lot) more obsessed with it?'*

For example, calorie counting may start as a way to eat healthily, but if it becomes a special interest, care needs to be taken to prevent it turning into an eating disorder. Research studies have found high rates of autism among adults with eating disorders, with some studies finding rates of 20–30% (Solmi et al. 2020).

A special interest I've seen become a problem is computer gaming. Modern, commercialised computer games are designed to be addictive, and thus play right into the autistic special interest mindset. Computer games can be so addictive, in fact, that the World Health Organization has added a new mental health disorder called 'gaming disorder' to the *International Classification of Diseases*, 11th edition (also known as the ICD-11). While gaming disorder is rare, addiction to games can lead to exclusion of other daily activities, negative changes in physical and psychological health, and reduced social functioning (World Health Organization 2018). A review of 12 research studies found that autistic children, teenagers, and adults are at higher risk of problematic video gaming compared to non-autistic people (Craig et al. 2021).

Other ideas of special interests that can become unhealthy include harmful political ideologies, social media, and gambling.

Research on Special Interests

A study of 443 autistic adults in 2018 found that having a special interest improved quality of life, as it improved leisure-time subjective well-being (Grove et al. 2018). Approximately two-thirds of the participants said they had a special interest, with more males than females having a special interest.

Most participants had more than one special interest. The most common special interests were computers, gaming, the topic of autism, music, nature, art, and gardening.

Participants did not see special interests as an obstacle to their functioning. However, 'a very high intensity of engagement with special interests' did correlate with reduced subjective well-being. The research paper suggests that when people have low levels of subjective well-being, they may engage in special interests as a coping mechanism rather than out of self-motivation.

This study mirrors my own experience. *Having a special interest improves my well-being, but when the special interest takes over or becomes too intense, it may suggest reduced well-being.*

KEY POINTS

◊ The PERMA model is an example of a model that can be used to identify what is important to bring meaning to your life.

◊ Autistic people can improve their well-being by making special interests part of their daily life.

◊ Making a daily routine can help ensure you find time for what's important to bringing meaning to your every day.

◊ Caution needs to be taken with special interests as they can become a problem when they are engaged in too often, or if they cause harm to you or others.

References

Attwood, T. (2015) *The Complete Guide to Asperger's Syndrome*. London: Jessica Kingsley Publishers.

Craig, F., Tenuta, F., De Giacomo, A., Trabacca, A., and Costabile, A. (2021) 'A Systematic Review of Problematic Video-Game Use in People with Autism Spectrum Disorders'. *Research in Autism Spectrum Disorders* 82 (3), 101726. http://dx.doi.org/10.1016/j.rasd.2021.101726

Grove, R., Hoekstra, R.A., Wierda, M., and Begeer, S. (2018) 'Special Interests and Subjective Well-Being in Autistic Adults'. *Autism Research* 11 (5), 766–775. https://doi.org/10.1002/aur.1931

Seligman, M. (2012) 'PERMA'. Accessed 11 June 2021 at: www.youtube.com/watch?v=iK6K_N2qe9Y

Solmi, F., Bentivenga, F., Bould, H., Mandy, W., Kothari, R., Rai, D., Skuse, D., and Lewis, G. (2020) 'Trajectories of Autistic Social Traits in Childhood and Adolescence and Disordered Eating Behaviours at Age 14 Years: A UK General Population Cohort Study'. *The Journal of Child Psychology and Psychiatry* 62 (1), 75–85. https://doi.org/10.1111/jcpp.13255

World Health Organization (2018) 'Addictive Behaviours: Gaming Disorders'. Accessed 10 October 2021 at: www.who.int/news-room/q-a-detail/addictive-behaviours-gaming-disorder

PART 2

SENSORY SELF-CARE

Chapter 5

The Sensory System and Autism

CHAPTER AIMS

› To explain what the sensory system is and how it works in the human body.
› To discuss how the majority of autistic people have differences in sensory integration, compared to non-autistic people.
› To recognise that no two autistic people have the same sensory system.

What Is the Sensory System?

> The aim of our sensory system is to tell us:
>
> 1. what's going on inside our body (e.g. if we are hungry, if we are in pain, if we feel sick etc.)
>
> 2. what's going on outside our body in the world around us (e.g. if the air feels cold on our skin, if there's loud music on, what food tastes like etc.).

Our bodies are full of senses which collect information from both inside and outside our bodies. These senses then send this information to our nervous system. The nervous system, which includes the brain, nerves, and spinal cord, decides what to do with the information. This system of collecting information, organising the information, and doing something about the information is called the sensory system.

Sensory Stimuli

Anything that activates our sensory system is called a sensory stimulus, i.e. the thing that makes one of our senses recognise that it is getting information. For example, if we hear an alarm ringing, the alarm is the sensory stimulus that activates our sound sense. The sound sense sends a message to the brain to tell it that there is an alarm ringing.

What Are the Senses in the Sensory System?

I remember being taught in school that there are five senses: sight, sound, taste, touch, and smell. However, these senses only collect information from *outside* our bodies, to tell us what's going on in the world around us, and how the world around us is affecting us.

But we also need to collect information from inside our bodies in order to function and survive. We need senses to tell us what our body needs or wants: if we are thirsty, if we are overheating, if we feel pain, if our body is off-balance and we might fall, and much more.

There are a lot more than five senses. For the purposes of this book, I will discuss the main eight senses that are relevant to autistic people. I use my own system of categorisation by naming groups of senses 'The Anchor Senses', 'The Basic Need Sense', and 'The Famous Five Senses'.

Senses That Tell Us What's Going On Inside Our Bodies
The Anchor Senses

1. *The Vestibular Sense*: Balance, and the position of your head.

2. *The Proprioception Sense*: This is the body's awareness of its own position. Another way to explain this is your ability to know where your body is in relation to the environment you are in. Sometimes referred to as 'where you are in space'.

The Basic Need Sense

1. *The Interoception Sense*: What you feel inside your body, including physical changes (e.g. heart rate, breathing rate), hunger, your temperature, thirst, pain, and your emotions.

Senses That Tell Us What's Going On Outside Our Bodies
The Famous Five Senses

1. *Sound (Auditory)*: What we hear in the world.

2. *Sight (Visual)*: What we see.

3. *Smell (Olfactory)*: What we smell.

4. *Taste (Gustatory)*: What we taste.

5. *Touch (Tactile)*: What we feel through touch.

Why I Categorise the Senses

I use my own made-up category names for the eight main senses, so if you go to an occupational therapist and say that you want to work on your 'Anchor Senses', your 'Basic Need Sense', or your 'Famous Five Senses' they will probably not know what you are talking about!

The reason I have categorised the senses in this way is to avoid focusing only on the Famous Five Senses, like so many people do without realising. This helps me to achieve greater sensory balance. *In my experience, if I focus on the Anchor and Basic Need Senses first, then the Famous Five Senses need a lot less attention.*

Regulating my Anchor Senses helps me to feel grounded, safe, and steady. Paying attention to my Basic Need Sense helps me to look after myself, and ensure my basic needs are met. This allows me to stay calmer, to achieve better emotional regulation, and also frees my attention up to look after my Famous Five Senses. Remember that the Famous Five Senses collect information about the world around us, and in my experience we cannot always control the world around us. We therefore need to be prepared and able to deal with stressors on our Famous Five Senses. *Once my Anchor Senses are grounded, and my basic needs are met, it is a lot easier to look after whatever the world throws at my Famous Five Senses.*

I use this system of categorising the senses for the general management of my sensory regulation, but of course sometimes the senses don't fall neatly into a sense either 'outside' or 'inside' the body. For example, if we smell our own breath, we are smelling something from inside our own bodies, but we are using the smell sense, which I categorise as a sense collecting information from outside our body. So I acknowledge that there are exceptions to my system of categorisation.

What Is Sensory Integration?

Sensory integration is the process of collecting information through our senses, organising that information, and responding to the information appropriately.

The steps of sensory integration include:

1. *Taking information in*: The senses gather information from inside the body, and from the world outside our body.

2. *Sorting information out*: The sensory system organises the information being collected through our senses, and makes sure that the correct part of the nervous system receives each bit of the information. Note that we can receive many pieces of information, from one sense or from multiple senses, at any one time.

3. *Processing information*: The nervous system tries to make sense of the information.

4. *Planning how to react*: The nervous system decides how to react to the information.

5. *Reacting*: The nervous system makes the body react through movement (this is called a motor response) or other appropriate responses.

Sensory Integration and Autism

Autistic people have a greater tendency to have difficulties with sensory integration, when compared to non-autistic people. Research has found that about 80–90% of autistic people have difficulties with sensory integration (Galiana-Simal et al. 2020). Sensory integration differences are not unique to autism however; they can also be found in non-autistic people, premature babies, people with ADHD and more.

Sensory integration differences or difficulties are considered an important factor when assessing a person for autism, and both the World Health Organization's diagnostic tool, the ICD-11 (*International Classification of Diseases*, 11th edition), and the American diagnostic tool, the DSM-5 (*Diagnostic and Statistical Manual of Mental Disorders*, 5th edition), include assessing sensory integration differences as part of their autism diagnostic process. It is, however, important to note that not all autistic people have significant differences in their sensory integration system.

The fact that autistic people often experience difficulties or differences in their ability to process sensory information is one of the reasons behind the saying 'Autistic people experience the world differently'. We do, actually, take in information about the world around us in a different way to non-autistic people. *Naturally, if we take information in differently, or if we process that information differently, we will react differently.* For example, a non-autistic person may see a bright glaring light and think to themselves, 'that light is very bright' and then continue about their business. An autistic person may see a bright glaring light and feel suddenly anxious, or under attack. Surely you can't go about your business if you feel under attack, and so you will react differently to the light; you might block out the light, or hide from it, or feel suddenly dysregulated.

Despite what some people think, autistic children don't conveniently grow out of their sensory differences when they become adults. *As autistic adults, we may learn to manage our sensory challenges better, but constantly working to manage an overwhelmed or stressed sensory system does take its toll.* Personally, I find my sensory system is getting more sensitive as I get older, and requires a lot more attention to keep it regulated. This can be exhausting.

Terminology: Sensory Processing Difference or Disorder

The terms sensory processing disorder and sensory processing difference are used somewhat interchangeably, and are both abbreviated to SPD. You may see these phrases in diagnostic reports, or as co-morbidities associated with autism. Increasingly, I've also noticed the term SID or 'sensory integration disorder' being used to mean the same thing. They are all terms to label having a different way of taking in, processing, organising, and reacting to sensory information.

In this book, when I say SPD, I mean sensory processing difference, so I can avoid using the word disorder. This is an idealistic choice of mine, because in an ideal world, the sensory environment would always be adapted to suit the needs of people with sensory processing differences. It is only when the environment is wrong that it becomes a disorder.

Unfortunately, the environment is often wrong, and so I often feel like my sensory processing differences are a disorder. They can, in fact, disable me from functioning or joining in with society. I have often had to leave situations, such as shops or social gatherings, because my sensory system became too overwhelmed. I have walked away from appointments because the smell of air freshener in the waiting room was so intense. I can't always join in with things that other people take for granted, such as skating in noisy ice rinks at Christmas, or watching a movie in the cinema when the cinema is full to the brim with people slurping soft drinks and rustling sweet packets and chewing popcorn. My SPD can therefore disable me from joining in with normal societal activities.

What Actually Happens in SPD?

Sensory difficulties or differences can show themselves in many ways. The difficulty can happen at any part, or multiple parts, of the process of gathering, organising, and reacting to sensory information. It's important to remember that if you do not gather information correctly, or process it correctly, you will probably not respond to it correctly. There are many ways that SPD can manifest, including the following:

- *A sense may not gather information correctly.* For example, if you go outside on a cold day, and your body doesn't gather the correct information about the air temperature, you will not know that it is cold and you won't put on a coat. This failure to react to the cold may cause you to feel distressed or dysregulated without knowing why; just because you don't know you are cold doesn't mean that your body is not cold.

- *Too much information can cause a traffic jam in your brain.* For example, if you go to a busy shopping centre, you might be bombarded with sensory information such as loud noise, bright lights, too many visual patterns, strong smells etc. Your brain may struggle to process all the information at once, and a traffic jam of information blocks up your brain. This makes it hard (or impossible) to think how to respond appropriately to each piece of information. When this happens me, I can find it hard to think at all, and have often automatically covered my ears and closed my eyes for a few seconds to restart my thinking (this is something that I do without even noticing, and it was actually my husband who pointed this out to me).

- *We may react inappropriately to sensory information.* For example, we may know we are hearing a loud noise that is hurting our ears, but our brain may be unable to come up with an appropriate response. I've experienced one of my autistic children reacting so inappropriately to loud noise that they jeopardised their safety. This happened when a loud truck drove past, and my daughter experienced such an intense over-reaction to the noise that she bolted onto the road and put herself in danger from the traffic. Thus her reaction to the loud noise is what became the actual danger, rather than the noise itself. This is an extreme example, but it's important to note that some reactions can be extreme. In my own daily life, my reactions are much more subtle, such as feeling panicked from white noise and having to turn the extractor fan off when cooking, or having to leave an environment with an intense smell.

- *Your brain may tell your body how to react to sensory information, but the body doesn't follow the brain's instructions correctly.* This is a particularly frustrating part of SPD for me, and only tends to happen me when I'm exhausted, very stressed, and anxious. For example, I hear a loud noise and think 'I want to walk away from the noise', but my body freezes and won't move away. Another example, and something that has happened many times, is that I pick up something hot, and I recognise it's hot, and I make the decision to put the hot thing back down on the table. But instead of reaching out for the table, my hand just drops the hot thing. I have dropped many potatoes on the floor from this! It rarely happens if I'm holding an object with both hands, it seems more common for me when an object is only in one hand. I know what to do, but my body doesn't do it.

Sensory Seeking and Sensory Avoiding

No two autistic people are the same, and all autistic people have unique sensory integration systems. For example, I hate white noise (especially the noise of an extractor fan) and so I avoid it as much as possible. But lots of autistic people love white noise, and seek it out by filling their environment with it, or by using it to help themselves get to sleep.

> SPD can manifest in many ways, sometimes through your need to avoid certain sensory stimuli, and sometimes to seek out certain sensory stimuli.

Sensory Avoiding

This means avoiding a sensory stimulus because you over-respond to it. For example:

- You may over-respond to a noise, and thus avoid it by covering your ears (sound avoiding).

- You may over-respond to tags on clothes, and avoid them by cutting them off (touch avoiding).

- If you over-respond to the taste of toothpaste, you may avoid it by not brushing your teeth (taste avoiding).

Sensory Seeking

This means seeking out a particular sensory stimuli because you crave it, or because you under-respond to it. For example:

- You may seek out movements that involve changing your balance, such as leaning your chair backwards to balance or swing on the back legs, or walking on the edge of curbs (vestibular seeking).

- You may seek out sensory stimulation to the joints in your body through deep pressure, such as crashing yourself down heavily on couches, or leaning into things like walls to feel the deep pressure against your body (proprioceptive seeking).

- If you under-respond to some tastes, you may seek out very strong flavours, for example by adding a lot of salt to your food (taste seeking).

Both Sensory Seeking and Avoiding

You can both seek and avoid stimulation of the same sense at the same time. For example:

- I often avoid certain smells I dislike by smelling scents that I love, such as soap or essential oils. In this case, I seek one smell in order to avoid a different smell.

- You may feel unable to tolerate gentle touch, but seek firm or deep touch. For example, you may dislike someone stroking your skin gently, but love them hugging you tightly. In this scenario, your touch sense over-reacts to the light touch and so you avoid it, but your touch sense may seek and love deep touch. Alternatively, your proprioceptive senses may be the sense that is seeking input here, and thus you crave a tight hug to bring deep pressure to your body.

SPD in Autistic People with ADHD

Out of all autistic people, 30–80% also have a diagnosis or symptoms of ADHD (attention deficit hyperactivity disorder) or ADD (attention deficit disorder), and the conditions are known to share genetic links (Knott et al. 2021). Autistic people and people with ADHD can experience differences in how SPD affects them, and for this reason, if you are both autistic and have ADHD, you may find some of your sensory differences particularly hard to figure out.

There is a high prevalence of SPD in people with ADHD and ADD (whether or not they are autistic), and this can have a significant impact on daily function (Engel-Yeger and Ziv-On 2011).

For example, a study that compared sensory processing patterns in higher education students with ADHD versus those with autism found that students with ADHD were significantly more likely to show sensory seeking patterns, and the autistic students were more likely to show sensory avoiding patterns (Clince et al. 2016).

I've had first-hand experience of this. When I was in university, I used to study best in quiet, empty, spacious areas. The library was ideal for this, but only if I could get the correct table away from other people, as other people are extremely noisy to me, even when they are 'quiet'. I hyper tune in to people clicking pens, whispering, tapping keyboards, writing with scrawly writing, opening doors, scraping chairs, breathing and rustling through bags. I need to shut out noise and people in order to get into a flow of work. However, a close autistic friend with ADHD was the complete opposite – his ability to study improved in busy loud places. While I avoided noise, he sought noise out, even creating his own noises when he didn't get enough from the environment. He wanted people around him, loud music on, and people talking to him. He was also constantly tapping his feet, swinging on his chair, humming, and he regularly shared his thoughts out loud. This just shows how no one size fits all, and this is the challenge in creating an environment that suits all people with SPD.

KEY POINTS

◊ Our body is full of senses, which gather information from both inside and outside our bodies.

◊ The main eight senses are sound, taste, touch, sight, smell, vestibular (balance and head position), proprioception (where you are in space), and interoception (what's happening inside the body including emotion, hunger, pain etc.).

◊ Our senses send information about our bodies and our environment to our nervous system. The nervous system comprises our brain, nerves, and spinal cord.

◊ Sensory integration is the process of gathering information through our senses, interpreting the information, and reacting appropriately to the information.

◊ Autistic people have very high rates of experiencing difficulty or differences in sensory integration.

◊ Sensory seeking means seeking out a certain experience for your senses.

◊ Sensory avoiding means your body over-reacts to a sensory experience, and thus you avoid exposure to that experience, e.g. covering your ears from loud noise.

◊ You can seek sensory stimulation at the same time as avoiding other sensory stimulation.

◊ Autistic people with ADHD may experience SPD differently.

References

Clince, M., Connolly, L., and Nolan, C. (2016) 'Comparing and Exploring the Sensory Processing Patterns of Higher Education Students with Attention Deficit Hyperactivity Disorder and Autism Spectrum Disorder'. *American Journal of Occupational Therapy* 70 (2), 1–9. https://doi.org/10.5014/ajot.2016.016816

Engel-Yeger, B. and Ziv-On, D. (2011) 'The Relationship between Sensory Processing Difficulties and Leisure Activity Preference of Children with Different Types of ADHD'. *Research in Developmental Disabilities* 32, 1154–1162. https://doi.org/10.1016/j.ridd.2011.01.008

Galiana-Simal, A., Vela-Romero, M., Romero-Vela, V.M., Oliver-Tercero, N., Garcia-Olma, V., Benito-Castellanos, P.J., Munoz-Martinez, V., and Beato-Fernandez, L. (2020) 'Sensory Processing Disorder: Key Points of a Frequent Alteration in Neurodevelopmental Disorders'. *Cogent Medicine* 7 (1), 1736829. https://doi.org/10.1080/2331205X.2020.1736829

Knott, R., Johnston, B.P., Tiego, L., Mellahn, O., Finlay, A., et al. (2021) 'The Monash Autism-ADHD Genetics and Neurodevelopmental (Magnet) Project Design and Methodologies: A Dimensional Approach to Understanding Neurobiological and Genetic Aetiology'. *Molecular Autism* 12 (1), 55. https://doi.org/10.1186/s13229-021-00457-3

Chapter 6

Getting to Know Your Own Sensory System

CHAPTER BREAKDOWN

CHAPTER AIMS

› To discuss the value of getting to know your own sensory system, as no two autistic people have the same sensory profile.
› To explore what might change your reaction to sensory stimuli, and how a sensory profile can change with different factors.
› To help you learn to identify your sensory triggers using the detective habit.

Introduction

I wasn't aware of how much sensory stress I had in my life until I began to truly understand autism and the sensory system. I couldn't understand why I seemed to get so stressed or exhausted from daily activities, and why I could go from feeling completely calm to feeling suddenly overwhelmed. What's more, I couldn't understand why this was getting more and more frequent the older I got.

Once I learnt about sensory processing and how autistic people are prone to having sensory differences, I began to investigate my own responses to sensory stimuli. I had to really pay attention to which sensory system was being triggered in different scenarios, in order to start to understand my sensory triggers. If you asked me five years ago if I had SPD, I would have said no, I'm just an anxious person. I didn't realise that a huge chunk of my daily anxiety was a direct result of my SPD.

Once I began to learn what my triggers were, I started to come up with ways to prevent myself becoming overwhelmed. I try not to avoid situations and activities just because there will be sensory triggers; instead I try to support myself and use strategies to allow me attend as many activities as I want to. Sometimes I feel like my sensory system is my fourth child, as it requires so much attention, planning, and care. Thankfully, once I give this attention to my sensory system, it thrives, and adult life becomes much easier.

I have learnt a lot about sensory integration through my children's occupational therapists, attending courses, doing training, and reading. However, *it is important to note that I am not an occupational therapist.* If, having read the sensory self-care chapters in this book, you feel you could benefit from more information about your own sensory system, then I recommend getting in touch with an occupational therapist who specialises in sensory integration therapy. A good occupational therapist, with this specialisation, will help you to identify your sensory needs, and make an individualised plan to support your own unique sensory system.

Discovering your Own Sensory Differences

By the time an autistic person is an adult, they probably know many of their sensory differences and difficulties. I knew I hated velvet, even though I didn't know this was because I have SPD. You might know that you don't like loud noises, or certain flavours or textures. But there might be other sensory differences that you have not yet recognised in yourself. You might be unaware of the unconscious reactions your body has to the sensory environment. Or you might be experiencing so many sensory stressors at once that you are only able to pinpoint your body's stress reaction to one or two sensory triggers, when in fact there may be many more.

I really recommend spending time and effort trying to get to know your sensory system. It can be difficult to start recognising your sensory triggers, and it doesn't happen overnight. It's a process, with every new experience giving you a little bit more information towards understanding your own sensory system. The more you pay attention to your sensory system and how you react, the more information you will gather. Chapters 7, 8, and 9 will discuss each of the groups of senses in more detail, to help you understand each sense and spot the signs that tell you which sense may need calming or regulating.

It's important to note that our sensory system is always changing. One day you may seek out loud music and flashing lights, and another day you may detest loud music, and get an immediate pain in your eyes from flashing lights. While this can seem inconvenient as it makes it harder to get to know a system that is always changing, I also think it's extremely positive as it means that we don't have to fully write off a sensory trigger just because we react negatively to it once, or sometimes. There are many factors that can increase our reactions to sensory stimuli, and knowing what makes you more sensitive to stimuli can really help you to manage your SPD.

WHAT CAN MAKE YOU MORE LIKELY TO REACT TO A SENSORY TRIGGER?

1. *An accumulation of sensory stress.* If you have been exposed to a lot of sensory triggers, and not had the opportunity to calm your sensory system between them, then your system can become overwhelmed more easily. This can make you sensitive to sensory triggers that you are not usually sensitive to. For example if I've just come home from a loud restaurant, I am much more sensitive to the loud noises and touches of my children. To support myself with this, I might sit in the car to listen to calm music with my eyes closed before I enter the house, so I can then enjoy my children's chatter and touch rather than feel overwhelmed by it.

2. *Cognitive stress.* When my mind is preoccupied, too busy, or under stress, I become much more sensitive to sensory triggers. I find it harder to calm my sensory system, and it's harder to notice that I'm feeling a build-up of sensory stress until it's too late and I'm overwhelmed. I believe this is because I am so focused on what is stressing my thoughts that I forget to pay enough attention to my body. I am also less likely to look after my basic needs when my mind is stressed, which increases my sensory reaction to triggers.

3. *Your basic needs not being met.* If your basic daily needs are not being met, including hunger, thirst etc., you are more

likely to react to sensory stimuli. If I am tired or hungry, I am much more likely to feel overwhelmed by noise and light. If I am in pain and haven't managed to control it, my body can feel hyper-sensitive, and so I react more strongly to external sensory triggers like gentle touch or balance changes.

4. *Hormonal changes.* Hormonal changes can affect our sensory integration. For women, the menstrual changes of oestrogen and progesterone have been found to affect the senses of smell, sight, sound, and taste (Farage et al. 2008). Hormones can also affect mood, and our mood can affect our sensory sensitivities. Puberty, menstruation, pregnancy, and menopausal changes can all cause changes in a woman's sensory integration. I notice a huge change in my proprioception for three days before menstruation, and my spatial awareness plummets, causing a deterioration in skills like parking the car or coordinating myself within a space.

5. *Anxiety.* When I am anxious, I need to work extra hard at regulating my sensory system. Anxiety hugely reduces my tolerance of sensory triggers, and makes me much more like to 'over-react' to sensory stimuli. A noise I can usually tolerate can become excruciating, and light can become blinding. I can find myself bumping into things, dropping things, miscalculating my distance from things, and I can get dizzy from the smallest movements.

6. *Ageing.* Some aspects of ageing can affect your sensory system. Our sense of taste can change as we age, as can our hearing, sight, and smell. Age-related joint changes can also affect your sensory system. We receive a lot of our proprioception information through our joints, but if you develop age-related joint changes such as arthritis, you can find it causes changes in your sensory system, especially in your proprioceptive sense (because our proprioception sense gathers information through our joints).

7. *Health changes.* When we experience changes in our health, we can experience differences in our sensory integration. For example, when I am in a flare of autoimmune arthritis, my proprioceptive sense deteriorates and I become clumsier.

My vestibular system also gets more sensitive and I become off-balance more easily. Another health change I've experienced is vertigo. When I experience vertigo, I become more sensitive to loud noise, bright light, and the feeling of clothes. People who smoke are more likely to experience changes to their taste senses. Diabetics are at higher risk of nerve damage, especially in their feet, and if their diabetes is not well-controlled, they may develop changes to their touch sense and their sight sense. Eyesight deterioration will affect your sight sense, but may also affect your vestibular sense, as we often assess or improve our control of our balance by using visual information (e.g. how we say to stare at one spot to get your balance when standing on one leg).

The Three Steps to Regulate Your Sensory System

Managing to regulate the sensory system when you have SPD is a time-consuming and thought-consuming task, but once you get the hang of it, it becomes second nature. I use a three-step approach to keep my senses as regulated as possible. This approach has made a huge difference to my well-being, and really helped me take control of my sensory system, rather than having it take control of me.

Three steps to regulate the sensory system:

1. 'How full is your cup?'

2. What sense or senses need soothing or regulating?

3. What sensory soothing strategies can I use to 'empty my cup'?

Step 1: 'How Full Is Your Cup?'

An excellent occupational therapist, Julie O'Sullivan, gave me the great advice to see the sensory system like a cup of water. Every new sensory trigger adds more water to the cup. If you don't empty out some of the water, the cup will eventually overflow, i.e. you get overwhelmed. Soothing and regulating your senses empties some water from the cup. The emptier the cup, the more you can fill it before it overflows.

This analogy really helps me to understand my sensory system, and I regularly ask myself 'How full is my cup?' The more attention I give to emptying my cup, the more I can tolerate sensory stimuli without becoming overwhelmed by them.

I know I need to 'empty some water from the cup' when:

- *I feel close to becoming overwhelmed*, or close to a shutdown or melt-down (see Chapter 11 for more on this).

- *One of my senses is under a lot of stress.*

- *Before I go to a new environment.* If I don't know what sensory triggers I will encounter, I prepare in advance by assuming there will be triggers.

- *Before I go to an environment that I know has a lot of sensory triggers* for me.

- *Before I go to a social event.* The less 'water in my cup' before I go, the more tolerance I will have for sensory stimuli, which will allow me to spend my energy on socialising rather than on an overloaded sensory system.

- *During a social event.* I use tools to keep emptying my cup during a social event, so I can manage the event better. If my cup starts to fill too high, my social skills go down, so it's important to use tactics and tools to keep myself as regulated as possible.

- *If I know I've been exposed to a number of sensory stimuli, even if I don't yet feel overwhelmed.* If I've been exposed to a lot of sensory stimuli, I can find it hard to predict which stimulus will be the one that fills the cup to overflowing. I therefore need to make sure I keep 'emptying the cup' so there's room at the top of the cup for more, or unexpected, sensory stimuli.

- *After a social event.* The more stressful the socialising, the more I need to take time to empty the cup. I might not notice the sensory stress building up when I'm at a social occasion, but the minute I leave and my brain stops having to work so hard at the socialising side of things, I will feel the aftermath of all the sensory stress in my body. Sometimes this can hit me like a sudden downpour of rain. I can go from thinking I feel fine, to suddenly feeling terrible, or even doomed, shaking, finding the light blinding, finding all noise painful, and feeling dizzy or crying.

Step 2: Identifying Which Sense or Senses
Need Soothing or Regulating

If I want to empty some water from my cup, I first try to pinpoint which sense, or senses, needs help. Another way to think of this is 'which sense can I soothe in order to empty some water from my cup?' It's not always easy to know which sense to soothe in order to increase your tolerance of sensory stimulation, so I ask myself these questions:

Identifying which sense to soothe:

- *Is it obvious which sense is being triggered?* If I know that loud music is triggering me, then I know I need to soothe my sound sense.

- *Is more than one thing triggering this sense?* For example, if I am suddenly reacting to a tag on my clothes, is the tag the only thing triggering my touch sense? For me, if my clothes become wet, I am more likely to over-react to all touch triggers. So if my trousers have damp patches from rain, my neck is more likely to react to a tag on my top. I need to soothe my touch sense, keeping in mind that the wet patch is the biggest culprit.

- *Is more than one sense stressed at the same time?* In a supermarket, I might think the loud noise is the sensory trigger making me feel stressed, but it might actually be an accumulation of noise, bright lights, strong smells etc. I therefore need to soothe as many of these senses as possible.

- *If you don't know which sense is triggered, look for clues*: If I can't identify the sense I need to soothe, but I know that my sensory system feel stressed, I use a version of the detective habit (Chapter 2) to try and look for clues to figure it out. If I feel dizzy, maybe my vestibular sense has over-reacted. If I feel nauseous, maybe I'm reacting to a smell. If I feel like my head is throbbing, maybe I'm reacting to a loud noise. *The more attention you pay to how you feel, and the more you record these reactions and the possible causes, the more you will spot patterns that will help you identify your triggers.*

- *If I still can't figure out the trigger*: If I can't figure out the sensory trigger, or if I'm feeling really overwhelmed and my brain just won't work for me, then I need to work on soothing as many senses as possible. If I'm at home, I might go to bed, close the blackout blinds, hug a hot water bottle, and put on a weighted blanket. If I'm not at home, I might go outside for fresh air, wearing sunglasses. This calms my sight sense, my sound sense, my smell sense, probably my touch sense. Leaning against a wall can ground my proprioceptive sense, and squatting down and putting my head down below my heart can soothe my vestibular sense. Alternatively I sit alone in the car with music on, close my eyes and allow my senses to calm.

Preparing for sensory triggers in advance:

- *If I am predicting that one of my senses will be stressed in an environment I am going to, I soothe that sense before I go*: For example, if I'm going to a party that I know will be noisy, I will make sure to soothe my sound sense with silence or calm music before I go. If I'm going outside on a very bright day, I soothe my sight sense before I go by having a rest in darkness, and preparing for the bright light by bringing sunglasses.

- *Pre-emptively soothing the sensory system in general*: If I am working on pre-emptively 'emptying my cup' before I go to an activity, and I can't predict which senses will be triggered, then I can choose which sense or senses to soothe. The more the merrier.

Step 3: Using Sensory Soothing Strategies

In order to regulate my sensory system, and 'empty my cup', I use one of my sensory soothing strategies. Chapters 7, 8, and 9 will explain each of the groups of senses in more detail, with sensory soothing strategies for each specific sense.

KEY POINTS

◊ No two autistic people have the same sensory differences, so it's important to spend some time figuring out your unique sensory profile.

◊ There are many factors that can affect how your sensory system processes information, such as your health status, your hormones etc.

◊ Seeing your sensory system as like a cup of water can help you become aware of when you need to soothe your sensory system by 'emptying some water'.

◊ Paying attention to and recording how your feel can help you spot patterns that will help you identify your sensory triggers.

References

Farage, M.A., Osborn, T.W., and McClean, A.B. (2008) 'Cognitive, Sensory, and Emotional Changes Associated with Menstrual Cycle: A Review'. *Archives of Gynaecology and Obstetrics* 278 (4), 299–307. https://doi.org/10.1007/s00404-008-0708-2

Chapter 7

The Anchor Senses: Vestibular and Proprioception

CHAPTER BREAKDOWN

CHAPTER AIMS

› To introduce the Anchor Senses: the vestibular and proprioceptive senses.
› To explain how regulating the Anchor Senses can also help regulate the other senses.
› To give ideas about how to regulate the Anchor Senses.

What Are the Anchor Senses?

The vestibular and proprioception senses are what I like to call the Anchor Senses. Thinking of them as anchors helps me visualise how important they are in keeping me grounded.

Regulating the vestibular and proprioceptive senses is like dropping an anchor to ground yourself. Once grounded, the other senses can be managed much more easily.

Without the 'anchor dropped', the other senses are harder to regulate, harder to recognise, and sensory stress will build up a lot faster.

To further explain this, I ask you to imagine you are on a boat in a choppy sea:

Imagine you are struggling to keep your balance, because the boat is swaying so much that it's hard to stay upright. While you feel so off-balance, and have to work so hard to stop yourself falling over, are you able to enjoy:

- The beautiful sight of the ocean and sky?

- The smell of sea air?

- The sound of the waves?

- The touch of the wind?

- The taste of salt sea spray?

No, of course you aren't. If your vestibular (balance) sense is challenged, then you can't use your other senses properly.

Now imagine the air is so full of fog that you can't find your bearings. You don't know where exactly you are on the boat; you don't know if you are close to the side of the boat and at risk of falling overboard, or if you're going to trip on something on the ground. You are not aware of where your body is in your environment. Your proprioceptive sense (the body-awareness sense) is challenged.

Now consider this: what happens if you hear a sudden loud noise? I know I would feel panicked, and assume the noise means that more danger is coming. The noise could even be the sound of a rescue helicopter, or a rescue boat beeping its horn, but for a few seconds all that noise does is send you into further anxiety.

If you live your daily life without a grounded sense of balance, and without a good understanding of where your body is, then it will be harder for your other senses to feel calm. *Even if you only experience mild difficulties in your vestibular and proprioceptive senses, it will still alter how you collect information through your other senses.* In order to really regulate the sight, sound, taste, smell, and touch senses, you first need to consider and regulate your vestibular and proprioceptive senses.

The Vestibular Sense

The vestibular sense collects information about balance and where your head is. It collects information through the inner ear, and also through other senses including the sight and sound senses. The vestibular sense tells us if we tilt our head to the side, if we bend forward, that we are standing up straight, how fast we are moving etc.

In autistic children, vestibular dysfunction can lead to delayed milestones including sitting and walking, poor posture, eye gaze differences, and poor gait. These can lead to coordination problems later in life (Mansour et al. 2021). The effects don't just wear off when we grow into adults, although they might affect us in different ways.

> A poorly regulated vestibular system will alter how you take information in through your other senses. It is therefore really important to work on regulating your vestibular system, so that your other senses can collect information about the environment and your body, and communicate this to your brain and nervous system.

Challenges with a dysregulated vestibular sense may include:

- *Accident prone*: More likely to fall, stumble, or be clumsy.

- *Coordination*: Difficulty working the left and right side of the body in a coordinated manner, difficulty planning and carrying out body movements.

- *Difficulty with sport*: Running, twisting, squatting, and moving direction or position quickly may feel wrong or frightening, or you may simply get it wrong.

- *Need to lean on something*: You may feel a strong need or desire to lean on people, railings, or walls to feel stable when walking or moving, especially if going up or down steps.

- *Housework difficulty*: You may feel anxious, dizzy, or off-balance when doing housework that involves leaning over, including filling the dishwasher, cleaning the bath, scrubbing a toilet etc.

- *Gravitational insecurity*: Feeling insecure or anxious when your feet are not firmly on steady or solid ground, for example on an escalator, if you are on a swing or a hammock, or if you lean backwards on a chair.

- *Poor postural control*: Poor posture, low muscle tone, difficulty standing up straight for long periods, difficulty sitting up straight and thus being prone to slouching.

- *Spatial orientation*: This is the ability to know the location of objects in relation to yourself, and to be able to tell what direction things are going in. Difficulties with this may include miscalculating the distance between your foot and a step, difficulty knowing how far to reach for something, and difficulty knowing how close you are to someone.

- *Manual work*: You may find manual work off-putting, or you may find yourself being very clumsy when doing manual work if it involves bending, crouching, squatting, or any movement that changes your head position.

Me and My Vestibular Sense

There have always been some movements that really frighten me, but there are other vestibular activities that only became a problem for me in adulthood. As a child I loved hanging upside down on bars in playgrounds, I loved the monkey bars and slides and swings. I even liked roller-coasters, which is so strange, as even the thought of going on one now makes me feel nauseous and dizzy.

Despite all this, I still had problems with certain vestibular activities, such as escalators.

I have a vivid memory of freezing at the top of an escalator as a child. I can remember watching my dad going down the escalator, and he thought I was right behind him. I remember my voice getting stuck in my throat so that I was unable to call my dad to tell him I couldn't step on. I felt dizzy even looking in the direction of the escalator. I just stood there, watching him disappear downstairs without me. Thankfully he noticed pretty quickly and came back upstairs to get me. I still have a problem with escalators, and can get really dizzy when on one. I have often had to put my hand to the side of my face to block myself from seeing escalators, as they can make me nauseous and dizzy.

Another strong memory I have is of walking on a big mountain. The people I was with jumped over a stream and kept walking. But I came to the stream and froze, because I had no idea how to get across. I remember reaching my foot out and immediately feeling like I was going to fall. I repeatedly did this, trying to figure out how to balance myself and get over the stream. It was not a big stream, but I just couldn't figure it out. And so I just stood there, staring at the stream and being unable to cross. The people I had been with walked on. I opened my mouth and tried to call out to them to wait for me, to help me, but no sound came out. It felt like there was a boulder blocking all sound from leaving my throat. I got lost on the mountain that day, and the people I was with had to call Mountain Rescue. Thankfully I was found before Mountain Rescue arrived.

Nowadays, I am someone who gets dizzy easily, and things like playground roundabouts and heights make me feel physically sick. My head continues to spin long after I step off a playground roundabout, and it doesn't take much to make me feel off-balance. This hasn't always been the case. As a teenager I used to walk on stilts, I used to love playing acrobatics on hanging bars and trapeze rings. I was good at balancing sports like surfing, and I adored roller-coasters and the waltzers at fun fairs.

But the less I practised these balancing skills, and the less I turned upside down for fun, the quicker I became dizzy or felt imbalanced from everyday activities.

Stopping playing as I grew older, along with my deteriorating joints, has led to more vestibular difficulties for me. When I'm in a flare of autoimmune arthritis, I feel like I'm going to fall a lot more, and so I have to work extra hard to regulate my vestibular sense.

Figuring Out Your Vestibular Sense

Getting to know your vestibular sense can be difficult, and figuring out what works for you to regulate this sense can take some trial and error. It can be challenging to find strategies to soothe this sense as *your vestibular needs and wants may be different in different moods, and on different days.*

The vestibular sense is the sense that I find the hardest to regulate. A lot of activities that regulate my vestibular sense don't come naturally to me, and it's not a sense that I intuitively know how to manage. I have to really think and plan to regulate my vestibular sense.

I tend to feel very off-balance when I'm anxious, stressed, or tired, and I have often had to lean on my husband's arm to steady myself. As a result, things like escalators and elevators can feel frightening and dangerous when I'm anxious. When I'm highly anxious and feel off-balance, I couldn't possibly sit on a rocking chair or sway in a hammock, as this would make me feel worse. Other autistic people I know are the opposite, and use their hammocks or rocking chairs in order to calm themselves.

One autistic person's vestibular soothing may be another autistic person's sensory trigger. While some people spin to soothe themselves, others can feel worse from spinning. Others may feel calm from short periods of spinning, but then quickly feel worse if they spin for too long, or if they don't incorporate some proprioception into the activity as well, such as lying under a weighted blanket after the spinning, or leaning into the wall, or getting a tight hug. It was an occupational therapist who taught me that combining proprioceptive soothing strategies with vestibular strategies can help you to tolerate vestibular changes better, and it has been really helpful to learn this.

When I feel calm and relaxed, I can tolerate a lot more vestibular activities, and even enjoy them. This is a great time to bring some rocking or swaying into my day, to build up my baseline level of vestibular regulation. The more I bring up my baseline level of vestibular regulation, the less I'm affected by unexpected vestibular changes, and the less dizzy I become if I become overwhelmed or anxious.

Sensory Soothing Strategies: Vestibular

- *Chewing and crunching*: Our vestibular system collects most of its information in our inner ears. Chewing and crunching food can bring alertness to this area, 'waking it up'. Some autistic people seek out chewing and crunching, and one of the reasons this may be is to regulate their vestibular sense, even if they don't realise that is what they are doing. They may be prone to chewing pen lids, pencils, sleeve cuffs etc.

  Healthier options to chew include sugar-free chewing gum, crunchy food like raw vegetables, and chewable jewellery or chewable pen-toppers.

- *Sucking*: Sucking though a straw can activate the inner ear to regulate the vestibular sense. You may find different textures work better for you, so sucking something thick through a straw like a smoothie may have a more calming effect than sucking water. If you don't like smoothies, you can test out other textures such as yoghurt drinks, milk, stewed fruit, or whatever else appeals to you.

  You might find different temperatures have a different effect on your vestibular system, so sucking ice cold water might make you feel more alert, whereas sucking a room temperature or warm drink might be calming.

- *Exercises* that work on your balance, or develop your ability to put your head upside down, for example the yoga positions downward dog or child's pose.

- *Swimming*: Swimming is a wonderful way to regulate your vestibular sense, as your body and head change position quite a lot in swimming.

- *Put your head lower than your heart*: This is my favourite vestibular strategy. I just love being upside down.

  Examples: Reach down as if tying your shoe (this can be done from a sitting position or a standing position). Lie on the bed on your tummy and let your head hang over the side of the bed, if safe to do so (please make sure you are stable and won't fall off the bed). I love headstands, and after years of not doing them, I recently started again once my physical trainer taught me how to do so safely.

- *Rolling head over heels*: If you are able to do these safely, head over heels somersaults are a great way to stimulate the vestibular system. I am not able to these any more, but I used to do them a lot as a child, and loved how they made me feel.

- *Shake or tilt your head from side to side, gently*: This brings alertness to your vestibular system, as it changes the position and direction of your ear.

- *Gently lean your head back, supporting your head and neck with your hands*: I advise doing this in a seated position on a stable chair, to prevent yourself falling backwards. This can be a gentle subtle movement, and there's no need to go so far back that you are at risk of falling off the chair. Even slight tilts in our head can have a big vestibular impact.

- *Spinning*: I like spinning when my feet are on the ground. I particularly love spinning on beaches, and have driven to beaches just so I can spin myself around in the gusty ocean air; pure joy. I do not like spinning when I have no control of the spinning, such as on funfair rides like waltzers, or playground roundabouts.

- *Swivel chairs*: These are a nice way to gently activate your vestibular system by small head position changes. I use a swivel chair for writing, to gently swivel my body side to side. As I don't like spinning when my feet are not firmly on the ground, I dislike spinning round and round on swivel chairs, but I know some people love this.

- *Rocking chairs*: I adore rocking chairs, but only when I'm not in a state of high anxiety. I love gently rocking back and forth – I find it very soothing and calming. But when I am anxious, I dislike rocking as it makes me dizzy.

  If you don't like the feeling of being on a rocking chair, you could try different variations of the movement; try rocking with your feet on the ground or on a stool, to help you get used to the movement. Alternatively, you might prefer rocking with your feet off the ground, by having your knees crossed up on the chair. You can also try rocking with a weighted blanket over you, or something heavy on your lap or shoulders, as this will help calm your proprioceptive sense; this can help you tolerate vestibular changes.

- *Hammocks*: We have both sitting and lying down hammocks in our house. I love them both, as long as my head doesn't tilt backwards below my shoulders. They are hugely calming. We had professional builders insert appropriate weight-bearing hooks to hang hammocks at home, and it has made a huge difference to the whole family.

The Proprioceptive Sense

Proprioception is the body awareness sense. The proprioceptive sense collects information through our joints and our muscles, to tell us where our body is in space. If we know where we are in space, we can tell how close we are to another person, how far away from a step we are, which part of a chair we are sitting on, how much distance we need to move our foot to walk through a doorway etc. It tells us about what pressure and forces we are feeling, such as how hard someone is touching us, or how tightly we are holding something.

> Regulating our proprioceptive sense not only helps our body awareness, but it can also help regulate all our other senses, as well as our emotions. It is a sense that should be considered and prioritised throughout the day, especially when you are having a hard sensory or emotional day.

Challenges with dysregulated proprioception may include:

- *Feeling disconnected from your body*: I get this a lot. It can feel as if my arms and legs are not attached to my body tightly enough, and I crave 'grounding'.

- *Lack of coordination*: If your proprioception is poor, you may be uncoordinated and feel as if the different parts of your body are not working properly together. This can make activities like riding a bike very difficult.

- *Movement planning difficulty*: You might find it hard to plan out your movements within the space around you, for example you may miss a step on the stairs, or you may miscalculate your distance from the curb and accidentally step onto the road. You might stub your toe a lot as you aren't aware of how far away the wall is.

- *Difficulty applying the correct force to objects*: This might include dropping things because you are not applying the correct force to hold the item, or you might hold things too hard and break them. You might be told you hug too tightly or shake hands too tightly, because you are not aware how much force you are applying to the other person.

- *Poor posture*: You might tend to slouch or sprawl across tables or chairs, and generally find it hard to hold your body in a position of good posture. You might notice that you are always leaning on things, or resting your head on your arm or hands when sitting, because your body finds it hard to sit upright.

- *Poor spatial awareness*: If you are unaware of where you are in space, it can make it difficult to calculate how far things are from your body. This leads to difficulty with spatial awareness. I notice huge changes in my spatial awareness at different times in my hormone cycle, and it can make me walk into door-frames, have difficulty parking, and bang my head on kitchen cupboards.

A Note on Hypermobility and Proprioception

There is a growing body of evidence that there is an overlap between autism and hypermobility.

Research has found that hypermobility syndromes such as HSD (hypermobility spectrum disorder) and hEDS (hypermobile Ehlers Danlos syndrome) can run in families that have a genetic predisposition to autism (Casanova et al. 2020).

Hypermobility is sometimes known as being double jointed, and may not cause any problems. But sometimes having hypermobile joints can be significant enough to affect daily life. One of the ways this can happen is if it affects your proprioception. More severe cases of hEDS can have a big impact on your daily activity through unstable joints, mobility difficulties, and joint dislocations.

If your joints are loose, and your connective tissue doesn't hold your joints in place as it should, then it naturally follows that you will receive altered information through your proprioceptive senses in your joints and muscles.

I have hEDS, and the older I get, the more affected I am by it. As I also have autoimmune arthritis, my joints are particularly complicated. My hypermobility was aggravated by pregnancy, as the pregnancy hormones loosen connective tissue (to get your body ready to give birth), which can temporarily increase hypermobility.

Female hormones have been found to affect the severity of hypermobile symptoms in women, for example during puberty, prior to menstruation, on oral contraceptives, and after pregnancy (Hugon-Rodin et al. 2016). I get more painful joints at certain times of the hormonal cycle, and my proprioception deteriorates during menstruation; I get clumsier, I walk into things, I sometimes stub my toe up to four times a day, and I crave more tight hugs (this is also because I get more emotional and crave affection). I therefore need to be more aware of my proprioceptive system at this time, as it needs more attention to stay regulated.

If you are hypermobile, you may need to be more careful with which proprioceptive activities you do, as you may be more likely to injure your joints. For example, I wouldn't use a very heavy weighted blanket, as it would be too much resistance for my joints if I needed to change position beneath the blanket. I therefore use a slightly light–medium resistance weighted blanket. It is not recommended to sleep under a weighted blanket if you have rheumatology conditions or weak joints, as the resistance from the blanket might put strain on your joints.

I am careful not to put too much pressure on a loose joint, and I work with a physical trainer who specialises in hypermobility to ensure I exercise correctly and lift weights in a way that will not cause damage to my joints.

If you think you might be hypermobile, or if you have other joint conditions such as arthritis, I recommend getting professional advice from a doctor, occupational therapist, or physical therapist who specialises in hypermobility before you engage in any proprioceptive activities that involve heavy lifting (including weight training) or deep pressure to your joints.

Sensory Soothing Strategies: Proprioception

- *Weight lifting*: I started weight lifting with a physical trainer to help me support my hypermobile joints and arthritis. I was pleasantly surprised to notice how calm I feel when he incorporates weight lifting into the session. It gives me a feeling of calm that lasts all day, as if my body is really connected within itself. There are right ways and wrong ways to lift weights, so I do advise getting professional guidance to teach you how to do this safely, especially if you are hypermobile or have any physical or medical illness or disability.

- *Weighted blanket*: I absolutely adore my weighted blanket. It is one of the main tools in my Quick Calm Plans (Chapter 3). Weighted blankets work on the proprioceptive sense. I find them so calming, and they can really help me switch from feeling very awake to sleepy.

  A study of 85 people with ADHD, autism, or both (48 children and 37 adults) found that using a weighted blanket improved the ability to fall asleep, stay asleep, and to relax during the day. Significantly more adults used the weighted blanket to relax during the day, whereas more children used the blanket to help them fall asleep at night; 81% of participants found that using a weighted blanket improved their ability to sleep through the night, 26.5% found it improved waking up in the morning, and 16.5% found it improved school/work performance (Bolic Barik et al. 2021).

- *Deep pressure*: Anything that brings safe, deep pressure to your joints will soothe your proprioceptive sense. I often ask my husband to hug me tightly around my shoulders and this is wonderfully calming deep pressure for me.

- *Chair lifts*: Sit on a chair and push your hands into the chair, as if trying to lift your torso up off the chair (you don't have to actually lift yourself up off the chair if you are not strong enough, or if you are at risk of injury, but you can still engage the joints and muscles to feel resistance). This puts deep pressure into your arm and shoulder joints.

- *Lean into walls*: I often find myself leaning into walls with my shoulders without consciously choosing to do this. This is a handy way to give yourself a quick burst of deep pressure. I have always been someone who needed to lean into things, and actually get quite dizzy if I'm standing and not leaning on something. Before I drove, I used to lean hard into bus stops, as queuing was particularly hard for me (I hated the unexpected touch, people standing too close to me, too many conversations around me), and I now recognise that I was regulating myself by doing this.

- *Tight spaces*: Sitting in cosy nooks and armchairs, or using cushions to tuck yourself in when sitting, can give tight deep pressure to your hips and lower back.

- *Swimming or water walking*: Water provides resistance for your body to push against, which is strong proprioceptive work. Either swimming or walking in water can be hugely calming to the whole body (swimming is a wonderful sensory tool as it also works on the vestibular and touch senses).

- *Weight on different body parts*: This might include wearing a heavy backpack on your back, or holding it on your lap when seated. You might find yourself drawn to heavy boots to increase the proprioception at your ankles. You can buy nice weighted ankle straps or wrist straps, or a weighted waistcoat or jacket to increase your proprioceptive feedback through the day. Some people like to wear tight compression clothing to achieve this deep pressure compression. There are many weighted products available from autism or sensory shops.

- *Weight-bearing exercise*: For example press-ups or pull-ups.

- *Roll yourself over a gym or peanut ball* and walk your hands on the floor, if safe to do so. If you have poor balance, I suggest starting off with 'peanut balls' or smaller gym balls, to avoid falling off. I really love walking with my hands with my body on a peanut ball – I find it instantly calming.

- *Room layout*: If you have poor proprioception and tend to walk into things, drop things, trip over bags, and stub your toes, it may help to re-evaluate your environment: can you move furniture to make clearer walkways around your house? Can you designate places for bags and shoes and ask people not to place things on the floor as you may trip on them? The less clutter and the fewer obstacles, the easier it is to navigate a space. I firmly believe in making your environment suit your needs, and putting a bit of thought into this is well worth it.

KEY POINTS

◊ Well-regulated proprioception and vestibular senses can help us feel 'grounded', like we are anchored in place.
◊ When the Anchor Senses are regulated, the other senses are easier to regulate.
◊ When the Anchor Senses are not regulated, this can lead to many daily challenges including clumsiness, movement problems, and poor posture.
◊ There are many sensory soothing strategies we can use to regulate our Anchor Senses.

References

Bolic Barik, V., Skuthalla, S., Pettersson, M., Gustafsson, P.A., and Kjellberg, A. (2021) 'The Effectiveness of Weighted Blankets on Sleep and Everyday Activities – A Retrospective Follow-Up Study of Children and Adults with Attention Deficit Hyperactivity Disorder and/or Autism Spectrum Disorder'. *Scandinavian Journal of Occupational Therapy.* doi:10.1080/11038128.2021.1939414

Casanova, E.L., Baezea-Velasco, C., Buchanan, C.B., and Casanova, M.F. (2020) 'The Relationship between Autism and Ehlers Danlos Syndromes/Hypermobility Spectrum Disorders'. *Journal of Personalised Medicine* 10 (4), 260. https://dx.doi.org/10.3390%2Fjpm10040260

Hugon-Rodin, J., Lebegue, G., Becourt, S., Hamonet, C., and Gompel, A. (2016) 'Gynecological Symptoms and the Influence on Reproductive Life in 386 Women with Hypermobility Type Ehlers-Danlos Syndrome: A Cohort Study'. *Orphanet Journal of Rare Diseases* 11 (1), 124. https://dx.doi.org/10.1186%2Fs13023-016-0511-2

Mansour, Y., Burchell, A., and Kulesza, R.J. (2021) 'Central Auditory and Vestibular Dysfunction Are Key Features of Autism Spectrum Disorder'. *Frontiers in Integrative Neuroscience* 15, 743561. https://doi.org/10.3389/fnint.2021.743561

Chapter 8

The Basic Need Sense: Interoception

CHAPTER BREAKDOWN

CHAPTER AIMS

› To explain what Interoception is.
› To explore how poor interoception can lead to difficulties, including our basic needs not being met.
› To share strategies to ensure our basic needs are met, and to regulate our interoception sense.

What Is Interoception?

The interoception sense gathers information about *how we feel, and what we feel inside us.* I think of this sense as the *Basic Need Sense* as it is what helps us to know what our body needs.

The interoception sense gathers information about:

- hunger

- thirst

- emotions

- pain

- body temperature

- feelings inside the body, for example wind, nausea, the feeling of 'butterflies in your tummy' etc.

- the need to go to the toilet

- energy levels

- tiredness

- changes in the body such as your heart speeding up, your breathing rate changing etc.

Interoception helps us to meet our basic needs. If your basic needs are not met, then you are more likely to hit:

1. Sensory overwhelm.

2. Emotional overwhelm.

3. Cognitive overwhelm (i.e. overwhelmed thinking, such as stress or anxious thoughts).

Interoception Difficulties

Autistic people can experience mild to drastic difficulties with their interoception sense. This can have a large impact on daily life, as it can inhibit our ability to recognise that we need to take action to regulate ourselves throughout the day.

Examples of How Poor Interoception Can Affect Daily Life

- *You might not recognise feelings of hunger*: This can lead to both under-eating and over-eating. If you don't feel hungry, you may not eat enough, and may end up deficient in nutrients. Under-eating can reduce concentration and energy levels, both because you may have vitamin or mineral imbalances and because our brain needs food fuel to work at its best.

    If you under-eat for hours, and then finally realise that you are hungry, you may end up eating much more than you need because the need for food has become so urgent that your body eats too much.

I often don't recognise early signs of hunger, and after a few hours of this I can end up shaking and feeling nauseous, because my blood sugar has dropped. When I finally realise I'm hungry, I can end up eating too much to try and get rid of the panicky shaky feeling, but actually it takes a few minutes after eating for this feeling to stop.

- *Difficulty with recognising the feeling of fullness, known as satiety*, and therefore being at risk of over-eating. If you don't feel full after eating, you are at risk of trying to reach that fullness feeling by eating excessive amounts of food. This can put pressure on the body, and can also contribute to obesity, which brings its own health risks.

- *Difficulty recognising thirst*: I know a lot of autistic people that don't recognise their thirst. It occasionally happens to me, but not regularly, possibly because I like the sensory feel of drinking water and therefore sip away at water throughout the day. Not recognising your own thirst can cause grumpiness, reduced need to go to the toilet, constipation, sluggish digestion (we need water to allow our digestive system to run smoothly), over-heating, and dehydration. Not recognising thirst during exercise or warm weather can be particularly problematic.

- *Not recognising that you feel cold*: If you don't feel the cold, it doesn't mean the cold doesn't affect you. One of my daughters does not feel the cold as part of her SPD, and as she also has big touch problems with the feel of certain clothes, she often goes out on cold days wearing too few clothes. She then gets goosebumps, turns blue, and gets really emotional. The cold affects her mood hugely, despite her not feeling the fact that she is cold, and she does not recognise that the cold is the cause of her becoming emotionally dysregulated.

- *Not recognising that you feel hot*: This may manifest in many ways, such as going outside on a warm day wearing a winter coat; you may have chosen to wear the cosy winter coat for the touch-seeking (craving the fluffy or soft lining of the coat) or proprioception-seeking element (craving weight or deep pressure of a heavy or tight coat). However, the side-effect of this is that you may overheat and not recognise that you don't feel well because you are too hot. This could increase risk of dehydration if the weather is very warm and you are sweating more, and might cause you to feel dizzy, cranky, or light-headed.

- *Difficulty or delay in recognising the signs of needing to go to the toilet*: This is more common in autistic children than adults but may present as bed wetting, constipation due to not recognising the urge to use the toilet, not reaching the toilet on time, going hours without going to the toilet as you don't recognise the urge etc.

- *Pain perception differences*: In my experience, some autistic people react differently to pain from non-autistic people. I have seen this in terms of small injuries causing enormous reactions, and more significant injuries causing a smaller reaction than you would expect.

  However, there have been very conflicting research findings about whether autistic people experience pain differently. There has been a popular belief that autistic people are under-sensitive to pain, but one study found that the autistic participants were in fact more sensitive to pain, which was possibly aggravated by a higher level of pain-related anxiety (Failla et al. 2020). A review of many research studies also found that autistic people are not insensitive to pain, but that they express their reaction to pain differently. For example, they may not show it in their faces or in their body language, and they might not communicate that they feel pain (Allely 2013).

  I am not someone who does not feel pain – I think I probably feel pain more than average. I get full body reactions to pain. I can get light-headed when I stub my toe, and I feel like I'm going to pass out. I feel things so strongly in my body that I can wake in the night with mild digestive discomfort, and I can find it very hard to ignore small pains. Since I developed autoimmune arthritis and now experience debilitating pain frequently, I have become even more sensitive to pain.

- *Possible differences in heart rate and respiratory rate recognition*: There is conflicting evidence about whether or not autistic people are less aware of their heart rate or respiratory rate. One study found that autistic children are less aware of changes to their heart rate and respiratory rate, but that autistic adults are not (Nicholson et al. 2019). Other research found that autistic children were superior at tracking their heart rate over long periods of time (Schauder et al. 2015). However, this was a small study, and I would like to see it replicated on a larger scale before I make my mind up about its conclusion.

- *Alexithymia*: This is a difficulty or inability to identify and name your emotions. It is not unique to autism, but is found in high percentages amongst autistic people. I will discuss this in Chapter 12.

- *Not recognising you are tired*: I sometimes start to shake in the evening, and my jaw clatters. I mistakenly think I'm cold, but my husband is usually the one to suggest that I'm tired. I therefore have a strict bedtime routine that I follow at the same time every night to try and get into bed before the physical signs of exhaustion kick in too strongly.

- *Confusion between emotional clues and physical changes in the body*: Our body gives us many clues to tell us what emotion we are experiencing. If you have difficulty recognising what's going on inside your body, you might misinterpret these clues and find it hard to know whether what you feel is a clue to an emotion, or if it's a purely physical change.

  An example of this that I have often experienced is stomach discomfort. Because stomach discomfort is a common symptom in anxiety, it can be hard to tell the difference between emotional stomach discomfort versus discomfort in your stomach caused by a physical problem such as the start of a stomach bug, or acid reflux.

  Another example is telling the difference between physical versus emotional causes of an increased heart rate. You might find it hard to tell if your heart rate is fast because you are feeling anxious, because you did exercise, or for a medical reason.

Self-Soothing Strategies: Interoception

- *Occupational therapy*: Occupational therapy is a profession that helps people to live life to the full through the teaching of skills, environmental adaptation, and the use of tools and aids to manage daily living. As it is a huge field, there are many different specialities within occupational therapy. If you want to work with an occupational therapist (OT) to improve your interoception, or any other sensory processing skill, it is vital that you work with an OT who specialises in sensory processing and interoception. The goal of interoception occupation therapy is to help you recognise the feelings within your body, to teach you what to do when you feel those feelings, and how to manage your basic needs in daily life.

- *Mindfulness*: Mindfulness practices are one of the most well-established interventions to improve interoception, and meditation is thought to activate the brain's interoception centre (Mahler 2022).

- *Learn how to identify and manage your emotions*: Learning to recognise and regulate your emotions will help you to manage your other basic needs. Identifying and managing your emotions will be explored in Part 3.

- *Exercise*: Exercise is a great way to get familiar with physical feelings within your body. Try to pay attention to how you feel when your heart rate speeds up, and when your breathing deepens or gets faster. Ask yourself which muscles are being used. Naming what you are feeling, for example 'That fluttering in my chest is my heart speeding up', may help you to identify physical changes, and start to notice earlier signs of physical change.

- *Check in with your body*: Regularly checking in with your body and asking yourself 'What do I feel?' or 'Does my body need anything?' might sound too easy, but it can actually make a huge difference to your self-regulation. It reminds you to notice what your body needs, such as whether you are thirsty, whether you are cold etc.

  One way to do this is to *set alarms* on your phone or watch to remind yourself to check in with your body and ask yourself if your body needs anything. Another way to do it is to *use little notes*, such as by having a sticky note on the kettle that reminds you to ask yourself how your body feels, and does it need anything to improve your self-regulation.

- *Make a routine*: This is a strategy I use constantly. Creating a routine around eating, drinking, sleeping, and other basic body needs helps me to ensure that I meet my basic needs, without having to rely on my interoception sense to tell me what I need. For example, if my routine includes eating lunch at midday, then I will automatically start to prepare food for myself at this time, whether or not I recognise my own hunger. This really helps me to maintain my energy levels, concentration, and my emotional regulation throughout the day. If you have significant difficulty with executive function (particularly initiation and time management) or if you have ADHD, I recommend making the routine visual, and possibly include alarms or other ways to prompt yourself to move onto the next task. Timers are something I also use to help myself understand how long I have before I must end the current task and move onto the next task.

Managing Specific Interoception Difficulties

Interoception is a huge sense, with many different elements, and so there's not just one strategy or tip that will improve all your interoception skills at once. It's worth spending some time assessing your own interoception to identify which areas of interoception you need to support more. For example, you might have no problem recognising hunger, but you might constantly find yourself going to bed much too late, which might suggest that you don't recognise signs of sleepiness or tiredness. It's important to note that interoception can change and be experienced differently at different times. So you might recognise exhaustion in the morning after poor sleep, and yet not recognise tiredness in the evening when you would benefit from going to bed. Equally, one day you might recognise your thirst, but another day you might not. I find that the more grounded all my other senses are, the better my interoception is in general. The more regulated and emotionally calm I am, the easier it is to recognise my basic needs.

Once you start identifying which elements of interoception you have difficulty with, you can start to develop support plans for each basic need. Here are some examples:

Eating and Drinking

- *Set alarms for eating and drinking.* If you are aware that you go hours without eating or drinking, then it may mean you are not feeling hunger or thirst. Setting alarms reminding you to eat and drink will ensure this basic need is met, despite you not recognising the feelings of hunger or thirst.

- *Prepare a lunch box of healthy snacks in the morning so you are reminded to eat well.* Leaving too long before eating can cause physical symptoms such as shaking, light-headedness, crankiness etc., and you will be more likely to grab an unhealthy snack to eat fast when you realise you need to eat. Or, when you finally realise you are starving, you may over-eat as your body will be crying out for an energy source, i.e. food.

- *Bring food with you in your bag if going out to remind you to eat.* This is especially important if you have food aversions, to ensure you will be able to eat even if the location you go to has no food that you like. I always bring non-perishable food with me as I am gluten intolerant, and it can be hard to get gluten-free food out and about.

- *If you realise you don't feel satiety (the feeling of fullness) it might be important to set rules for yourself about your meals.* Using a reputable food pyramid can be a helpful way to make sure you have a balanced diet and take care of portion size. If you are unable to do this yourself, consider getting professional help from a dietician or medical professional with experience of autism.

Temperature Regulation

- *Pay attention to whether you react the same way to temperature as others around you do.* Do you notice you are the only one not wearing a coat? Are other people sweating and wearing t-shirts and you are shivering under a coat and blanket? Paying attention to what the majority of others are wearing might give you a clue about the actual temperature. I suggest not taking your clothing cues from teenagers and young adults who are out socialising at night, who often freeze themselves for the sake of fashion!

- *Question whether temperature changes have more of an effect on you than you think.* You might think you are not cold, but if your hands go blue, your skin gets goosebumps, and you start to feel unsafe or grumpy, perhaps you are cold and don't realise it.

- *Question whether you are reacting to temperature or something else.* I shiver when I'm tired and anxious. I used to think this was because I'm a cold creature, but I now recognise that shivering doesn't always reflect temperature for me, and thus putting on more clothes doesn't solve the root cause; I need to address the tiredness or anxiety.

- *Wear multiple thin layers.* I find that wearing layers can be really helpful when going to a day-long event, especially if there will be temperature changes. For example, it might be really warm in a room full of people, but cold outside, or cold in the bathrooms. Having layers of clothes can allow you to adjust your clothes to avoid sudden temperature changes which may affect your mood.

KEY POINTS

◊ The interoception sense tells us what is going on inside our body.

◊ It helps us to meet our basic needs, such as telling us when we are hungry or thirsty.

◊ It helps us regulate our emotions by telling us how we feel.

◊ Poor interoception can lead to many difficulties with everyday life including difficulty recognising your own emotions, not recognising thirst, hunger, or fullness, and difficulty regulating your temperature.

◊ There are many strategies to help you to care for your interoception sense, which will help you to regulate it.

◊ Having a regulated interoception sense will help the other senses stay regulated also.

References

Allely, C.S. (2013) 'Pain Sensitivity and Observer Perception of Pain in Individuals with Autistic Spectrum Disorder'. *Scientific World Journal*, 916178. https://dx.doi.org/10.1155/2013/916178

Fallia, M.D., Gerdez, M.B., Williams, Z.J., Moore, D.J., and Cascio, C.J. (2020) 'Increased Pain Sensitivity and Pain-Related Anxiety in Individuals with Autism'. *Pain Reports* 5 (6), e861. https://dx.doi.org/10.1097/PR9.0000000000000861

Mahler, K. (2022) 'What Is Interoception?' Accessed 9 July 2022 at: www.kelly-mahler.com/what-is-interoception/

Nicholson, T., Williams, D., Carpenter, K., and Kallitsounaki, A. (2019) 'Interoception Is Impaired in Children, But Not Adults with Autism Spectrum Disorder'. *Journal of Autism and Developmental Disorders* 49 (9), 3625–3637. https://dx.doi.org/10.1007/s10803-019-04079-w

Schauder, K.B., Mash, L.E., Byrant, L.K., and Cascio, C.J. (2015) 'Interoception Ability and Body Awareness in Autism Spectrum Disorder'. *Journal of Experimental Child Psychology* 131, 193–300. https://doi.org/10.1016/j.jecp.2014.11.002

Chapter 9

The Famous Five Senses: The Good, the Bad, and the Soothing Strategies

CHAPTER BREAKDOWN

CHAPTER AIMS

› To introduce each of the Famous Five Senses.
› The highlight some of the good things about sensory differences in each of the Famous Five Senses.
› To highlight some of the bad things about sensory differences in each of the Famous Five Senses.
› To give soothing strategies for each of the Famous Five Senses.

What Are the Famous Five Senses?

The Famous Five Senses are:

- The sound (auditory) sense.

- The taste (gustatory) sense.

- The smell (olfactory) sense.

- The sight (visual) sense.

- The touch (tactile) sense.

How the Famous Five Senses Affect Our Lives

> While the Anchor and Basic Need Senses are mostly responsible for us feeling grounded in our own bodies, it is often the Famous Five Senses that affect how we join in with society, other people, and the world around us.

How we respond to the sensory world around us can have a significant impact on everything in our lives, from what might seem like small-scale decisions, to major life decisions. On a small scale, our Famous Five Senses will impact what we eat (taste, smell, and touch senses), what clothes we wear (touch and visual senses), what deodorant or fragrance we choose (smell and touch senses) etc. On a larger scale, how we experience our Famous Five Senses can affect our ability to socialise, our relationships, and what career choices we make (if the sensory environment of a job is too stressful, you might find the job too challenging, despite it being your chosen career).

How we experience our Famous Five Senses can also affect how we navigate our daily lives, such as whether we are able to use public transport (does the close proximity of strangers and the potential for unexpected touch mean you can't possibly use a tram or a train?), whether you can meet your friends at a social event (or does the loud music or bright lights turn you off joining in?), or whether you can go shopping in a supermarket (or is the environment too loud, too bright, too demanding?).

A lot of the ways we portray ourselves, or the ways in which we identify ourselves, are based around our Famous Five Senses. Just look at teenagers and you will see that they often group together and identify with each other based on sensory information: what type of music they listen to (sound sense), what style of clothes they wear (visual sense), what movies they watch (visual and sound senses).

Sometimes it can be hard for an autistic person to join in socially based on their sensory challenges with one of the Famous Five Senses. For example, if the social group you want to belong to socialises by meeting in loud bars, and you can't stand loud music, then you may feel unable to join in. Or if you want to go to one of your friend's houses to play board games, but their house has a smell you can't stand, you may end up avoiding joining in despite really wanting to. This might look like you are avoiding socialising for its own sake, but in fact you might really want to socialise but just be unable to tolerate the sensory elements of socialising.

You might experience social rejection based on your sensory difference. For example, if you can't tolerate the clothes (due to your touch sense) that your social group sees as necessary fashion, you might experience rejection (I experienced this in my childhood and teenage years). Social rejection can also happen if you seek out certain sensory movements or behaviours that are deemed 'socially unacceptable' or odd (e.g. having to smell every item of clothing in a shop because you seek smell so much, or if you have a habit of rubbing everything against your cheek because it helps you process how it feels). Having sensory differences with self-care and hygiene can also cause social challenges or rejection, such as if you have bad breath because brushing your teeth feels torturous to your touch sense.

I have often refused to go somewhere because I know that the environment will stress one of my Famous Five Senses, and I can end up feeling frustrated and upset that I have to miss out on something because I have overly sensitive hearing, or because I can't bear certain fabrics (I have honestly turned down invitations if I know that all the furniture in a room is covered in velvet).

Although I do use a lot of sensory soothing strategies for my Famous Five Senses, I unfortunately don't have a magic wand that can switch off my strong sense of smell, or my sensitivity to loud noise. I have, however, started to accept my differences, adapt my activities, and look at the positive side of my differences.

The Benefit of Differences in the Famous Five Senses

Although having differences in how we experience the Famous Five Senses can be challenging, I also believe they give us many strengths. The more I take the time to notice these strengths, the less I resent my differences, and the more I see them as a positive thing in my life.

For example, my visual strength of spotting patterns helped me in my nursing career, as I could see patterns in a patient's vital signs that helped me notice early signs of deterioration, especially in heart rhythm analysis. I could spot subtle changes in a patient's pallor, or other signs of deterioration, before others. My strong sound sense also helped, as I could hear tiny differences in a patient's breathing, or tune into sound differences in patient monitors, which allowed me to intervene early and avoid a patient becoming more unwell. I was often praised for this ability, and I really believe my sensory difference enhanced my intensive-care nursing career.

Many of my sensory differences are the things that bring the most joy to my life. When I go outside in my garden, I don't just hear traffic; I hear the birds, the wind rustling, and the different sounds of different vehicles. I don't just see trees and flowers, I see each blade of grass and spot patterns in them. I see each new flower bud popping up and I spot patterns of colours throughout the stones and sticks around me. This sounds strange, but just looking at nature makes me feel as though my eyes are taking nourishment into my body. I don't just see nature; I feel it.

I used to struggle with my challenges to join in with certain things socially, but I am now more confident at expressing my sensory needs, and I don't see it as a flaw. I can tell people that I won't join them in a noisy pub, but I will meet them for coffee or a walk instead. I prefer this environment anyway, and so by speaking up for my sensory needs, I actually get more enjoyment out of socialising.

If I'm going to a party, I ask the host in advance if there's a quiet part of the house that I could go to for a small break if I need it. This not only soothes my sensory system, but also gives me time to process conversations and time to reflect on what I want to do next or whom I want to talk to, which all enhance my social experience.

1. The Smell (Olfactory) Sense
The Good Differences

- *Ability to gather smell information quickly and before others*: This was really helpful to me in nursing, as I was able to notice subtle differences in odours such as in wounds, and therefore know a dressing needed changing earlier than scheduled. It also helped when I worked with the elderly in a nursing home; I could walk past a room and immediately know if a patient needed hygiene or toileting attention, despite the other carers being unable to smell anything. The early care and attention to hygiene and toileting needs helped me to prevent skin damage, and promoted the dignity and comfort of my patients.

- *Smell detection*: Some people with strong senses of smell can break down the individual scents in an odour, i.e. they can pinpoint the ingredients. This is beneficial for chefs, people working in forensics, people working with perfumes or perfumed products etc. This skill makes me think of Sherlock Holmes identifying the type of poison hidden in a drink! Alas, this is not a skill I have.

- *Scent creativity*: The ability to deeply understand scents and how different scents work together would be a wonderful skill for someone working in scent creations, such as designing perfume, scented body care products, scented craft making such as candles etc.

- *Smell and memory*: Our sense of smell is highly linked to our memory. I have met people with a very poor smell memory, for whom smells don't trigger memories, and this helped me see my strong smell memory as a gift. I often use smell to create memories, almost like taking a photograph with my nose. To access the memory, I first access the smell memory, and the rest follows.

- *Smell and emotions*: Our sense of smell is closely linked to our emotions. Research has found that odours can play an important role in mood and emotion, and while this can be problematic when an odour is unpleasant, it can also be hugely beneficial when used to support emotions and improve mood (Kontaris et al. 2020).

The Bad Differences

- *Having a very strong sense of smell can make social occasions difficult*: Being surrounded by multiple people with multiple scents can be very overwhelming, and can make me nauseous. I distinctly remember the smell of one boy in secondary school who always smelled of sweat. I could smell him from the next corridor, and felt so dizzy that I thought I would faint from the smell. This led me to avoid him, which I knew was not a socially kind thing to do, but I couldn't bear to be close to him.

- *Reacting physically to bad smells*: I can vomit or gag from bad smells. I have walked out of venues if the smell makes me nauseous, when other people can cope fine with the smell. I have been unable to use a public toilet if the smell is bad, despite an urgent need to use the bathroom, because the smell makes me feel like I'm going to faint. Chores like cleaning out an old tub of food or cleaning the fridge can be hugely challenging to me, and can cause me to gag and feel faint.

- *Difficulty with environments*: Some environments can be full of unpleasant smells, and if you have a very strong sense of smell, it can be unbearable to enter. I've experienced this with canteens, take-aways, pubs, butchers, cheese shops, swimming pools, gyms, perfume and body-care shops, pet shops, petting farms, houses that smell strongly of pets, and public toilets.

- *Difficulty with food*: If you are very sensitive to smell, it can be very hard to eat food that smells strong. The smell alone can turn you off even tasting it.

- *Making friend challenges*: If you are very sensitive to smell, you may notice the natural smells of other people. If you meet a new person that you detest the smell of, it can be really hard to expose yourself to that person. They might be the perfect friend for you, but if their smell stresses you (whether it's their natural odours or a perfume they wear), it can make it really hard to be around them.

- *Difficulties with physical intimacy*: Being intimate with someone can be full of strong smells. Strong breath, body odour, and other natural body smells can make intimacy challenging, as being very close to someone physically makes escaping smells difficult. This can lead to a lack of physical closeness and a resistance to intimacy, which can put pressure on a relationship.

The Soothing Strategies: Smell

- *Seek out smells you love, and carry them with you*: I bring a small bar of unopened rose-scented soap with me in my bag, and take a sniff if I feel dizzy or anxious. I also keep a little bottle of bergamot oil on my desk, and every now and then I pause work to smell it, which revives my energy and helps me focus.

- *Identify a smell you love and make it part of your daily routine*: For example, if you like lavender, you might hang a bag of lavender in your car, or use lavender bags in your sock drawer. I treat myself to soaps I love the smell of, or I ask for fancy soaps (I specify which one as I don't like all soap) for my birthday. This allows me to smell a beautiful scent every time I wash my hands, which is something I find very regulating.

- *Plan ahead for environments that might upset your sense of smell*: Plan to sit next to open windows or doorways to get blasts of fresh air to dilute smells. Sit far away from the kitchen area in cafes or restaurants, if that's the source of the smell you dislike. When I worked in a hospital, I found the smell of the canteen very off-putting, but it was the only place we were allowed to eat. I therefore used to sit as far away from the food serving area as possible, and I would leave after eating to sit alone in the hospital chapel to calm my senses before returning to the ward.

- *Use something to block your nose*: For example, holding a scarf over your nose when walking past a cheese counter. I've been told by many people that they have the physical ability to block the back of their nose by using their soft palate, as if they are closing their nose to stop smell entering. Some people use this to stop water entering their throat when it goes up their nose when swimming. This is not a skill I have, but I am very jealous of those who do! It would have made nursing a lot easier.

- *Use unscented or reduced scent hygiene products*: Pharmacies, health food shops and children's autism or special needs online stores often sell these.

- *Smell before you buy*: Most shops will allow you to smell a product before you buy it. Pharmacies or body care shops often have tester bottles that you can bring home, so that you can smell before you buy.

- *Gradual exposure*: I don't think this will work for everyone, and if it's tortuous then I don't advise it. Gradually exposing myself to a smell has often helped me desensitise to an odour, but only when I've been determined to do it myself.

When I began training as nurse, I found it hard to cope with the smells involved, and regularly had to go to the bathroom to retch over smells. I vomited over the smell of a bedpan on more than one occasion, but thankfully I was always able to hide this from patients and staff (I was very good at pretending to be fine when inside I was struggling enormously, because it was extremely important to me that my patients never felt that I was appalled by a smell, and that their dignity was always maintained). Amazingly, I eventually got used to the smells of the human body. I would force myself to endure a smell, and would distract my brain by counting while I walked away from the patient. I would then immediately go and smell soap to replace the bad smell with a good one. Interestingly, I only desensitised to these smells in the context of nursing, and can still react severely to the same smells outside of nursing. When I became a mum, I had to desensitise to these smells all over again, in the context of mothering. It's as if my smell desensitisation comes with specific instructions for the context it will work in.

Smells I have never been able to force myself to endure are those of animal's bodily functions, and the smell of cat or dog vomit will inevitably make me vomit.

Please please never try to force another person to desensitise to a smell that is offensive to them. Desensitisation has only ever worked for me when I have chosen to do it myself, and I am in control of it. If someone else put pressure on me to desensitise to a smell, it truly would be akin to torture, and would not work anyway.

- *Fresh air*: Taking breaks from a smell to inhale fresh air can act like lovely odour rinse.

- *Wash out a bad smell with a good smell*: This really does work. Hence why carrying a strong pleasant smell with you is helpful, as you can wash away the lingering smell of whatever it was you disliked. I carry mandarins or tangerines (I love the smell of citrus fruit). I also bring soaps still in their wrappers with me to smell.

- *Communicate about intimacy difficulties*: While this can be difficult, as it's a sensitive topic, I believe it's really important to communicate your smell difficulties so that you can plan for intimacy around times that smells are least offensive, for example after your partner has brushed their teeth, not first thing in the morning as body and breath smells are strong at this time, after your partner has a shower, when the bed sheets have just been changed and smell fresh etc. Asking your partner to use smells you love such as colognes, perfumes, deodorants or shampoos might mask their body odours, and might even become a smell that you seek. Obviously you need to be sensitive and kind in how you discuss this, and avoid using hurtful language. See Chapter 10 for more on intimacy and sensory care.

2. The Sound (Auditory) Sense
The Good Differences

- *Sound creativity*: Some people with a strong sound sense can understand music and sound at a deep level, and are able to understand how sounds work together, and design sound into music. I do not have this strength, but my brothers do, and it truly is remarkable. This strength will benefit musicians, songwriters, DJs, radio presenters, theatre directors, those working in television and movies, and those working in advertising and sound technology design.

- *Heightened pitch discrimination*: Autistic people are more likely to have excellent pitch discrimination and pitch memory (Stanutz et al. 2014). This strength will benefit singers, musicians, composers, music teachers, and music appreciators. Again, not a strength I have.

- *Having a 'good ear'*: This can be beneficial for people who wish to learn and speak new languages. It would also be highly beneficial to linguistics specialists, translators, and interpreters. It is also a great skill for impersonating voices, which can benefit comedians, musicians, or musicians doing tribute acts or impersonations (think Elvis impersonators).

- *Safety services*: Having excellent hearing would be a huge benefit for people working in health and safety, for example fire fighters will benefit from being able to pinpoint sounds of danger or people calling for help.

- *Excellent auditory discrimination skills*: Being able to pinpoint individual sounds in a mass of sound will benefit musicians, orchestra conductors, sound editors, sound technicians, sound engineers etc. There have been many jobs over the years that relied on auditory discrimination, including telephone operators who needed to rec- ognise the sounds that different coins made in the phone box, and people working in sound signal analysis.

The Bad Differences

- *Social difficulty*: Being overly sensitive to sound and noise can make social situations overwhelming. If the noise of a pub is overwhelm- ing to you, you may be turned off socialising, despite wanting to. Listening to other people eating is full of sounds such as chewing, slurping, swallowing, biting, talking with their mouth full of food etc. – these might sound very loud and offensive to you, and might even make you nauseous or gag. This can make socialising difficult in restaurants, cinemas, or anywhere that people eat. Listening to other people eat popcorn and slurp soft drinks in a cinema is a big deterrent for me going to the cinema with other people, and I much prefer going alone at quiet times.

- *Inability to enjoy experiences due to sound quality*: For example, if you are a music lover, but you can hear hisses or other unpleasant noises from bad recordings or poor-quality speakers. This can affect your enjoyment of music in public places, or places with poor acoustics.

- *Inability to focus on one sound*: If you are so sensitive to noise that you hear every single noise in the environment, it can be hard to focus on the one sound you are supposed to hear, such as a lecturer speaking at the front of the room, or your friend talking to you in a noisy pub.

- *Daily living skill difficulties*: There are many activities in modern daily life that can be overwhelmingly noisy. Shopping centres, busy roads, road works, working environments, and travel systems are examples of environments that can be overwhelming if you are sensitive to noise. Household items can also produce noises that can overwhelm a sound sensitive person, including vacuum cleaners, cooling fans, extractor fans, electric razors, liquidisers, food processors, kettles, televisions, radios etc.

- *Hearing what others don't*: There are certain pitches and sounds that most people don't hear, but people with a heightened sound sense may hear. I can hear a high pitched whine from some technology when it is charging, which makes it really difficult to relax or sleep. This can be very irritating, especially in a work environment, where you need to be able to focus, but are constantly distracted by noises that no-one else hears.

- *Being unable to filter out background noise*: I have spoken to a number of autistic people who really suffer from this. Examples including being unable to zone out from the noise of someone tapping on a keyboard, chewing gum, breathing through their mouth, or clicking a pen. Being unable to stop listening to these noises can be frustrating and overwhelming.

- *Sensitivity to voices or accents*: I am really sensitive to the accent and voice of narrators of audiobooks, and presenters on the radio or TV. If I don't like the voice, I can't listen to them as I get a feeling of vulnerability or irritability.

The Soothing Strategies

- *'Loud noise' warning*: In our house, we say 'Loud noise' before we turn on loud machines like blenders or vacuum cleaners, so we all have a second or two of a warning. Unexpected loud noise bothers me much more than expected loud noise. We also give each other a chance to leave the room if we don't want to hear the noise. It is a basic sign of respect to prepare someone who has sound sensitivities before you start hoovering, or using other loud household items.

- *Block out noise*: If a sound is triggering sensory stress, then block it out. Ear buds, noise cancelling headphones, ear defenders, noise reducing products, or wearing a thick hat that covers your ears can all help to reduce or block out noise. Thankfully there are a lot of options to reduce noise, once you start shopping and asking around. I use ear defenders at home, and ear plugs away from the house. Unfortunately, I really dislike noise cancelling headphones, but I know many autistic people love them.

- *Drown out a bad sound with a good sound*: For example, listening to music, an audiobook, or meditative sounds such as waves. Some people like white noise (personally I can't stand it) and find it helps them sleep as it blocks out other noise.

- *Seek out silence after the sound sense has been triggered*: If I've been overwhelmed by sound, I crave silence. My sound sense needs calm and quiet to reset.

- *Manage the amount of sound:* By this I mean limiting when different sounds occur around you. If you are aware that you dislike the sound of the extractor fan, and you dislike the sound of the TV, then don't start cooking while the TV is on. This sounds so obvious, but this exact scenario has happened many times in my home, and it took me ages to figure out that it's not a combination that works for me.

- *Flexible thinking to avoid sounds that trigger your sound sense*: There will always be bothersome sounds in life, and sometimes there's no escaping them. With a bit of intentional flexible thinking, it is often possible to come up with a solution. I say intentional because I often forget to try to think flexibly, but when I tell myself to do it, I can come up with good solutions. For example, when I worked in a hospital, the cleaners would vacuum-clean every morning. I found it extremely difficult to focus on my work with the vacuum cleaner on. I therefore made subtle changes to how I followed the ward routine, to avoid being in the same room as the vacuum cleaner.

- *Meet people outdoors*: I find it a lot easier to meet people outdoors as I am so calmed by the sounds of nature, and it means avoiding coffee shop noises (other people talking, chairs scraping, milk frothers, coffee machines etc.), and bars or busy restaurants.

3. The Taste (Gustatory) Sense

This sense takes information in through the taste buds in the mouth and throat. Our smell can also affect how we taste things, so these senses often work together.

The Good Differences

- *Advanced flavour discrimination*: For example, being able to pinpoint subtle flavours in food. This would be a great skill for wine or alcohol tasters, chefs, and food critics.

- *Food creativity*: Advanced taste senses may lead to creative skills in cooking, with enhanced ability to pair food or invent recipes. This would be extremely helpful for chefs and people working with food.

- *Advanced ability to collect information through taste*: For example, detecting changes to quality of food, which will benefit chefs and people working in food quality control. Also useful in security and forensics (again I'm thinking of a detective tasting a powdery residue to determine what poison it is, which is possibly fiction but it still seems like a great skill to me!).

The Bad Differences

- *Food aversion*: If you cannot tolerate certain tastes, it will probably lead you to avoid these tastes. If there are multiple tastes you cannot tolerate, it can lead to a very limited diet.

- *Dietary deficiencies due to food aversion*: Research has found higher levels of vitamin and mineral deficiencies in autistic people compared to non-autistic people, including low levels of A, D, and B vitamins, iron, calcium, and more (Ranjan and Nasser 2015).

- *Fear of new foods*: If you have a very sensitive palate and certain tastes make you gag or feel unsafe, it can be very difficult to try new foods for fear of how you will react. This can make things like travel or eating out difficult.

- *Difficulty with eating food cooked by other people*: One of my autistic children will only eat meals if I cook them, as she associates the flavours of a meal with how I cook it. This can really limit your activities such as socialising, joining in family meals etc., and can add a huge organisational challenge to going out.

- *Difficulty with taking necessary medicine*: I have had huge difficulty with the taste of some medicine, especially fish oil capsules. It can be so hard to swallow them: I can gag, and have to really force myself to swallow them.

- *Aversion to the taste of toothpaste*: This can lead to reduced teeth brushing, poor oral health, and bad breath (also known as halitosis). I am very sensitive to other people's bad breath, and have had to walk away from talking to people because of it, and so I am keenly aware that having bad breath can taint your social experience.

- *Over-eating specific tastes*: This may lead to an excessive consumption of salt or sugar, or one specific food.

- *Over-eating and obesity*: If you are constantly seeking out the taste sensation, or the specific taste of sugary or processed food, you might end up eating more than your daily food requirements, which can lead to health problems such as becoming overweight or obese.

- *Under-eating and low weight*: If you dislike the taste sensation and avoid many foods, you may not eat enough to meet your daily requirements. This can lead to being underweight.

- *Eating non-food objects*: If you constantly seek taste in your mouth, you might find yourself chewing or tasting non-food objects, and this can be unhealthy or even dangerous. Pica is an eating disorder that includes compulsively eating non-food items, and can cause stomach upset and serious harm if the items eaten are poisonous or harmful. Medical treatment is recommended for Pica.

   Chewing non-food objects, without craving the taste of that object, might suggest that you are vestibular seeking rather than taste seeking, as chewing can regulate the vestibular senses.

The Soothing Strategies

- *Identify foods you seek*: I seek salty food when I'm tired, anxious, or overwhelmed, so I keep a packet of salty crisps or salty rice cakes at home for emotional emergencies. I also bring salty snacks to events like conferences, as they work well to perk me up and draw attention back to my sensory system. I used to seek sugar when upset, but I forced myself to cut out sugar for my health and gradually stopped craving sugar. Strong flavours like pickles can also really help perk me up and focus, whereas creamy food like Greek yoghurt and honey help me calm down.

- *Look up the menu online in advance*: If going to a restaurant, make sure there's something on the menu you can eat before you go. If there's nothing, ring ahead and see can they prepare something that you can eat.

- *Warm drinks*: These are famously comforting. If you don't drink tea or coffee, it's worth experimenting with other warm drinks to find one that you like the taste of. I bring decaf tea bags with me in my purse so I can have a warm drink without increasing my anxiety through caffeine.

- *Easy food for when you are overwhelmed*: I tend to keep a zero-effort meal at all times in the freezer, so I know that if I'm overwhelmed, there's an easy to prepare meal in the freezer. This is important, as I can avoid eating if overwhelmed, but having food I like at home makes it easier to meet this basic need.

- *Bring food with you when you go out*: If I'm going out I try to always bring a snack with me. If going to a conference or a day-long event, I bring my own lunch to ensure I will tolerate the food. This is particularly important for me as I don't tolerate eating gluten, and so I have to be prepared.

Tips for Taste Aversion

- *Experiment with texture*: Sometimes we can think we hate the taste of a food, but the problem is actually the texture rather than the taste. If there's a food you want to include in your diet, consider hiding it in baking, or trying out different recipes or ways to cook it. Changing the texture can hugely affect how we taste food.

- *Experiment with temperature*: Changing the temperature of food can lead to a big difference in how we perceive the taste. For example, there's a big difference between yoghurt straight from the fridge and yoghurt that has warmed up in a lunch box for hours.

- *Consider if the aversion is caused by inflexible thinking*: By adulthood, most autistic adults know what food they can or cannot tolerate. But if food restriction is leading to an unhealthy or imbalanced diet, it might be worth challenging your tolerance to different tastes. Sometimes we can form preconceived ideas that we will never eat anything that has a certain food in it, but it's worth questioning if this is actually a sensory issue or is the aversion due to inflexible thinking? I often have to challenge my flexible thinking to open up new experiences.

- *Keep trying*: Some foods can trigger sensory aversion the first time you try them, but if you keep on trying, perhaps masking the flavour with other foods, you may eventually desensitise to it. I have gagged over medication drinks, but forced myself to drink them by masking the taste by alternating with sips of a strong drink I do like. I kept doing this until I could drink a whole glass of the medicine without the alternative drink. Please don't force another person to this, as it is very challenging. I only advise trying to desensitise yourself to a taste if you know the benefit to yourself outweighs the challenge of the process.

- *Find alternatives*: If you can't stand the taste of toothpaste, there are flavour-free toothpastes available (mostly in shops that market to parents of autistic children), or you can experiment with different flavour toothpastes. You can also speak to your dentist for suggestions.

- *Nutritional supplementation*: If you have a limited diet due to taste sensitivities, it's worth checking your vitamin and mineral levels with your medical professional, and supplementing the nutrients you are deficient in.

- *Try to include variety in case you suddenly get turned off a food*: I am very repetitive with certain meals, and tend to get stuck eating one breakfast for extended periods. Then one morning I wake up and the thought of it makes me feel sick, and I can't eat it again for months or years. I therefore try to have a different breakfast once or twice a month, usually at the weekend when I have more flexibility to eat later and in a different venue (such as in the garden, or in bed, or even in a café).

- *Calm your other senses*: The more regulated your other senses are, the calmer your taste system will be. If you want to try a new food, a loud busy bright restaurant may not be the ideal environment to try it, as your senses will be on high alert. I suggest grounding your Anchor Senses before you try a new food.

- *Professional help*: Dieticians, occupational therapists, or your doctor may help you widen your diet.

4. The Sight (Visual) Sense

The sight sense takes information in through the eyes, including light, patterns, and images.

The Good Differences

- *Advanced ability to spot visual patterns*: This isn't just helpful for things like interior design, but can also be helpful in collecting information. I used to work in coronary and intensive care and was quick to spot patterns in heart rhythms and blood pressure, and thus was able to spot changes early, which allowed me to intervene early.

- *Advanced ability to spot visual detail*: The ability to notice visual detail that others might miss can be helpful in many careers, including design, information gathering, data analysis, quality and inspection etc.

- *Advanced understanding or use of colour*: Advanced creativity and understanding of colour is a wonderful skill for artists, designers, architects, and more.

- *Advanced visual categorisation and organisation skills*: I am quite preoccupied with visual organisation and get great pleasure from re-organising and rearranging things into visual categories. From the crockery on my kitchen dresser, to books on my bookshelves, to how my clothes are stored, I get a lot of pleasure from creating visual categories. I like to change these around, and organise things in new patterns or categories. Being able to organise things in a visual way can be hugely helpful to improving the function of a space, especially a work space or a filing system.

- *Visual memory*: Having a strong visual memory can make information recall much easier. In school and university, I had good exam success as I could recall my study notes visually, but only if the information was written in my own writing and with my own colour coding system.

- *Visual thinking*: Many autistic people think in visual images, or in pictures, rather than in words or sentences like the majority of people. This can be a wonderful skill for enhancing memory, problem solving, and being able to visualise exactly what you are thinking about.

The Bad Differences

- *Overwhelm when faced with too many patterns, or clashing patterns*: Clutter and clashing patterns can make me feel genuinely stressed, and even nauseous.

- *Preoccupation with patterns*: This really affects me; I can become unable to focus on my task because I can't stop noticing or counting patterns, especially if there's a repeating pattern like on a carpet or wallpaper, or if the pattern lacks symmetry.

- *Difficulty with bright lights*: Bright lights are a well-known trigger for many autistic people. They not only make activities like shopping in bright shopping centres difficult, but they can also affect tasks such as driving at night when cars use glaring headlights, and working in environments with bright lights. They can also cause headaches and eye strain.

- *Difficulty with different types of light*: Some people have difficulty with certain frequencies of light, such as that in fluorescent bulbs. This can make working in places with fluorescent light difficult, such as in some restaurant kitchens or factories.

- *Difficulty with moving or flashing lights*: If an environment has moving or flashing lights, I can find it hard to focus on a task. Waiting in line somewhere with flashing Christmas lights can be uncomfortable for me. As a teenager I loved strobe lights, but now they make me feel nauseous – I have no idea why this changed.

- *Feeling stressed from unexpected visual changes*: When things are out of place in a visual scene, or things are not where they belong, I can become preoccupied with this. If I'm used to seeing an environment one way, I can get upset or even angry if it has changed without me knowing. Furniture being moved in a room without me knowing it's happening can really throw me. This is strange in a way because I am constantly rearranging the furniture in my house, but because I am the one controlling it, it is not an unexpected visual change.

The Soothing Strategies

- *Dimness or darkness*: Low lighting or darkness can be very soothing, and will reduce the amount of visual stress you see. Closing the curtains, turning off the lights, and using blackout blinds can all help.

- *Use an eye mask*: I often put on an eye mask when I am resting after an outing. Not only does it block out light, but it also blocks out patterns. This is a relief to me as I can find compulsive pattern-counting exhausting. I sometimes bring an eye mask in my handbag, and if my husband is driving, I put the eye mask on in the car to calm my eyes as I transition away from a social situation.

- *Calm lighting*: Using lamps or candles instead of bright lights can be visually calming in the evening.

- *Colourful lights*: Coloured bulbs or lava lamps may be calming to you. Twinkling colourful lights can also be enjoyable to some people. A flickering fire (either real or fake) is famously cosy.

- *Looking at images of beautiful things or your special interest* may produce calm feelings. I love looking at Jane Austen TV shows, and sometimes put them on just to look at the house decor in them. I also keep Jane Austen books by my bed, and things I associate with Jane Austen such as embroidery and fabrics that remind me of the shows and movies.

- *Block out bright light*: Wearing sunglasses or a light-blocking hat can help manage bright light. Using desk screens in your work environment can reduce light glare, or you can move your desk so you are facing away from glaring light. Many operating systems, web browsers, apps, and other software now support an optional 'Dark Mode' to reduce screen brightness.

- *Try to have one visually calm space or corner at home*: This means there is one place you can sit without looking at visually overwhelming mess, even if the house is untidy. I avoid fully open plan living for this reason. I could not relax in the evening if my sofa faced a messy kitchen, and as my arthritis often makes it impossible to tidy in the evening, my kitchen is often messy at this time. Positioning a chair to face a window can also work, if the view is pleasant. Sitting here for a few minutes may allow your visual sense calm down.

- *Sparkling objects, or objects that reflect light*: These can be very re-laxing for visual seekers. Fairy lights, crystals hanging in windows, and prisms that reflect light can be a lovely way to seek calm light. When I was a teenager I used to collect glitter globes, and I am still mesmerised by them. I adore how light reflects off the glitter as it spins around the globe. Glitter globes that play beautiful music are a perfect match for my seeking senses.

5. The Touch (Tactile) Sense

The touch sense gathers information through the skin, including type of touch, vibrations, fabric type, temperature of what you touch and the environment, whether it's a light or strong touch etc.

The Good Differences

- *Information-gathering hands*: Having sensitive touch in your hands can be a wonderful skill, and there are many careers and roles that benefit from the ability to gather extra information through your hands. Many caring professions would really benefit from this, including physiotherapists, osteopaths, massage therapists, doctors, and nurses. I have always been able to use my hands to gather extra information, and have often noticed that I can feel things that others don't, like whether a baby's tummy is full of wind, or whether someone has a tight muscle knot on their back (I studied Swedish body massage before I did nursing, and my tactile strength was wonderful for this).

- *Heightened sensitivity to fabrics*: Some people can use their touch sense not only to gather information, but to inform them how to use materials in a creative manner. This would be a wonderful skill for carpenters, fashion designers, interior designers, and more.

- *Advanced ability to manipulate materials using touch*: This would benefit sculptors, jewellery makers, people who work with electronics etc.

- *Seeing the world through touch*: When I was a child, I touched everything and smelled everything. I didn't feel like I'd truly seen a thing until I'd touched it; almost like it wasn't real until I knew how it felt. I touched everything, and dragged my hand along walls and bushes and railings constantly. I still love to touch things more than most people, and it helps me turn the memory of an object from a 2D memory to a 3D memory. I also get a huge amount of joy from touching things, as I have a strong link between my emotions and my touch sense.

- *Navigating in low light*: A helpful skill for campers, renovators, rescue workers, and for when you want to navigate at night in a home or hostel without waking anyone. It is valuable, too, for finding things

THE FAMOUS FIVE SENSES

that are simply out-of-sight, such as when finding items lost under a car seat or behind furniture.

- *Physical information for empathy*: We often gather information that sparks our empathy through touch. We may sense the emotional state of a person through the grip of their hand, or by the temperature and perspiration of their skin, or the set of their back and shoulders when we embrace or sit with arms over one another.

The Bad Differences

- *Uncomfortable touch*: When you are extra sensitive to touch, it can make it hard to relax when your skin touches something that feels uncomfortable. For example, I find it hard to stay focused if my clothes get wet, and have vivid memories of the torture of sitting in school with wet tights after walking to school in the rain. It felt like actual pain, rather than discomfort.

- *Sensitive touch can make it hard to touch certain things*: I find touching slime or play-doh really difficult, but my children love it, so I inevitably have to touch it to clean up. Other things I've noticed some autistic people find hard to touch include raw meat, certain foods, insects, soil, and sand.

- *Eating and drinking*: The texture of food (which is touch and not taste) can make eating or drinking difficult. Things like shellfish, sauces, lumps in mashed potato, and orange juice with bits in rather than smooth can all feel like an assault in the mouth if you are sensitive to food texture. I am very lucky I don't have an overly sensitive palate, but members of my family can be hugely restricted in what they eat due to texture. The temperature of food or drink can also affect your touch sense, and you may, for example, find water from the tap difficult to drink, but manage tap water out of the fridge no problem.

- *Difficulty with seams or tags on clothes*: This can make picking clothes very challenging, and can be very difficult if you have to wear certain clothes, such as a work uniform that has prominent seams.

- *Difficulty finding clothes that feel comfortable*: This is particularly hard when a social norm dictates what clothes are appropriate in a social situation. For example, you may be most comfortable wearing joggers, but this won't look appropriate for most job interviews. You may be asked to wear a uniform or a suit for work, but you may have an extreme aversion to the material involved, the tightness of the fabric, or the seams.

- *Difficulty with certain fabrics*: For me, I can't wear or sit on velvet. If I'm near velvet, or any material than feels like it might physically get under my nails, my hands tense up like claws and I feel acutely stressed. One of my daughters can't touch me if I wear wool (her whole body tenses up). If I'm very stressed I can't wear denim jeans as I feel claustrophobic in them.

- *Extreme difficulty with wearing creams or lotions*: This can include sun lotion or medicated creams, which can lead to an increased risk of sun burn, skin damage, or the inability to treat medical conditions.

- *Difficulty with medical treatment*: A lot of medical treatment involves some sort of touch, whether it's having your blood pressure taken, your heart rate listened to, a dressing or plaster being put on your skin, or the touch involved with having a medical procedure or having an operation.

- *Difficulty with the dentist*: Going to the dentist can highly challenge the touch sense (and other senses for that matter!). I find this is intensified because someone is touching inside my mouth, which is an area totally unused to touch from other people's hands. Dental treatment can also bring unusual touch or vibrations from the instruments and tools used.

- *Challenges with touch during pregnancy*: Being pregnant involves a huge amount of touch changes, from the actual feeling of a baby moving around inside you (personally I loved this), to the midwives or doctors touching your body to assess your and your baby's health. I found the frequent touch by other people during pregnancy quite disconcerting at first, but thankfully I adjusted to it quickly. Also, having a large pregnant belly seems to attract people to rub your belly, including strangers, which can be very uncomfortable.

- *A dislike of being touched by other people*: There are different degrees of this, and everyone will be different. For some autistic people, they can't bear any physical touch with another person. Others can tolerate it only on their terms, and when they are in full control of the touch. Some autistic people love touch from some people, usually family members, but can't tolerate it from other people. Others may love touching others, and constantly want to touch other people. One of my daughters wants to be constantly touching me, hugging me, leaning on me, but if I go to hug her, she tenses up. The touch must be on her terms.

Having an aversion to touching other people can be very challenging. It can make crowded places and social situations stressful as you don't know if someone will touch you. It can also make accessing healthcare stressful if you are worried health professionals will touch you, or if you don't know when to predict touch.

Other stressful activities include using busy public transport where a lot of people stand in close proximity, or sitting next to strangers in cinemas or on airplanes. I really dislike when someone puts their elbow on the armrest between seats, and tense up in fear that their elbow will touch me. I don't have a high level of touch aversion, but it explodes in small or confined spaces, especially when there's no way to quickly escape. Squashed elevators are a nightmare.

- *Difficulty with physical affection and intimacy*: Having an intimate relationship can involve various forms of touch (from sitting beside each other with thighs touching or an arm draped around your shoulder, to holding hands, to kissing, to sexual activity), and exploring intimate touch may be uncomfortable at times if you experience unexpected discomfort around touch, or fear of discomfort. Chapter 10 provides further detail on this challenge.

- *Discomfort with 'shoulder-taps'*: In many parts of the world, it is customary for people to tap your shoulder if they want your attention and cannot get your attention through audible cues (e.g. if you are in a loud setting, or if you failed to hear them the first time, or in places where audible cues are inappropriate such as libraries). If you are deaf, perhaps people feel that a shoulder-tap is the only means to attract your attention. Because of these external factors and usual social conventions, this can be a form of unexpected personal touch that it is hard for you to express discomfort with.

The Soothing Strategies

- *Try clothes on before buying, and notice your mood*: This is to make sure that they don't aggravate your touch sense. Don't try on clothes when you're really stressed as your touch sense may be extra sensitive. I have certain clothes I can wear happily when I feel calm, but not if I'm feeling stressed, as I feel like the seams are cutting into me, the tags are scratching me, and the fabric is claustrophobic against my skin. It is sometimes worth trying the clothes on at home instead of in the shop, but leave the shop tags on so you can return them if they aren't comfortable.

- *Assess which materials or objects are pleasing to your touch sense*: I love the feel of smooth round stones, and when I rub them between my fingers they help me feel calm. I therefore keep one on my desk, and I hold it during stressful phone calls, or as a way to seek touch.

- *Prepare for sensations you know you dislike*: For example, if you dislike sand and are going to the beach, you could bring fresh water to rinse your feet after the beach, a towel to dry them and talcum powder to get any leftover sand off before you put your socks and shoes on.

- *Communicate your difficulty with physical touch*: It's perfectly fine to tell healthcare staff that you dislike touch. You can ask them to tell you if they need to touch you, so you can prepare yourself and use a technique like counting to distract yourself. You can ask them to hand you equipment and allow you put it on yourself so they don't have to touch you. You can ask them to touch you over your clothes and wear a vest for abdominal examinations (this isn't always possible, but even if the exam was mostly done over a vest, it might prevent your touch sense getting totally overwhelmed). I so dislike the touch in dental treatment that I listen to music using earphones, I wear sunglasses, I wear very comfortable clothes, and I repeat the mantra 'It's a sensation not a pain' in my head. These tactics really help me endure dental treatment.

- *Communicate your difficulty with fabric*: I have phoned or emailed hotels and asked for a room with no velvet. I have also asked for allergy-safe pillows as I dislike the feeling of feather pillows (I feel as though each individual feather is digging into me, and it distracts me from sleep). If there is a choice of chairs in an environment, I request the non-velvet one.

- *Alter your clothes*: Cut off tags. Wear socks or vests inside out to avoid the seams against your skin. Get a tailor or seamstress to line uniforms with a material you can tolerate such as soft jersey. Sew a desired material into your pockets for a lovely sensory sensation, such as satin or soft fleece.

- *Put a barrier between you and the thing you dislike to touch*: Lay a coat on a chair you dislike the feel of. Wear plastic gloves if you dislike play-doh or baking. Roll out your baking between layers of baking paper so you can shape pastry, cookies etc. without it sticking to your hands (and the table and rolling pin so the tidying up is less tactile too). Use tools to avoid touching something with your hands, e.g. use kitchen tongs if you dislike touching raw meat.

- *Arrive early to social gatherings*: This allows you to choose a chair you can tolerate, and choose a quiet corner so people aren't going to be brushing past you physically.

- *Tips for wet clothes*: If you can't change out of wet clothes, try putting a tissue or cotton handkerchief between you and the wet fabric, or using a hand dryer to dry the fabric. I often bring spare socks in my bag as I can't relax when I have wet socks, and often bring cotton handkerchiefs or muslin cloths with me, to use as a barrier between my skin and wet fabric.

- *Pay attention to temperature changes against your skin*: I really over-react to cold air, and can start to shake if cold air touches my skin. I therefore try to wear warm clothes (sometimes even gloves) in a shop when I'm picking food out of fridges or freezers.

- *Warmth*: I adore warmth against my skin (although I dislike very hot sunshine), and use a hot water bottle as one of my main soothing strategies. I find the warmth extremely comforting, and I hold it against my tummy, my heart, or areas of discomfort. I also hold a hot water bottle when going to sleep; it helps bring my attention to the warm spot rather than the fact that my body can get jittery in bed.

- *Water*: People use water for different reasons. For example, sea swimmers feel re-energised from the cold water shock (personally I hate really cold water). Many people turn the shower to cold before they get out as it wakes them up and helps them focus. Warm baths and showers are known to calm and relax the body. I often run warm water on my wrists to help me calm down. If I'm at a lecture or conference and have lost focus, I run cold water over my wrists in the bathroom, as it sends an alert feeling up my arm. I also splash cold water on my face to bring back my focus.

- *Experiment and ask for advice if you can't tolerate medical equipment or creams*: Communicate your problems and ask for alternatives. Pharmacists have a lot of knowledge about products, and you might discover that while you can't tolerate a sun cream, you can tolerate a sun-protection mist, oil, or a rub-on sun-stick.

- *The Wilbarger Protocol (aka brushing)*: This is an occupational therapy technique that aims to improve tactile defensiveness (which means avoidance of and sensitivity to touch). It involves using a specific type of brush at certain parts of the body, along with joint compression. While I was unable to find any research into autistic adults using this technique, there is a very small amount of published evidence about its benefit in children. Despite the small amount of research, in my experience it is widely used for autistic children with good effect. The technique needs to be taught by an occupational therapist trained in doing so.

- *Get creative about controlling touch from other people*: There are many types of relationships that carry the expectation of touch. It is worth exploring what touch feels safe in each relationship, and what you can do to improve your tolerance of touch if you want to. You might tolerate one type of touch with members of your family, but not tolerate it with friends. You might love unexpected kisses and cuddles from your child, but dislike it intensely from anyone else.

Sometimes I get 'touched out', which means I've hit my maximum tolerance of being touched, and can't take any more without hitting a point of overwhelm. If my children have needed a lot of physical attention and touch one day, I sometimes feel unable to touch, or even be very near, other people. Setting boundaries and taking some time alone can help with this.

You can also get creative about reducing the chances that someone will touch you. For example:

- Set up your environment to deter people touching you. This may include sitting on an armchair rather than a couch, as a couch invites more people to sit near you.

- Draping a blanket or your coat over you can act like a barrier to other people touching you. Positioning your desk so that you are cordoned off from people walking by can help avoid people touching you.

  I've had friends who always wanted to link arms, and this has made me uncomfortable as I didn't feel in control of the touch. I didn't know how to ask them to stop, but I figured out that if I linked their arm instead of them linking mine, I was in control, and this felt fine, as long as our skin didn't touch. Nowadays I would have no problem communicating that I'd rather not link arms, but as a teenager or young adult I didn't have that confidence.

- *Increase your proprioceptive and vestibular sensory feedback*: When my proprioception sense is grounded, I am able to tolerate more touch. If my children are having a day in which they need a lot of cuddles and touch, I often increase my proprioception feedback, for example by using a weighted blanket or lifting small weights. Regulating my vestibular sense also helps me feel calmer in myself, so I often try to do some yoga poses like downward dog, or eat some crunchy raw vegetables like carrots or celery. This really helps me ground myself, and can even reset my touch tolerance.

KEY POINTS

◊ The Famous Five Senses include the sound sense, the taste sense, the smell sense, the sight sense, and the touch sense.
◊ How we react to each of the Famous Five Senses being stimulated can have a significant impact on our lives. It can affect how we experience the world, how we join in with society, our relationships, and the decisions we make.
◊ Having a difference in how you experience any of the Famous Five Senses can bring challenges, but also strengths.

References

Kontaris, I., East, B.S., and Wilson, D.A. (2020) 'Behavioural and Neurobiological Convergence of Odor, Mood and Emotion: A Review'. *Frontiers in Behavioural Neuroscience* 14, 35. https://doi.org/10.3389/fnbeh.2020.00035

Ranjan, S. and Nasser, J.A. (2015) 'Nutritional Status of Individuals with Autism Spectrum Disorders: Do We Know Enough?' *Advances in Nutrition* 6 (4), 397–407. https://dx.doi.org/10.3945/an.114.007914

Stanutz, S., Wapnick, J., and Burack, J.A. (2014) 'Pitch Discrimination and Melodic Memory in Children with Autism Spectrum Disorders'. *Autism* 18 (2), 137–147. https://doi.org/10.1177/1362361312462905

Chapter 10

Looking After Your Senses during Intimacy and Sexual Activity

CHAPTER BREAKDOWN

CHAPTER AIMS

› To discuss how to look after your Famous Five Senses, especially touch, during intimacy and sexual activity.
› To explore consent, and how it is vital to protect and support your senses, especially your touch sense.
› To look at how important it is to ensure you have a method of giving and withdrawing consent.

Introduction

Intimate relationships and sexual activity are an important part of life for many autistic adults, just like they are for non-autistic adults. Sensory differences can have a significant impact on how you experience intimacy and/or sexual activity. SPD can cause challenges in intimacy, from small difficulties (such as not being able to enjoy intimacy unless the lights are off) to major challenges (such as extreme levels of touch aversion so that intimate touch makes you feel unsafe or anxious). Alternatively, for some people with SPD, their sensory differences can improve their experience of intimacy or sexual activity, in that they experience enhanced pleasure from the sensory experiences involved.

As autistic adults, we often need to think 'outside the box' in order to adapt activities to suit our sensory needs (rather than adapting ourselves to suit the activity!). Intimacy and sexual activity are no different.

In this chapter, I have included suggestions for managing the Famous Five Senses, in particular touch, during intimacy or sexual activity. I also explore the power of consent to set intimacy boundaries, both to protect yourself and your partner, and to increase your enjoyment of intimacy. If you cannot find the strategies you need in this chapter, I recommend spending time thinking about how you can develop your own strategies, discussing any issues with your partner to see if they can come up with a strategy that works for you both. If you continue to have difficulties with your senses during intimacy or sexual activity, I recommend seeking out professional help and advice.

Our emotions are very tied up with our senses, and if you continue to have sensory challenges during intimacy or sexual activity, it might be worth exploring if the problem is actually sensory, or if it is psychological. Talking to a psychotherapist, psychologist, sex counsellor, or counsellor might help you explore this. Intimacy and sex can be very important in our lives, and need to be treated as important (unless they are actually not important to you, for example if you are asexual or aromantic); do consider seeking help if you experience difficulties in this area.

Set the Scene for the Senses

Intimacy and sexual activity need to feel safe in order for you to enjoy them. If you don't feel safe and secure, the experience will probably end up feeling uncomfortable, upsetting, and perhaps even traumatic.

When I say you need to feel safe, I don't only mean that you should feel safe with your partner; I also mean that each of your senses needs to feel safe within the activity. In order to do this, I advise you to spend some time thinking about what sensory soothing strategies will help each of your senses feel safe. You can then 'set the scene' for your sensory comfort, to maximise your enjoyment and feeling of safety within whatever intimate or sexual activity you choose to engage in.

- *Proprioception*: Regulating your proprioceptive sense before and during intimacy can really increase your feeling of safety and your tolerance of sensory stimulation, especially touch. Perhaps you can lie under a weighted blanket before intimacy, or you can try creating the sensation of tucking parts of your body in with pillows, to help your body feel cocooned, grounded, and safe. You could also try weighted products, such as weighted ankle or wrist straps or jewellery, or draping a weighted blanket over your shoulder (weighted blankets come in different weights, so you can test which one will work for you in this situation).

- *Vestibular*: If you have difficulty with your vestibular sense, you might not like certain positions involved in intimacy. For example, you might dislike lying flat on your back, or leaning your head back. You might feel off balance if you don't feel connected to a solid surface, such as if you cannot feel your limbs on the ground, or the full length of your body on a bed. Trying different positions, or using pillows or blankets to prop up parts of your body or your head, can help reduce the feeling of vestibular dysregulation during intimacy.

- *Smell*: There are many things that can trigger the smell sense during intimacy, and it can present a significant challenge. You can't exactly put a peg on your nose in order to kiss someone (unless you are extremely creative with your position!). Intimacy and sexual activity usually involve being in very close proximity to your partner, thus making it impossible to walk away from the smell you dislike without walking away from the intimacy (which has the potential to make your partner feel rejected). Difficult smells can include natural body odours, bodily fluids, your partner's breath (especially if it smells of alcohol, cigarettes, or unbrushed teeth), the smell of food your partner has eaten (think garlic), perfumes or hygiene products your dislike, and more.

  A smell can have an overwhelming effect, and can make you feel repulsed by your partner's close proximity, no matter how much you want to be near them. If you or your partner has not had a shower lately, it can intensify the smell of body odours and bodily fluids. Making sure you are both clean and fresh can really help with intimacy comfort. Having a window slightly open or having a smell you like in the room (e.g. a scented candle) can help.

You could also include scents that you love or seek, for example choosing a deodorant or perfume/cologne with your partner. Fresh sheets on the bed can also improve the overall smell in the room. Communicating with your partner is so important when it comes to smells. Having a polite conversation of what smells you do and don't like can really improve your experience of intimacy. If this is done in advance of intimacy, it can avoid situations of rejection.

- *Sight*: The light in the environment can have a big impact on whether you feel safe and calm. If the light is glaring or too bright, and you feel bothered by this, it might make you more sensitive or resistant to other sensory inputs such as touch or smell.

  It's worth trying out different types of light, from daylight to lamps, candles to darkness, and seeing which one feels safe and comfortable to you. You might also like to have a light that appeals to your senses, such as a lava lamp, coloured lights, or flickering candlelight. Bed linens can move around a lot during sexual activity, so make sure any candles are secure and contained safely.

- *Taste*: Depending on how you and your partner choose to be intimate, there can be taste sensations involved in intimacy and sexual activity, and these can be challenging if you have taste aversions.

  Kissing with bad breath can taste unpleasant, and bodies and bodily fluids can also have strong and changeable tastes, depending on what your partner has been doing that day (e.g. if they have been doing manual labour or are not clean!). Some foods, such as garlic, onion, or asparagus can significantly change bodily smells and tastes, so it's worth paying attention to what foods turn you off being intimate with your partner, and communicating this in a respectful and kind manner.

- *Interoception*: As with all sensory self-care, meeting your basic needs will greatly improve your ability to tolerate touch or other sensory inputs during sexual intimacy. This includes making sure you are not hungry, thirsty, too cold, too hot, in pain etc. How we feel emotionally will also have a huge impact on our ability to be intimate, so checking in with your emotions can help you know what activities you feel safe engaging in and what you are comfortable consenting to.

- *Sound*: Sexual intimacy naturally brings sounds, and some of these sounds can be unsettling or uncomfortable. I have heard of people who can't stand the sound of two materials rubbing on each other, and I've heard of people who are so terrified that their own body will make a strange or embarrassing noise during intimacy (e.g. a fart) that they can't relax and enjoy it. Using music, recorded sounds, or white noise might increase your enjoyment of intimacy.

  The best advice I have to deal with embarrassing body sounds is to laugh at it. It's really no big deal, we are all human, and the human body is noisy; coming to terms with this, or preparing a funny phrase in advance, can help you relax about it.

Sensory Soothing Strategies for Touch during Intimacy or Sexual Activity

It can be very hard on a relationship if you have difficulty with touch during intimacy or sexual activity. The more senses that are challenged during intimate or sexual activity, the harder it is to manage any one sense. Keeping this in mind can really improve your ability to enjoy touch during intimacy. There are also things you can do specifically to support your touch sense during intimacy.

- *Reduce skin-to-skin contact*: If you find it overwhelming to touch another person, or to touch too much of a person at one time, it can help to reduce the amount of skin-to-skin contact you have. Using clothes, sheets, cushions etc. can help achieve this.

- *Increase skin-to-skin contact*: If you find the feeling of clothes rubbing against each other difficult, it might be helpful to reduce the amount of clothes between you and thus increase skin-to-skin contact. Skin-to-skin contact can also improve emotional connection, which can help your sensory tolerance.

- *Experiment with fabrics*: Trying out different materials may help you tolerate the feel of sheets, or your partner's clothing against you. Your choice of fabric is very personal, and in my experience, autistic people can differ widely on which fabrics they can tolerate. For example, silk and satin are often associated with being a desirable fabric for intimacy, but it might feel awful to you. Personally, I find synthetic fabric difficult, and so I avoid polyester sheets, nylon tights, acrylic clothes etc. I love woollen jumpers, but not if it touches my skin directly, and so I need a layer between myself and wool, and certainly couldn't lie on a woollen blanket.

Lycra and fleece are two materials that I've seen people be very divided on; some people find Lycra clothes very appealing to the touch sense, and others hate it. Fleece is highly comforting to some people, and you can even buy fleece bed sheets. Other people can't stand the synthetic, unbreathable nature of fleece, and would have difficulty lying on a bed with fleece sheets. It is therefore worth planning out what fabrics, or lack of fabrics, will help you to enjoy intimacy.

- *Deal with perspiration*: Perspiration during sexual intimacy may alter how you respond to the touch of your partner, so it may help if you have an absorbent sheet between you, or even a damp towel to quickly wipe off the perspiration if it becomes too uncomfortable (this could be a bit startling to your partner if it's unexpected, so it might be worth letting your partner know that you plan to do this in advance, especially if you're cleaning it off their body and not your own!). If you want to avoid clammy skin, you can try using hygiene products such as talcum powder to reduce clamminess. However, it's important to note that talc is not to be inhaled or used on intimate parts of the body due to possible risk of health problems.

- *Experiment with environments*: Different environments and rooms may affect how you experience intimate or sexual touch. You might dislike being touched on the sofa, but enjoy it in a dark bedroom. You might feel anxious in a bedroom in case the activity goes further than you want it to, and so you might feel more relaxed to be intimate with your partner in a less personal room of the house, if appropriate to do so. You might find that you can tolerate more touch in water, so taking a bath or shower with your partner might be a pleasant or calm place to begin intimacy.

The Power of Consent to Set Intimacy Boundaries
Everyone has the right to give or withdraw consent during sexual or intimate activity, at any time or stage. Knowing that you are in control of your

own consent is extremely important for your sensory system to feel safe, and to keep it regulated during sexual activity. To know that your touch sense is safe during intimacy, you must first ensure that you have the ability to communicate your giving and taking away of consent.

Consent during sex or intimacy means that you agree to the activity (the activity can range anywhere from holding hands or kissing, to sexting or sending sexual photos, to engaging in sex or sexual activity). Consent should be sought from both partners in a sexual relationship, and you both have the power not only to give your consent, but also to take away your consent.

If someone acts in a sexual manner towards you, knowingly within view of you, or with your body, without your consent, this may be considered sexual assault. Equally, if you do not have your partner's consent and you engage in sexual activity with them or in front of them, this may also be considered sexual assault.

Consent to do one activity doesn't automatically mean consent to do another activity. For example, if you give consent to kiss, this doesn't mean you are giving consent to have sex. Consent to one kind of sexual activity does not mean consent to another or to all kinds of sexual activities. Consent is therefore not something that happens once at the start of sexual intimacy, it should be a continuous part of intimacy, constantly sought out each time the sexual activity progresses or changes, to ensure nothing makes one of the partners uncomfortable. This is particularly important for autistic people who have touch sensitivities, as you might not know that a touch will feel uncomfortable until it happens. You should therefore always be able to communicate that you want a touch to stop, or change.

Consent is given or taken away through communication, and because autistic people can have difficulties or differences with communication, it is extremely important that before you engage in sexual activity, you first establish a method of communication to ensure you both maintain your power of consent. This is the best way to ensure you stay comfortable with any touch during sexual intimacy, and the best way to ensure you feel safe.

There are many methods with which to give and take back consent, but the method needs to be clear to both partners. Consent is not always spoken; sometimes it is implied through physical movement, for example moving towards your partner, or responding encouragingly to their touch advances by using encouraging body language, or by making sounds that suggest you are pleased or feeling pleasure. Spoken or written denial or withdrawal of consent, of course, always supersedes what might seem like approving body language.

Consent is sometimes looked for in facial expressions. For example, your partner may look at your face to see if you look like you are enjoying the activity and want to continue, or to see if you want them to progress towards more intimate activity. *As autistic people can have difficulty with body language and facial expressions, it can get confusing at times to communicate consent through these methods, both to give consent yourself, or to read whether your partner gives consent.*

If you do not feel able to use body language or facial expression to give or take away your own consent, or to read your partner's body language or facial expression, it is advisable to explain this to your partner in advance of any sexual activity. You can then discuss which alternative method of communication you can use to express or withhold consent.

It's always okay to take away consent during sexual or intimate activity, but you need to communicate this to your partner. This will involve pre-arranging a way to communicate when you want to withdraw consent in any activity, at any time.

If you plan on using verbal communication for consent, it can be helpful to prepare what you will say in advance. This is because if you feel stressed or unsafe during an activity, it can be hard to come up with a phrase or to think of how to say what you want to say. Examples of useful phrases might include, 'Let's take a break', 'I'd like a break', 'I'm not comfortable with that', 'I need a minute', or even 'Stop'.

If you find it difficult to or cannot rely on words to communicate, you can use alternative methods of communication, such as guiding your partner's hand away from where they are touching, or using a 'Stop' or 'Time Out' hand gesture. You could also agree on a signal like turning on the lamp to show that you want to stop. You could use a visual system to control your consent, such as having a visual flashcard that says 'Stop' or 'Not That' or 'No Thanks'. You could equally have a notebook on your bedside table and you can write out what you give consent to do, and what you don't give consent to do.

An alternative is creating a visual traffic light type system, such as having a green object, orange object, and a red object on your bedside locker. When you want your partner to change activity, or stop touching you somewhere, you can hold up the orange object. When you want to take a complete break you can hold up the red object. For this to work you need to explain the system to your partner. Types of objects to use in a traffic light system could include pillows, scarfs, or ribbons in green, orange, and red, and you simply have to hold up the colour that communicates your preference.

I've heard people saying that asking for consent 'kills the mood'. Personally, I'd rather 'kill the mood' than engage in a sexual activity that I don't feel safe with. Nothing kills the mood more than feeling unsafe, or realising too late that your partner has started doing something to your body that you don't want them to. I believe that being asked for your consent is the total opposite of a mood killer; to me, it improves the mood, and is a basic right. I would feel a lot more attracted to a person knowing they value my sense of safety and comfort.

Plan It, and State It

A study of the sexual experiences of autistic adults found that planning was a helpful tool when it comes to engaging in sexual activity, as it helps autistic adults to manage and establish expectations, and to prepare for any particular needs (Barnett and Maticka-Tyndale, 2015). Preparing when you and your partner will engage in sexual activity can allow you to incorporate many of the sensory activities mentioned in this chapter, such as by ensuring your basic needs are met, getting the scene ready for your senses, and grounding your proprioceptive and vestibular senses beforehand. Obviously some of these will work better for people who are in an established relationship, rather than if you are having a spontaneous one night stand, or if you don't yet know if your desired partner will want to engage in sexual activity.

It's important to note, however, that just because you agree and plan ahead with your partner, this doesn't mean that either partner can't change their mind and withdraw consent at any point.

The same study also identified that autistic people found it helpful to state ('Literal Declaration' as per the research article) their intentions, agreement, and feelings, and to avoid innuendo-based language or euphemism when it comes to sexual activity. This was found to be the key to successful use of sensory strategies, such as using barriers like blankets or latex gloves (for the touch sense), or to negotiate sexual activities that they wish to engage in or not engage in.

KEY POINTS

◊ Intimacy and sexual activity can bring their own unique challenges to the sensory system.

◊ Setting the scene for the senses can help each sense feel calm, and thus increase your ability to enjoy intimacy or sexual activity.

◊ There are a number of sensory soothing strategies to support your touch sense during intimacy or sexual activity.

◊ The power of consent is a very important part of managing the senses during sexual intimacy.

◊ It is important to establish a method of communication for giving or taking away consent during intimacy or sexual activity.

References

Barnett, J.P. and Maticka-Tyndale, E. (2015) 'Qualitative Exploration of Sexual Experiences among Adults on the Autism Spectrum: Implications for Sex Education'. *Perspectives on Sexual and Reproductive Health* 47 (4), 171–179. https://doi.org/10.1363/47e5715

Chapter 11

Managing Sensory Overload, Shutdowns, and Meltdowns

CHAPTER BREAKDOWN

CHAPTER AIMS

> To discuss sensory overload.
> To explain my experience of shutdowns and meltdowns.
> To look at the good and the bad of meltdowns.
> To explain the need for Sensory Soothing Plans.
> To explore the use of having a portable sensory toolkit.

What Is Sensory Overload?

Sensory overload occurs when one or more of your senses becomes over-stimulated. During sensory overload, your nervous system becomes unable to process the information that your senses are taking in. Because autistic people are more likely to have difficulties processing sensory information, we are more likely to reach a point of sensory overload than non-autistic people, or people without SPD.

> To explain sensory overload: Imagine you see a toddler screaming and screaming at their parent. At first the parent can cope with the screaming; they try to reason with the toddler, and they try to distract the toddler with a toy. The child keeps screaming. This continues for a while, but eventually the parent starts to lose patience; they start to look stressed, and they start begging the child to stop screaming at them. The child continues to scream. Eventually the parent can no longer cope with the screaming. They reach their limit. They cover their ears, they close their eyes, they clench their jaw. They cannot think rationally any more. They are overloaded, and they feel out of control.

This feeling of hitting your limit and being unable to maintain control is similar to the feeling autistic people can get when we experience sensory overload. *If we can't take back control once we've hit our sensory limit, we may experience shutdown, or have a meltdown.*

Sensory Overload Is Not 'All in Your Head'

It's important to remember that an overloaded sensory system is not in your head, it's not a thought pattern, and it's not the same as anxiety (although it does act like a 'welcome in' sign for anxiety). It is physical, it's in our bodies. However, if the sensory system is overloaded, the overwhelm can easily spread into other areas of function, including cognitive function (the ability to think), and executive function (including thinking, planning, problem solving etc.). Sensory overwhelm can reduce your ability to communicate, your social skills, and your ability to plan and organise. It can also cause emotional distress and anxiety.

Because your sensory system is part of your body, it needs to be treated like any other part of your body. If you twisted your ankle, would you tell yourself this is all in your head and force yourself to walk on it? If you did, you would not be caring for your body. Sensory stress can build up, just like walking on a sprained ankle will increase your pain. People with SPD need to recognise when their sensory system needs care, just like the rest of the body. If you don't check in with your sensory system, and if you don't allow your sensory system to calm down when it's under pressure, you will increase your chances of becoming overwhelmed.

If I try to force myself to keep going when my sensory system is over-loaded, I become anxious, shaky, and am likely to cry or lose my temper. I stop being able to think properly, I get a feeling of doom, and become nauseous, dizzy, and experience an increased heart rate. If I am exposed to something that triggers my sensory overwhelm for too long, or if I don't have the tools to deals with an over-stimulating environment, it can lead me to shut down or melt down.

What Are Meltdowns and Shutdowns?

A meltdown is an intense response to becoming overwhelmed. The cause of overwhelm can be sensory, emotional, or cognitive. A meltdown can be described as the loss of control of yourself, or of your emotions.

Meltdowns are different for every autistic person. They might involve intense emotional release such as crying uncontrollably or shouting or screaming. They might involve certain functions of your body shutting down, such as losing the ability to speak or think. They might involve run-ning away or hiding. They might include physical changes such as shaking, trembling, or repetitive movements such as rocking back and forth.

For some people, a meltdown can involve the 'fight' response, causing them to lash out. Some people lash out through words (this might include verbally attacking yourself, other people, or be aimed at no-one), others through physical actions (this might include actions such as pinching your arm, pulling hairs out of your head, clenching your fists so tight that your nails cut into your skin, smashing things, punching walls, being physically aggressive to another person, banging or striking your head etc.).

During a meltdown you may be unable to process or recognise the fact that you are doing any of these behaviours, and cannot simply tell yourself to stop. This doesn't mean that you aren't aware it's happening, and it doesn't mean you won't remember what happened after the meltdown. In fact, guilt and shame after a meltdown can be very common, as people do usually remember what happened.

A shutdown, on the other hand, is more like the 'freeze' response to stress, where you tend to go in on yourself, and your brain feels as though it has shut down. In a shutdown, an autistic person may lose the ability to communicate, or seem detached from people or the environment around them. Almost like they are 'hiding in a shell' and can't come out, because their ability to function has switched off.

My Shutdowns

Just like all autistic people experience differences in their sensory integration, we also all experience differences in how we shut down or melt down.

I can go a few weeks without a shutdown, or I can shut down once or twice a week, or once or twice a day. It all depends on what I am doing and how I'm feeling. If I am at home all week, feeling mostly calm, spending my time on my special interests, seeing no-one or very few people socially, I am unlikely to shut down. If I have a busy week with multiple appointments, jobs to do outside of my home, and a lot of balls to juggle (metaphorically), then I am more likely to experience shutdown. *My sensory system becomes more sensitive the more emotional stress I am under.* Another thing that makes me more likely to become overwhelmed easily is exhaustion, especially if I'm going through a bout of insomnia.

Sometimes I will have what I call a '*mini shutdown*'. I can recover from a mini shutdown quickly, usually within an hour, as long as I can take the time to calm my sensory system. This can feel like my brain and body just need a rest as they aren't in sync, and my thinking is struggling. I always crave my bed when I have a mini shutdown. My body may feel stressed or like there's an itch that I can't scratch unless I rest. This may happen after a social outing or a trip to a shopping centre. I hit a point where I know I need to rest and switch off my brain and body in order to recharge, so that my body can feel safe and calm again, rather than threatened or under attack.

A *full shutdown* may affect me for a whole day or more, and I need to completely rest. A full shutdown, for me, feels like I become detached from my surroundings and feel unable to function. This would never lead to a dangerous situation for me, as I am always able to postpone shutting down until it is safe to do so, but I do need to get away from the sensory stimulus that is causing my overwhelm. For example, if I become aware that I am about to shut down, I know to turn off the cooker. I know to pull over the car if I am too overwhelmed to drive safely, which has only ever happened once or twice. If I am alone with my children, I know I cannot shut down while I am responsible for them, and so I can push back shutting down until my husband is available to mind them. Only when it is safe to do so, do I go to my bedroom and allow myself to shut down. This postponement takes huge effort and causes a lot of stress in my body, and I will certainly end up with a clenched jaw and a headache. Postponing a shutdown makes the shutdown more intense, and it might last longer.

To cope with a shutdown, I basically lock myself in my house and reduce all demands on me as much as possible. I need a lot of physical rest and I need to be very caring to myself. Once I've had an hour or two alone in bed, I can then talk to my family and do the basic jobs like cooking, but I can't meet other people, I can't face demands, and I need to physically rest as much as possible.

My Meltdowns

The cause of me having a meltdown is usually from forcing myself not to shut down for too long a time. Then when I finally do allow myself to shut down, it turns into a meltdown of uncontrollable crying, deep and intense dread, and feelings of doom, nausea, difficulty breathing without hyperventilating, feeling completely unable to cope, and feeling like I will faint.

Another way I can melt down is that I can start laughing, and the laughter becomes intense and uncontrollable. This leads me to feel afraid, and I end up crying, possibly hyperventilating, and can then become dizzy, faint, and nauseous. This *laughing meltdown* is more likely to happen to me when I am emotionally stressed or exhausted, whereas a regular shutdown or meltdown can be from sensory overwhelm alone.

I find the laughter meltdown the hardest of meltdowns. It sounds so ridiculous, and even funny, but in fact, it feels like that horrible laughter you get when you are being tickled, and yet there is no-one to stop tickling you. It tends to start with me actually laughing at something funny, but the laughter escalates to hysteria. It then just goes on and on, and switches from laughing to crying to laughing to crying. I have absolutely no control over it; I cannot push it back to happen another time. I feel like I cannot breathe when it happens, and it really feels like I've lost all control of myself.

Despite the fact that I look like I'm laughing, and other people find it hilarious and will contagiously laugh at me, it is actually terrifying to be inside that laughing meltdown, because it is hard to catch my breath. Thankfully, it doesn't happen in public, although it did happen in public a few times in my teenage years. I have always struggled to stop laughing (even when not in a meltdown), and regularly had to leave the classroom in school to finish laughing, alone in the school bathrooms. My husband is wonderful when this horrible laughing meltdown hits me; he guides me to bed, puts a weighted blanket over me, closes the blinds, and stays with me; a soothing presence. This helps enormously. I nearly always sleep afterwards as it is completely exhausting.

The Bitter and Sweet of Meltdowns

The bitter side to meltdowns is that it can make you feel like you've lost control, and you might feel embarrassed that you 'couldn't hold it together'. This can lead to feelings of shame or guilt. I know I have certainly felt ashamed of myself in the past after a meltdown, and chastised myself for 'not being able to deal with things like other adults'. Thankfully now that I understand I'm autistic, I no longer feel this way. Instead, I become com-passionate towards myself and kick into self-care mode, using my sensory soothing strategies to calm myself.

Meltdowns can also lead to physical discomfort and exhaustion. You might develop pain in your body due to a meltdown (I get a headache, jaw pain, and pain in my neck and shoulder muscles from shaking). Some autistic people can hurt themselves during a meltdown, for example by banging their head against the wall, or punching a hard surface.

Another bitter side to meltdowns is that they make some people behave in ways that they normally wouldn't. They might scream, shout, or say hurtful things in the heat of the moment. I used to feel afraid when my sensory system was overwhelmed, and this would come out as anger. But that is in my past, I no longer get angry, because I no longer feel afraid in a meltdown. Instead I see my meltdown as a giant wave; I know it will pass, and I just have to hold on and ride the wave.

The sweet side to meltdowns is that they release pent-up emotion or pent-up sensory stress. To simplify it, they 'clear the air' in an overloaded sensory system. There can be a huge sense of relief after a meltdown, almost as though something has been released. The more you accept your melt-downs, and don't chastise yourself for them, the more of a release it will be.

Five Steps to Deal with Sensory Overload

When you feel yourself approaching overload, shutdown, or meltdown, it's important to take the time to think what you can do to calm your sensory system. I ask myself five questions to get back in control:

- *What sensory soothing strategies can you use* to help you deal with the sensory trigger? Do you have sensory soothing tools with you, for example a sensory kit with ear plugs, an eye mask, a squeeze ball, a soft scarf to rub your fingers over, a favourite song etc.?

- *Are your basic needs met?* Hunger, thirst, pain, and exhaustion can all make you hit your sensory limit a lot faster than usual. It's also a lot harder to come back from your limit if you don't meet these basic needs, so it's really important to prioritise eating, drinking etc.

- *Do you need to remove the sensory stressor from your environment?*

- *Do you need to remove yourself from the environment?*

- *Are you heading towards a shutdown or a meltdown?* If the answer is yes, what is your Sensory Soothing Plan?

Sensory Soothing Plans

To reduce or recover from sensory overload, and to stop sensory overload turning into a meltdown, I use a Sensory Soothing Plan. If I am engaging in an activity that I know will challenge my sensory system, I make my Sensory Soothing Plan before I go. The bigger the event, the bigger the plan needs to be.

If I'm going out for a small outing, such as popping to the local shop for a few groceries, I may only need a *small Sensory Soothing Plan*. My plan may simply include having a rest and a cup of tea when I get home. I may not even need the cup of tea after the shop, but knowing the option is there is hugely reassuring to me. It may involve simply putting a weighted blanket on my lap, or having nice music on in the car home. It may be to just check in with myself and ask myself how I'm feeling, and whether I need to do something about how I'm feeling.

If I'm going to a bigger event, like a social gathering, a trip to a number of shops, or a large family gathering, then I need a *big Sensory Soothing Plan*. I need to plan time to recover for an hour or two after the event. I may plan to go to bed and listen to an audiobook for an hour, or watch a favourite show, or take a walk in the fresh air.

If I'm going to a major event, like a wedding, then I need a *major Sensory Soothing Plan*. This requires planning a whole afternoon to rest and recuperate, and may spill into the following day as well as the day of the event. I need to be very prepared for this sort of plan, as I need to reduce as many demands on myself as possible, to reduce my need to think flexibly. I also need to allow my body to rest in order to recover from sensory overwhelm. This may include having a dinner pre-prepared in the fridge or freezer, having no appointments or things I need to leave the house for, having a favourite book or a TV show ready, and having the housework in good order before the event so I don't have to try to catch up on laundry or hoovering when I need to be resting. I might borrow a toy from a friend so my children have the novelty factor of having a different toy to play with, or plan a movie afternoon for them, so that I can rest. Or I might ask for babysitting help in advance so I know I can fully switch off.

Sensory Soothing Plan Ideas

Everyone will have different ideas of what to put in their Sensory Soothing Plan. It's worth trying out different things to see what works for you. As sensory overwhelm is a physical thing, I do think it's important to involve a physical element in your plan, but that doesn't have to be all you have. Combining your special interest with something physical can be a great combination to achieve both mental and physical calm at the same time.

Here are some of the things I include in my plans:

- *Change into very comfortable clothes*: I sometimes even lay out my post-event clothes before I go out, so when I come home I don't have to think about what to choose. When I am overloaded, I find choice very difficult, so the more planning I do in advance, the better. Comfortable clothes act like a soothing balm to my body.

- *Lie down under a weighted blanket*: My limbs can feel almost disconnected from my body when I'm overwhelmed, and the weighted blanket makes me feel connected back together. It also stops me shaking.

- *Hold a hot water bottle to your heart or tummy*: I tend to get the shivers and can feel extremely cold when my sensory system is overwhelmed, and for that reason I really need to warm myself up to calm the horrible shivering. Holding a hot water bottle to my tummy helps settle the gut clench I get, and holding it to my heart helps settle a racing heart.

- *Eat and drink*: Before an event, I plan what I will eat when I come home, and will get it all ready so when I return I can eat and drink easily. This is usually something easy like toast and a decaf tea. Caffeine when I'm overwhelmed makes me feel worse.

- *Close the curtains*: I love darkness when I'm overwhelmed.

- *Listen to music or an audiobook*: I listen to the same audiobooks repeatedly when I need calming or comforting, and I have certain songs that I associate with calm too.

- *Shower or bath*: I find water very calming when my sensory system is stressed.

- *Turn off my phone*: This helps me disconnect, but also ensures I don't increase my visual stress by scrolling through my phone, as this can worsen my sensory challenges.

- *Engage in my special interest*: This helps my mind feel calm. Calming the mind helps calm the body.

- *Watch a favourite TV show*: I have about three TV shows that I watch repeatedly, and when I feel overwhelmed, they are my best friends; safe, predictable, and lovely.

- *Read beloved books*: If I'm not calm, I can find it hard to read new material, so I often go back to old beloved books or poems that I associate with calm or happiness.

- *Sensory box*: This a box I keep under my bed with sensory tools: soap to smell, a postcard or book of beautiful images, an eye mask to block out light if I have a headache, something soft like a silk scarf to touch, and a list of songs I love to remind me to listen to something to calm the sound sense. I don't keep food in the box but I do keep salty crisps always at home as they give my taste sense a lovely burst of stimulation, and for some reason the salt helps me feel better.

Portable Sensory Toolkit

I always bring sensory tools with me when I go somewhere, to ensure I can use my sensory soothing strategies. Whether it's just sunglasses to block out light, or a backpack full of different sensory tools, knowing I'm prepared for the sensory environment helps me feel calm leaving home. Everyone's tools will be different, but it's important to remember that we can both seek and avoid sensory sensations. It's therefore good to bring tools that give you the sensory feedback your body craves, and not just tools to block out the sensory feedback you want to avoid.

IDEAS FOR A PORTABLE SENSORY TOOLKIT
Visual

Visual avoidance: Sunglasses, tinted glasses, or hat to block out light.

Visual seeking: A keyring torch, or a fidget with a light or something that you feel calm looking at. A photo, postcard, video, sensory app on phone, or image of a special interest or something that is beautiful or calming to you.

Smell

Smell avoidance: A scarf to breathe through to dilute environmental odours. A strong smell like eucalyptus to overpower a bad smell in the environment.

Smell seeking: Unopened soaps, small bottle of a body wash, or food that you love the smell of (I choose mandarins or oranges). I have often held an orange against my nose in a lecture, or at a conference, and nobody has ever seemed to noticed. I also frequently bring something with menthol or eucalyptus scents, as smelling this is hugely awakening and refreshing to me.

Taste

Taste avoidance: If you don't know if there will be appropriate food, then bring your own. It is so important to ensure your basic need of eating is met, to avoid hunger making you more sensitive to other sensory triggers.

Taste seeking: Bring food that makes a strong impact on your taste senses, for example something salty, or peppermint.

Sound

Sound avoidance: Ear buds, noise cancelling or over-ear headphones, or a thick hat to muffle and reduce the noise reaching your ears.

Sound seeking: Earphones to listen to music, audiobooks, podcasts etc. on your phone, MP3 player, or car radio.

Touch

Touch avoidance: Identify the main areas of touch you dislike, and then bring things to act as a barrier between you and the tactile offender. For example, bring a large coat that can be draped over a chair if you can't stand the texture of the chair material. If you can't stand wet socks, then bring a spare pair in case your socks get wet from rain. Wear long sleeves that can be pulled over hands to avoid skin touch, or wear gloves.

Touch seeking: Bring fidgets, for example: keyrings, dice, smooth stones, stress squeezy balls, Chinese meditation balls, tennis balls or baseballs (to catch from hand to hand), fidget cubes, fidget spinners, spinner rings (designs are available for 3D printers if you cannot buy one), and handheld pocket bean bags.

Besides fidgets, you could also bring materials you like to touch, e.g. a silky scarf, or line your coat pockets with material you love, such as fleece or satin.

I have often left a well-wrapped-up hot water bottle in the car to put on my lap after an event, as I find warmth very soothing. Pocket hand warmers are an alternative.

Vestibular

Vestibular seeking: As our balance is controlled behind our ear, we can activate our vestibular sense by crunching or sucking. This can be achieved by bringing crunchy food, a bottle that you need to suck to get the drink out, or sugar-free chewing gum. You could also use chewable jewellery (available in some lovely designs for parents to wear for their teething babies, and also available in many designs from shops specifically for people with SPD).

Proprioception

Proprioceptive seeking: Wear a heavy backpack, wear heavy boots, or bring something heavy to hold in your pocket. If sitting down, a coat can be squished between you and the sides of the chair to create a cosy deep pressure around your hips. Pocket bean bags or weighted ankle or wrist straps can also be used.

Interoception

Interoception awareness: Bring snacks and a bottle of water, as having these prepared will remind you to eat and drink. Drinking water also acts as a soothing tactic as it brings awareness to the feeling in your throat, which is calming. Wear layers of clothes so you can regulate your temperature. Set alarms on your phone to remind yourself to eat and drink.

KEY POINTS

◇ Sensory overload can occur when our sensory system becomes overwhelmed or over-stimulated.

◇ Sensory overload can lead to shutdowns or meltdowns.

◇ Shutdowns or meltdowns can also be caused by emotional or cognitive overwhelm.

◇ Shutdowns and meltdowns are different for every autistic person. They might involve physical, verbal, emotional, and cognitive reactions or behaviours.

◇ Using the five steps can help you spot if you are getting close to a meltdown or shutdown.

◇ Having a Sensory Soothing Plan can help you prepare for environments and activities, to reduce your sensory overwhelm.

◇ Bringing a portable sensory toolkit with you can ensure you have the equipment you need to calm your sensory system.

PART 3

EMOTIONAL REGULATION

Disclaimer

It is so important that I emphasise that I am not a psychologist, psychotherapist, or any other kind of emotional therapist. Throughout this section, I am simply sharing what works for me, what I've seen work for other autistic people, what I have learnt from research literature, or what I've learnt through attending psychotherapy.

I highly recommend getting professional help to manage your emotions if you feel uncomfortable with your emotions to an extreme, serious, or continuous level.

Chapter 12

Recognising and Naming Your Emotions

CHAPTER BREAKDOWN

CHAPTER AIMS

› To explore my own personal journey with recognising and naming my emotions.
› To introduce alexithymia, which is a difficulty recognising and naming your emotions.
› To explain that if you can't recognise and name your emotions, it can very hard to regulate them.
› To discuss therapies that can help you learn how to recognise and name your emotions.
› To discuss how therapy can be adapted for your autistic needs.

Introduction

Before you can learn to regulate your emotions, you first need to question whether you can, in fact, recognise and name your own emotions. This is something a lot of autistic people have difficulty with. This chapter will bring you through my journey of learning that I didn't recognise my own emotions as well as I thought I did.

If you can't recognise and name your emotions, it will be very hard to learn to regulate your emotions. For this reason, I believe that the first step to learning how to regulate your emotions is to check if you know how to recognise and name your own emotions.

My History of Recognising Other People's Emotions

I used to think I was someone who really understood my emotions, because I was deeply interested in emotions as a topic. I have spent a lot of my life watching other people's emotions, and always made a huge effort to make other people's emotions make sense.

As a young child, my teacher named me 'Nurse Niamh', as whenever a younger child was upset or hurt, I was first on the scene to try and help them. I remember sitting on the yard bench, watching the smaller children, waiting for one of them to cry, or fall, or to need my help. This distracted me from the fact that from the age of nine and up, I struggled socially with my own peers. I often chose to sit alone on the yard bench rather than try and fail to join in with my peers.

As a teenager, I regularly misread other people's emotions, and was occasionally chastised for reacting inappropriately to someone's emotions. Even when I didn't misread emotions, I often reacted inappropriately, such as laughing hysterically if I saw someone hurt themselves. I had no control over this, but once I started laughing, I just had to walk away as I could not stop the laughter. This looked extremely unempathetic, but in fact I would feel deeply upset for that person (plus guilt that I had laughed at their pain). I felt such strong empathy that it caused a hysterical reaction in me.

In my early teens, I began buying books and magazines on psychology, the human body, and medical diagnosis. I knew that I needed to figure people out, as they were baffling me. I thought that if I understood the body, I could understand the brain, which would help me understand people. Reading books and magazines about psychology helped me to realise that there were many reasons that people act the way they do. This helped me to start seeing things from other perspectives, and becoming more aware of other people's emotional motives.

My training in nursing also taught me a lot about other people's emotions. Patients open up to nurses. Their emotions hit peak points, they cry, they break down, and they express relief out loud in words. In nursing, I learnt how to ask people how they feel, and I learnt to listen. I had the enormous privilege of being allowed to see people at their most vulnerable. I also learnt that people don't always feel the emotion that they display on their face. I saw people put on a brave face in front of their ill loved one, acting brave and cheerful, only to fall apart in the corridor where their loved one couldn't see them. It was an enormous learning curve, and I am deeply grateful that my 18-year-old self was given that opportunity.

As an adult, I am constantly on the lookout for changes in other people's emotions, as this is what has helped me to navigate social relationships. By carefully watching other people's faces and body language for emotional cues, I can often pick up on social clues such as that I've said the wrong thing, or that I need to stop talking about the same thing, or that I need to listen (rather than talk on and on).

All this studying and reflection on emotion led me to believe I was an emotionally intelligent human being, with a good emotional understanding of myself. But I was completely wrong. I eventually learnt that *being able to read other people's emotions doesn't automatically mean you can read your own emotions.*

Realising That I Didn't Know My Own Emotions

In my late twenties, I hit rock bottom with anxiety, and had a horrible bout of depression when my second child was a few months old. I can now understand that I was completely overwhelmed by the demands of motherhood. I didn't know that I was autistic, and thus had no strategies or support systems in place for my autistic self. I began psychotherapy after numerous attempts at counselling that hadn't helped. It was in psycho-therapy that I realised that despite being reasonably good at reading other people's emotions, I really struggled to read my own.

Attending psychotherapy has been the kindest thing I've ever done for myself and my family. It changed how I live, how I react, and how I care for and inter-act with my husband and my children. It also taught me how my past affects my present emotions, and finally, what to do when I feel certain emotions.

In psychotherapy, I learnt that I was able to recognise when I felt a major emotion, like fear if I thought a car was above to drive into me, or happiness if I got good news. But even happiness left me feeling overwhelmed and sometimes uncomfortable. In each session, my psychotherapist would ask me how I felt, and all I could answer was 'bad' or 'I don't know'. I regularly had no idea which actual emotion I was feeling, I just knew that my gut felt like it was tied in a big knot that was pulling on my chest.

The more stressed and anxious I became, the less I was managing to 'mask' my emotions, and so people started commenting on how I displayed emotion. I've been told that I don't know how to hide my emotion, and I've had people say that they're afraid to tell me things because I'm so bluntly honest. Other people have thanked me for my blunt honesty, when I had no idea I was being bluntly honest. I've had people tell me that I'm the most judgemental person they know, when inside my head I'm not judging them at all.

Other people have told me I look cross when I didn't think that I felt cross. But when someone pointed it out, I then realised that I didn't know if I felt cross, and ended up second guessing whether or not I was cross.

I've been told I have no 'poker face' and thus can't pretend to approve of something someone has said, when I thought I could hide it very well. I therefore realised that there was a disconnect between what I thought I was feeling and what my facial expression was displaying, This caused a lot of confusion, both for others and for myself.

It took a lot of therapy and a lot of self-reflection to finally start getting to know my own emotions.

Once I started naming what emotions I was feeling, I was able to get comfortable with them. I won't pretend I always now know which emotion I'm feeling, because I don't. It's an ongoing process, but one I'm getting better at. Thankfully this new knowledge has warded off extensive bouts of depression.

Alexithymia

Alexithymia is defined as 'the inability to recognise, describe and understand emotions' (Collins Dictionary 2019). Research has found that approximately 50% of autistic people experience some degree of alexithymia (Poquereusse et al. 2018). Alexithymia is not exclusive to autism, and can be experienced by non-autistic people, including people experiencing usually transient mental health difficulties such as depression, as well as people without any clinical diagnosis.

Alexithymia isn't necessarily a case of you either have it or you don't, as some people can score low on the alexithymia rating scale (meaning you have a low level of alexithymia), and others may score high (meaning you have a high level of alexithymia). I find my own ability to read my emotions can change, and if I'm very stressed or overwhelmed I find it harder to recognise my emotions.

Alexithymia can manifest in different ways, including:

- Difficulty recognising that you are feeling an emotion.

- Difficulty naming the emotion you are feeling.

- Not recognising early signs of emotion, and thus only realising you feel an emotion when it has hit an extreme level.

- Difficulty reading other people's emotions.

If you don't know that you are feeling an emotion, it makes it very difficult to regulate that emotion. For example, you might not recognise the early warning signs of anger, and thus you will do nothing to calm that anger. The anger will continue to build until you feel overwhelmed by extreme anger, or by extreme feelings in your body that you don't know are anger. To use a metaphor, you may hit melting point without ever noticing that you were heating up.

I have often experienced this. I often thought I went from 'o to 90' with my emotions. But when I actually examine those situations, I now recognise that I simply didn't notice that my emotions were climbing to 90. I might have felt an increased heart rate, or a tightening of my jaw, or a knot in my gut. I might have ignored those feelings, or been so focused on processing a conversation, trying to fit in socially, or trying to organise my thoughts, that I didn't give time to the emotional clues that were happening in my body.

Some people have extreme experiences of alexithymia. I've read accounts of people who are severely debilitated by not recognising or feeling any emotion at all, or people who are unable to recognise any emotional changes in other people. I've heard accounts of autistic people who say the only emotion they feel is anxiety, and that anxiety takes over every part of every day. I know myself that when my anxiety is high, it dampens all my other emotions and takes all my mental focus.

If you experience challenges in emotional recognition, emotional regulation, alexithymia, or anxiety, I highly recommend getting professional help to teach you how to manage these challenges. It is not shameful to need this help, and not something to put off, as every single day of your life matters. If it works, it can mean an enormous improvement to your quality of life.

I wish I had a magic wand, or an immediate strategy to help you recognise your emotions, but unfortunately learning to recognise your emotions is a complex endeavour. Thankfully, there are therapists trained in supporting, and teaching adults with their emotional regulation. Chapter 14 will go through the types of therapies that might help, and what adjustments therapists can make to ensure their services are more accessible to autistic adults.

KEY POINTS

◊ If you don't know how to recognise your emotions, and name what you are feeling, it will be much harder to learn how to regulate your emotions.

◊ Our ability to recognise and name our emotions can fluctuate, depending on how stressed we are.

◊ Alexithymia means finding it hard to recognise and name your emotions.

References

Collins Dictionary (2019) 'Alexithymia'. Accessed 2 February 2022 at: www.collinsdictionary.com/dictionary/english/alexithymia Harper-Collins Publishers

Poquereusse, L., Pastore, L., Dellantonio, S., and Esposito, G. (2018) 'Alexithymia and Autism Spectrum Disorder: A Complex Relationship'. *Frontiers in Psychology* 9, 1196. https://dx.doi.org/10.3389/fpsyg.2018.01196

Chapter 13

Getting Comfortable with Uncomfortable Emotions

CHAPTER BREAKDOWN

CHAPTER AIMS

> › To explain how all emotions are relevant and important.
> › To discuss how having difficulty managing one emotion can lead to a domino effect of other uncomfortable emotions.
> › To explore the importance of getting comfortable with uncomfortable emotions.
> › To share strategies and ideas of how I manage individual uncomfortable emotions.
> › To look at creativity as a tool for emotional management.
> › To look at the impacts of long-term uncomfortable emotions.

Emotional Regulation and Me

Of all the parts of my autism that challenge me, emotional regulation is by far the hardest. Emotional changes often come unexpectedly for me, and I intensely dislike things that I can't predict, as they feel like a hovering permanent threat. One day I can feel calm, and the next day I can wake up with a deep emptiness, despite nothing upsetting happening in the interim.

One day I can feel accepting of everything in life, and then suddenly whack, anger hits me and I feel overcome with rage at the unfairness of life. I can be enjoying a movie, and then one quick scene or image can make me feel vulnerable and unsafe in the world, and this feeling can linger for days.

All emotion can be uncomfortable for me. It's not just the typically uncomfortable emotions like sadness and anger that cause me anguish. I can feel just as awful when I feel intense excitement as I do when I feel anxious (to be honest I'm not sure I can actually tell the difference). I can toss and turn unable to sleep because I feel immensely happy, or because I feel frightened. Extreme excitement can cause me to burst into tears, or feel too nauseous to eat. Very good news can lead to sheer joy followed by crippling anxiety followed by shutdown.

I used to think that there were positive emotions (happiness, calmness, excitement etc.) and negative emotions (sadness, anger etc.). However, the first psychotherapist I went to explained there are no positive and negative emotions; instead we can feel comfortable or uncomfortable feeling any emotion in any one moment. This had a profound effect on me and completely changed my view of emotion. It also brought huge relief to me, as I was someone who often disliked feeling what I thought were supposed to be positive emotions.

Through therapy, I learnt the importance of allowing myself to feel all emotions, instead of forcing uncomfortable emotions away. I realised that if I didn't feel anger, I wouldn't stand up for myself. If I didn't feel fear, I wouldn't know to protect myself. If I didn't feel disappointment, I wouldn't feel the desire to strive harder for things after failure.

I often used to say that my perfect emotion was to feel neutral; neither good nor bad. I longed for neutrality. This was because I found both extreme happiness and extreme sadness terribly uncomfortable, and so I wanted to sit in the space between the two, feeling blissful nothingness. But feeling nothing leads to numbness. While numbness can be protective in the short term, it can then turn into an uncomfortable emotion in itself. So now I try to achieve calmness, rather than nothingness.

Thankfully, I am now able to feel each of my emotions to a certain degree without becoming emotionally dysregulated. I can even feel deep sadness without freaking out about it, although that doesn't mean I like it. I have learnt to sit with sadness and be calm in that sad space. The greatest thing I've learnt is that I need to allow my emotions to be felt, so that they can move on. I often see recognising and accepting my emotions as similar to paying bills. The longer I ignore them, the bigger the consequences.

Deal with them on arrival, and you save yourself a lot of bother, stress, and accumulation of cost.

Autism and Uncomfortable Emotions

Autistic people often feel emotions at more extreme levels than non-autistic people. When the emotions are uncomfortable, it can be difficult to manage those extreme emotions.

There are some uncomfortable emotions that are felt at higher rates by autistic people, and this can make it hard to feel emotionally regulated. For example, one study found that shame is more frequently felt by autistic adults than by non-autistic adults, and there are also high levels of guilt amongst autistic adults (Davidson et al. 2017). The researchers found that shame can lead to other uncomfortable emotions including anger, and behaviours that include blaming others, aggression, or hostility.

Shame is different to guilt, although it's easy to mix the feelings up. Guilt is an uncomfortable feeling that we have done something wrong, or against our values. Shame has been described as a painful feeling that we are flawed as a person, and unworthy of belonging or love (Brown 2013). When you've always felt on the outside and unable to fit in, or when you're aware of people looking at you as if there's something very odd about you, or if you can't join in with society as much as you want to, it is easy to see why shame is a commonly felt emotion amongst autistic people.

Other emotions that are felt more frequently in the autistic community are fear and anxiety. Fear is a response to a known and immediate threat, whereas anxiety is the anticipation or apprehension of an uncertain or unpredictable threat (Naaz et al. 2019). For example, if you see a car speeding towards you, you may feel fear as there is a real threat that you will get knocked over. But if you are walking safely along the footpath, and you feel apprehensive that a car may knock you down, despite no evidence that this might happen, this is anxiety.

In my experience, fear can be a common feeling in autistic people, and this can naturally lead to anxiety. For example, if you feel fear when you hear a loud noise, then it is easy to see how you might feel anxious every time you go into an environment that may have unexpected loud noises. If you have experienced fear from direct bullying or being treated poorly in a social situation, then it is easy to see how you could develop anxiety around social situations.

I believe that living with the core traits of autism, including sensory sensitivities and communication challenges or differences, can lead to an increase of uncomfortable emotions in everyday life. For this reason, it is important we develop our own strategies to manage these emotions.

Emotional Dominoes

Something I've noticed about myself is that when I feel one uncomfortable emotion, another uncomfortable emotion often follows. If I don't validate the initial emotion, and manage this emotion, I am much more likely to experience an emotional domino effect, with one uncomfortable emotion leading to another and another.

The initial emotion can often turn into the weakest emotion being felt, and the secondary emotions can become the dominant emotions. I have often found that the secondary emotions cause the bigger social problems for me. I'll explain this by using scenario examples.

SCENARIO 1

I remember once going out for a walk before I remembered that I had not wanted anyone to see the outfit I was wearing, because it was very peculiar and unflattering. I then bumped into someone I knew. I felt extremely embarrassed that they had seen me in this ridiculous outfit. Embarrassment was my first, or primary, emotion. But then shame, which was the secondary emotion, arrived. The shame was a much stronger emotion, and brought negative thoughts with it. This led me to feel angry at myself, and to try and rush away from the person I knew as fast as I could. I then felt guilty that I had rushed away from them, and spent the whole day second guessing how I had acted and what I had said, which caused anxiety. Had I been able to just accept that I felt embarrassed, and managed that feeling, I could have avoided the domino emotions of shame, anger at myself, guilt, and then anxiety.

SCENARIO 2

I was once in a restaurant with a friend of mine, who is autistic, and she ordered a meal from the menu. The waiter returned to our table after we had ordered to explain that there were no more portions of the meal that my friend had ordered left. My autistic friend was initially disappointed, which was the primary emotion, but soon became angry.

The anger was the secondary emotion here. Her anger caused her to say things that I deemed to be quite rude, and the waiter became extremely uncomfortable and I thought they would start to cry. It was clear to me that there really was nothing that the waiter could do, and no matter how hard they tried to offer suggestions, my friend was completely shut down to flexible thinking (which can happen with autistic people when we feel stressed). My friend then lost her temper to the point that she was shouting and caused quite a scene. This anger ruined the restaurant experience for all of us, but I found it interesting to see how the initial feeling of disappointment had turned into something much more detrimental. After the event, my friend was anxious and down, and vowed never to go back to that restaurant again. So the primary emotion of disappointment caused a domino effect leading to anger, anxiety, and feeling down. I believe that if this friend had been able to 'deal with' her initial feeling of disappointment, then she would not have spiralled to feeling the other uncomfortable emotions.

In both these scenarios, I have shown how the inability to manage the primary (first) emotion caused the scenario to deteriorate, and a spiralling of uncomfortable emotions. The intense emotions also triggered a stress response, caused flexible thinking to deteriorate, and led to poor social outcomes.

The impact of being unable to deal with the primary emotion didn't just affect the moment, but lasted long after the event.

The long-term side-effects of the first scenario were a triggering of recurring shame, and anxiety that I had offended the person I had met, which led to weeks of worry and an avoidance of that person.

The long-term effect in the second scenario was that my friend refused to ever go back to the restaurant. Additionally, I was a bit turned off going to any restaurant with this friend in case it happened again, as I had not enjoyed the experience and found the negative attention from onlookers in the restaurant very stressful to my own emotions.

Four-Step Strategy to Manage Uncomfortable Emotions

When I feel a strong uncomfortable emotion, I follow this four-step strategy:

1. Name the emotion.
2. Scan the body.

3. Ask yourself, do you know the cause of this emotion? If not, just move straight on to step 4.

4. What can you do about it?

1. Name the Emotion

Sometimes just naming the emotion you are feeling is enough to gain control of it, and stop the domino effect of uncomfortable emotions. This may sound simple, but sometimes the simplest actions have the most powerful impact. And actually, it's not as simple as it sounds, because naming your emotions is a skill in itself, as explained in Chapter 12.

Naming the emotion, by which I simply mean stating to yourself 'I feel sad' or 'Right now I feel angry' or 'In this moment I feel giddy' , means you come face to face with the emotion and acknowledge that it is there.

I first heard about naming the emotion you feel from a play therapist, who advised my husband and me to try a strategy called 'Name It to Tame It' with one of our daughters. This strategy was developed by Dr Dan Siegal, who is a Professor of Psychiatry at UCLA and Director of the Mindsight Institute. I saw how powerful this strategy was at helping my daughter to regulate and get comfortable with her emotions, and so I began using it myself to regulate my own emotions. I couldn't believe how powerful it was. Just like how children like an adult to listen to them and validate their emotions, we also want our emotions to be heard and validated; starting with being heard and validated by ourselves.

The more often you name your emotions throughout the day, the more often you will start to recognise how often your emotions fluctuate. I got into the practise of trying to name every single emotion I felt, all day long. I find this extremely helpful as it allows me to see that all emotions come and go. This reminds me that I won't get stuck feeling any uncomfortable emotion forever. I really needed to learn this, as I was prone to being overwhelmed by uncomfortable emotions, and failed to see when a more comfortable emotion crept back in, or when the uncomfortable emotion went away.

Getting Started with Naming Your Emotions

It is much easier to start the practice of naming your emotions by first practising naming the comfortable emotions you feel throughout the day, instead of the uncomfortable ones. This is because when we feel intense or uncomfortable emotions, we are often overwhelmed, and may be experiencing a lot of physically bothersome feelings in our bodies as well.

Physically bothersome feelings tend to steal our focus, and can be frightening, or even terrifying. For example, if your physical reaction to an emotion makes you feel like you are going to vomit, you are going to find it hard to take a moment and think 'What emotion do I feel? Oh yes, I feel anxious.' You will be too preoccupied with the nausea. Or if your heart is pounding and your jaw is clenched and you feel like you're full of hot steam ready to blow, it is very hard to stop and say 'What emotion do I feel? Is it sadness? No. It's anger.' *The more overwhelmed I am, the harder it is to name my emotion. This is why it is easier to start off with comfortable emotions.*

Once you are managing to name the comfortable emotions throughout your day (which took me a number of weeks), I suggest moving on to slightly uncomfortable emotions. This will help you to recognise the early feelings of each uncomfortable emotion. This is an enormously powerful skill, as if you can start to recognise the early signs of each emotion, you can do something about it before the emotion builds to intense levels, or melting point. *It is also easier to recognise and name uncomfortable emotions before they get too strong, and are taken over by intense physical reactions in your body.*

Once you master naming the comfortable and slightly uncomfortable emotions, it's time to move on to stronger uncomfortable emotions.

2. Scan the Body

Scanning the body for physical changes gives you three major pieces of information that can help in emotional regulation:

- *It can help you to identify the emotion*: Sometimes it can be hard to name the emotions we are feeling. If we know we feel an emotion, but are not sure what it is, it can help to scan the body for clues about the emotion. For example, if I notice that I'm light-headed and nauseous, this may indicate anxiety. If I feel full of heat, my jaw is clenched and my fingers are tense, this is a clue that I feel angry.

- *It can give you information about how intense the emotion is*: For example, if you know you feel fear, and your heartbeat is slightly faster than normal, then this may indicate a minor amount of fear. But if your heart is racing, you are sweating, you feel light-headed, or your body feels frozen to the spot, then this tells you that the level of fear you are feeling is very intense. Knowing how intense the emotion is can help you identify whether you need to do something very small to calm down, or if you need to take bigger steps to soothe yourself.

- *It can help you identify where in your body needs to be soothed*: By finding the areas of your body that are having a physical reaction to the emotion you are feeling, you can then use your sensory soothing strategies to soothe those parts of the body. For example, if I feel a clench in my gut from anxiety, I get great relief from holding something hot to this area. *Soothing the body can help soothe the emotion.*

3. Do You Know the Cause of This Emotion Right Now?

It is not always important to immediately know why you feel an emotion, and sometimes it is better to wait until after you have calmed down and can think clearly about what has triggered it. But sometimes we need to know what triggered the emotion so that we can do something about it in that moment.

There are some situations where it is more important to look at the cause of the emotion, rather than dealing with the emotion in that moment. For example, if you are in a dangerous situation that is causing you to feel fear, then it's more important to get out of the dangerous situation than to name and validate your fear. The naming and validating can happen later.

Another reason to identify the trigger of an uncomfortable emotion is to help you build your understanding of your emotional triggers. Sometimes we don't know what has caused an uncomfortable emotion, but when we look back at the situation later, we realise that there was something in the sensory environment that may have been the trigger. This knowledge can help you develop a Sensory Soothing Plan for the next time you are in a similar environment. The more you get to know your sensory triggers, the quicker you will notice if an uncomfortable emotion was caused by a sensory trigger.

I can often identify what triggered an uncomfortable emotion, but sometimes I can't. I can suddenly experience an uncomfortable emotion and be totally unaware of what triggered it. If I don't know the cause of the uncomfortable emotion, I move on and stop trying to figure it out in that moment, as it can be a fruitless task that achieves very little. Over-focusing on the cause can prevent me from reaching step 4, which is 'What am I going to do about it?' Therefore, I simply skip trying to figure out the cause, and instead move on to what I'm going to do about it (my current psychotherapist taught me to do this, and it's been game-changing as I used to ruminate on finding the cause of every emotion). However, if I have a repetitive or persistent uncomfortable emotion that I can't explain, I bring it up with my psychotherapist so I can explore it in a safe and supported environment. I am usually able to get to the bottom of what is causing the emotion with my psychotherapist.

4. What Can You Do About It?

In my experience, naming my emotion is often enough to calm the emotion. But if the emotion is intense, or if I'm having a strong physical reaction to the emotion, then I need to do more than just name it. I need to do something to soothe myself.

When I feel an uncomfortable emotion, I ask myself:

- *Do I need or want to do something about the cause?*

    Example: If I'm having a conversation with someone, and they say something hurtful to me, I know the cause of my sadness is the hurtful comment. I need to question what will really help me in that moment. This is a classic example of a situation that could lead to the emotional domino effect. If I don't calm the sadness, it may spiral to anger and I could end up having a big fight, and the anger will cause huge discomfort and possibly physical distress. If I believe the hurtful comments, it may lead to shame, self-loathing, guilt, and despair. Neither situation has a good outcome.

    However, if I can take control of the feeling of sadness, and decide to deal with the cause later, I can reduce this emotional domino effect. I firmly believe in giving myself time to process another person's comments that have caused me distress, and telling them that I will respond later, or tomorrow. Responding in the moment merely escalates the distress, and makes me more likely to say something I will regret.

    I therefore focus on myself rather than on the other person. *Focusing on the emotion in my body, rather than on the other person, is the key to managing my emotion when it's caused by another person.*

- *What Sensory Soothing Strategy can I use to calm the physical reactions to emotion in my body?* This involves identifying the part of my body that feels distressed, and picking an action that will directly soothe that part of my body. Reducing the distress in the body will reduce the overwhelm caused by a strong emotion.

    Example 1: If I feel discomfort in my chest, I can take a deep breath in to soothe it, and make a warm drink.

    Example 2: If I feel the tingly threat of tears in my eyes, I might go outside and focus on feeling the sensation of wind on my eyelashes, which I find very soothing.

    Example 3: If I'm caught for breath, I can focus on my breathing.

- *What can I do if a sensory trigger is causing the uncomfortable emotion?* When the cause of an uncomfortable emotion is sensory, you need to decide if you are equipped to deal with it, or if you need to avoid the trigger in order to calm your emotional reaction.

  Example: If a noise is making me feel rage, I ask myself: do I need to walk away to a quiet place, and thus reduce the risk that I will lose my temper? Or do I need to use something from my portable sensory toolkit to help me stay in the environment?

- *Ask yourself if you are comfortable to continue feeling the emotion or do you want the trigger to stop? If I choose to continue feeling the uncomfortable emotion, what can I do to support myself while I feel it?* We don't always mind feeling an uncomfortable emotion, and sometimes we might even choose to. It's important to ask ourselves whether we feel capable of managing an uncomfortable emotion right now, or whether we do not want to feel it in this moment.

  Example 1: If I'm watching a heart-breaking movie and it's making me feel extremely sad, I need to question whether I want to keep watching it, or would I feel better if I turned it off? This boils down to whether or not I am comfortable feeling the uncomfortable emotion in that moment. I can ask myself, do I feel overwhelmed by the emotion? If I am not overwhelmed, and I want to continue watching the movie, can I use a Sensory Soothing Strategy to help manage the emotion (e.g. hot water bottle against my chest, fluffy or weighted blanket, fidget in hand, warm drink, crunchy snack)? Sensory soothing strategies will help to soothe the physical reactions I'm experiencing, so that I will feel more comfortable watching the movie.

  Example 2: I sometimes feel a sudden wave of sadness when I think of people who have died in my life, especially my dad and step-brother, who both died when I was a child. Sometimes I am comfortable feeling this sadness and grief, and choose to delve into it by looking at photos of them or talking about them. This helps me to feel as though I'm remembering them, and can be comforting and even cathartic. But if I'm not feeling emotionally strong enough in that moment to feel the sadness about them, I might choose to distract myself from the feeling. I don't think it's healthy to always distract yourself from grief, and the more I allow myself to feel it, the easier it gets. But sometimes I'm just not feeling strong enough, so I think about what I can do to release the feeling, or move it on.

- *What can you do to regulate this emotion?* The next chapter will give you ideas of how to regulate individual emotions.

KEY POINTS

◇ Autistic people can feel emotions more intensely than non-autistic people, and are more prone to certain uncomfortable emotions including shame, guilt, anxiety, and fear.

◇ If you don't validate and manage the first uncomfortable emotion that arrives, it is more likely that other uncomfortable emotions will follow, in an emotional domino effect.

◇ The four-step strategy for emotional regulation includes:
  1. Naming the emotion.
  2. Scanning the body.
  3. Asking yourself, what is the cause of the emotion? If you don't know the cause, just move straight on to step 4.
  4. Asking yourself, what can you do about it?

References

Brown, B. (2013) 'Shame vs. Guilt'. Accessed 12 January 2022 at: https://brenebrown.com/articles/2013/01/15/shame-v-guilt/

Davidson, D., Vanegas, S.B., and Hilvert, E. (2017) 'Proneness to Self-Consciousness Emotions in Adults with and without Autism Traits'. *Journal of Autism and Developmental Disorders* 47 (11), 3392–3404, https://doi.org/10.1007/s10803-017-3260-8

Naaz, F., Knight, L.K., and Depue, B.E. (2019) 'Explicit and Ambiguous Threat Processing: Functionally Dissociable Roles of the Amygdala and Bed Nucleus of the Stria Terminalis'. *Journal of Cognitive Neuroscience* 31 (4), 543–559. https://doi.org/10.1162/jocn_a_01369

Chapter 14

Emotional Regulation Plans

CHAPTER BREAKDOWN

CHAPTER AIMS

› To introduce the need for Emotional Regulation Plans for individual uncomfortable emotions.
› To share ideas of how to regulate individual uncomfortable emotions, including anger, sadness, emptiness, nostalgia, loneliness, shame, anxiety, disappointment, excitement or extreme happiness, and embarrassment.
› To discuss how creativity can be used to support emotional regulation.
› To discuss long-term emotions.

Emotional Reactions

We all react to different emotions in different ways. But how we react when we feel a particular emotion isn't always the most helpful way that we can react. For example, if you punch a wall when you feel angry, you will hurt yourself (and possibly damage the wall). If you bite your fingernails when you feel scared, you can damage your nails and introduce infection to your nail-bed skin. If you fight the urge to cry every time you feel sad, you might be repressing the release that your body craves, and thus the emotion will remain unresolved.

We learn to react to individual emotions through a variety of influences. How our parents or guardians react to their own emotions, and react to our emotions, will play a part. Our social and school experiences will play a part. How intensely our body feels each emotion, and what our body craves when it feels an emotion, also has a role; it is easy not to hit a wall when you are angry if you don't feel the physical rush in your body telling you to hit a wall!

There are also cultural influences that can influence how we react to emotion. For example, there can be gender differences in how we are taught to manage our emotions, starting from a young age. Historically, males have experienced a cultural upbringing that discourages healthy management of some emotions. For example, boys are sometimes discouraged from showing fear, anxiety, or upset. Uncomfortable emotions such as anger may be talked about as things to be 'controlled' rather than 'soothed', 'managed', or simply 'felt'. The notorious line 'big boys don't cry' teaches boys that it's not okay to acknowledge and express their upset, and thus they are basically being told to suppress it.

Girls can also experience cultural judgement over their emotions, such as by being compelled to internalise anger, turning it into sadness or disappointment, rather than releasing it. When boys get out their anger or solve an argument with a friend through rough horse-play, I have often heard the phrase 'boys will be boys'. But if girls engage in rough horse-play they are more likely to be told off, or judged as a tomboy or a child with anger problems. I'm not saying that I think rough horse-play is a good thing, but I am saying that culturally girls and boys are treated differently when resolving arguments or expressing anger, and thus develop different reactions.

It is worth considering how you react when you feel an emotion, and question if that is how you want to react? Does your reaction to the emotion release the emotion, or suppress it? Do you feel better after you release the emotion? Do other people feel safe with how you release or manage (or don't manage) your emotion?

Sometimes we don't know how to react, or what to do, when we feel an emotion. If you have alexithymia, you might not even know what emotion you are feeling, let alone how you react to it. Once you work on recognising and naming your emotions, it is well worth thinking about how you want to manage and react to your emotions. I'm not sure if anyone in the world is fully in control of how they react to all emotions, but I do know that we can change how we react, and we can take steps to ensure we manage our emotions as best as we can. This is where an Emotional Regulation Plan comes in.

Emotional Regulation Plans

An Emotional Regulation Plan is a plan of action to help you deal with, and release, uncomfortable emotions.

Each emotion affects us differently, so we need different strategies to deal with individual emotions. When we feel very distressed from an emotion, it can be hard to think of a solution, because our flexible thinking reduces or shuts down under stress (see Chapter 2). For this reason, I recommend brainstorming what would help you deal with different emotions when you are calm, or just after you have calmed down while the feeling is still fresh in your mind. Making a visual plan for how to manage each emotion can reduce the need to think up a solution when you are feeling emotionally distressed.

What to Do When I Feel _____?

Here I share some strategies that I use to release different emotions, but of course everyone will have different strategies. What calms me may aggravate another person, and this is why this has to be very personalised. I am only including the most common emotions that I experience, to show how I approach managing them, but there are many more emotions that you might experience, and I advise you to make your own individual plan for each emotion.

Please note that I include sensory soothing strategies for each emotion I discuss, because soothing the physical discomfort that uncomfortable emotions bring can be a really helpful way to reduce the effect of emotional overwhelm.

What to Do When I Feel: Anger?

- *Feel it, don't fuel it*: There is a big difference between allowing yourself feel your anger and fuelling your anger, although it can be hard to tell the difference at times. Acknowledging and validating your anger can be helpful, as it helps you release the anger. Doing something to make your anger worse, like shouting or having an argument with someone, can be unhelpful as it can make the anger grow, and even cause new anger to arrive.

- *Stay away from social media*: I don't write about my anger on social media or anywhere online, as there's such a high risk of offending someone, facing a backlash, or regretting it afterwards. We can't think properly when feeling angry, and so our internal filter weakens, increasing the risk of misjudging what we are writing.

I also find that social media can end up fuelling my anger, or adding to my anger, rather than validating it. You may think that you are releasing your anger as you are talking about it, but from what I've observed of other people getting angry on social media, it actually builds the anger rather than releasing it.

- *Deep breath*: I know that taking a deep breath when angry is a cliché, but it's a cliché that works. It physically widens the chest, reduces muscle tightness in the ribs, and improves air flow, which helps the body feel calmer, and gives you a moment to process the feeling and the cause of the anger.

- *Angry music*: I find that listening to music that conveys anger or deep beats helps me to validate my anger, without directing it at another person.

- *Sing an angry song*: I have one song that I sing when I am angry. It helps me feel the anger, and I always feel a little less angry after I finish.

- *Write it down*: Getting the words out of my head and onto paper is one of the best ways for me to process anger.

- *Write an angry letter but don't give it to the person*: If I'm angry at a person, I sometimes write a letter to them explaining my anger but I don't give it to the person. I then leave it hidden overnight, and the next day I read it again, and often find the angry feelings have disappeared. I then tear up the letter. If I still feel the anger and realise that I do need to talk to the person that I'm angry with, at least I've had time to calm down and didn't act rashly in the moment.

- *Practise not acting in haste*: When I get angry, I sometimes want to confront the person I'm angry with. This achieves very little, other than possibly making that person feel unsafe. Walking away and counting to ten, or breathing to the count of ten, can really help me in this situation. To help me develop this habit, I stuck a piece of paper on the kitchen cabinet telling me what to do when I feel anger (i.e. walk to my bedroom counting my breaths out loud), and this visual helped me learn what I could do with my anger.

- *Exercise the anger out*: Exercise is a fantastic way to calm anger. I used to love going for a jog to run out the anger, but now I am very limited in what exercise I can do due to my rheumatology conditions. I often cannot walk, let alone jog, which has made me notice just how useful exercise used to be for my anger. I do still use my body however I can, whether it's a bit of gardening, yoga, weight training etc. Swimming is a great way to calm anger, as its repetitive nature can be soothing and regulating. Using my body takes my mind off the anger, and feels grounding.

- *Symbolise letting it go*: As important as it is to validate the anger, it's also important to let it go. Holding onto anger can be detrimental, to our bodies and minds. I've heard of a few techniques to symbolise letting your anger go, such as lighting a candle, writing out what you're angry about and then putting it in the fire, or blowing the angry thoughts into the wind. You might prefer something more physical, such as 'punching out' your anger by punching a cushion, couch, or bed.

- *Sensory soothing strategy*: Using a sensory soothing strategy can really help me process and calm my anger. My preferred strategies for anger are taking a shower, getting proprioceptive feedback such as weight lifting, or punching a punch bag. Once I've released the anger, I often like to lie under a weighted blanket to bring calm back into my body.

What to Do When I Feel: Sadness?

- *Nature*: By far the best thing for me when I am sad is to go into nature. I usually choose to go into the woods, or to the ocean. Sometimes I just go into the garden. Fresh air and nature have an uplifting effect on me.

- *Talk about it*: When sadness feels like a heavy weight inside me, it gets lifted up and out by talking about it. I talk to my husband, family, and close friends. It is just as important for men to talk about their sadness as it is for women, but if it is new to you, it might take practice.

- *Cry*: I am a big believer in the power of a good cry, as it releases the pent-up sadness. Crying is a natural body reaction to sadness, which starts from infancy and lasts throughout life. But some people are taught to, or make themselves, suppress their tears. If you have been brought up to force yourself not to cry, you might find crying difficult or impossible. Working with a psychotherapist might help you to address this, if it is something that you would like to re-learn how to do.

- *Exercise*: The last thing I want to do when I'm sad is to exercise, but exercise is a great way to get myself out of my head, and to stop thinking about the sadness, if I can find the motivation to get up and do it.

- *Get creative*: Being creative during a sad moment can help the sadness pass, or act as a comfort to the sadness, so I often do something like drawing, mindful colouring, or writing a poem when I feel suddenly sad.

  If I find myself sad for a prolonged period, I often realise that I've not done anything creative recently. I have to be creative regularly to keep sadness away. I've no idea why, but I know that's not uncommon.

- *Laugh*: Watching comedy shows and reading funny books are wonderful ways to help me feel uplifted. There is nothing better than a big belly laugh to push away sadness. I return to one movie in particular when I need to laugh, and I have a few short TV shows that I am guaranteed to laugh at.

- *Sensory soothing strategies*: I try to counteract sadness by increasing my sensory comfort. My preferred strategies for sadness are tasting wholesome foods (these make me feel safe), smelling pleasant smells like soap, aftershave, perfume, or herbs, wearing soft comfortable clothes, wrapping up in fluffy blankets, and looking at visually beautiful things such as art, images, or TV shows.

What to Do When I Feel: Emptiness?

- *Get out in nature*: Feeling connected to nature is hugely soothing to me, especially if I see beauty. It helps me feel more connected to the world, so I feel more 'whole' rather than 'empty'.

- *Help someone else, or do something kind for another person*: I get a boost of fulfilment from doing a kind act, which is a great way to counteract emptiness.

- *Get creative*: I use many forms of creativity to lift me back up from emptiness. Writing is my first choice in general, but painting and sewing are two hobbies that can also help me perk up when I feel empty.

- *Engage in my special interest*: When I feel empty, I often feel like I don't want to read or write. But I force myself to sit down and do ten minutes of writing or editing. I set a timer so I know that it's not indefinite, there's a beginning and an end. Once I begin, I find that I can get lost in my writing and after the ten minutes I don't want to stop, and so I don't. This helps me feel a connection to something I love, which reduces my feelings of emptiness.

- *Social connection*: Sometimes social interaction can be the thing that causes me to feel empty, but sometimes social interaction is what cures my emptiness. Meeting friends or family is really important to me when I feel empty. If I don't feel able to commit to social plans, then small quick social connections can be enough to lift my emptiness, such as talking to a librarian for a few minutes about a book (one of my favourite topics), or having a small chat with a shopkeeper.

- *Sensory soothing strategies*: I tend to focus on my visual senses when I'm feeling empty. Looking at beautiful things, or things to do with my special interest, helps me feel a sense of belonging. I try to wear cheerful clothes with fabrics that look beautiful to me. I know a lot of people find music very soothing (sound sense) when they feel empty, but there are very few songs that help me with this. However, audiobooks and the sounds of nature do soothe my sound sense. I can lose my appetite when I feel empty, so I have to make an extra effort to eat, even if my taste sense resists food. I choose strong flavours to alert my taste senses, including salty crunchy snacks (the crunchy snacks also alert my vestibular sense), or spicy foods. Alternatively, I might choose comfort foods from childhood, which can be soothing and remind me of my family, thus helping me feel connected.

What to Do When I Feel: Nostalgia?

I get bouts of nostalgia, and it can be a really strong and uncomfortable emotion. It usually happens during a time of stress, transition, or hardship, and I get a wretched longing for things in the past.

- *Poetry*: Reading poetry helps me to validate my nostalgia. I have one poem in particular that I read whenever I feel nostalgic, and it really helps me feel better.

- *Keep a diary*: I have kept personal diaries since I was about nine years old. These are really helpful for when I get into a nostalgic mood, as when I read back over a time I'm nostalgic for, I realise that it wasn't all sunshine and rainbows back then.

- *Let nostalgia come and then flow away*: Nostalgia is a feeling that I don't like hanging about, and so once I've acknowledged it and thought about why I'm nostalgic, I then let it go. Holding onto the past has proven dangerous for me by prolonging emotions and mixing up facts about the past. I therefore distract myself out of it by keeping busy.

- *Meditation*: I sometimes meditate and imagine myself throwing the thing I'm nostalgic for into the depths of the ocean. I then visualise myself turning and walking away from it. This is a powerful meditative visualisation, and it's one that took me a lot of practice to get comfortable with, as I can find meditation quite hard (because I can get very jittery, physically, when doing meditation).

- *Sensory soothing strategies*: I often think about the senses from the time that I am nostalgic for, so I can recreate them. I might play the music I used to listen to, smell something from that time, eat something I associate from the time. I often find that this helps me to recreate what was nice about that time, without over-indulging in thoughts that relate to it.

What to Do When I Feel: Loneliness?

- *Loneliness when with other people*: When I feel lonely when surrounded by people, I plan what I will do when I get away from the other people. I remind myself that I love time alone, and I will treat myself to time alone when I leave. I allow myself to look forward to a nice TV show, nature, or my special interests.

- *Get creative about connection*: Just meeting other humans doesn't necessarily make me less lonely. On the contrary, it often makes me feel more lonely, as I can feel outside the group, or feel confused by the social interaction and whether I'm interpreting it and responding correctly. But when I connect with other like-minded people, or people who have a shared interest or hobby, this does work to reduce loneliness for me.

   I joined a painting class a few years ago. I wasn't trying to make friends, I simply wanted to learn a new skill. This class allowed me to feel part of something, and thus feel connected, but I felt no social pressure. I could choose whether to talk or not talk, I had my own workstation, I could get lost in the art. I never felt lonely there, and that feeling would last long after the class had ended for the night.

- *Plan something to look forward to where I will connect with others*: This might be a social event with like-minded people, or it might be a course or a class in an area of interest. I love having a conference or a webinar to look forward to in the area of autism, writing, and reading, and so I space events out over the year. There are often free events at book or writing festivals, and sometimes the workshops and paid events are very reasonably priced, which makes this manageable. I often find meeting strangers with similar interests easier than meeting people I know well, as there can be a social freedom with strangers.

- *Find an online community, but be careful about it*: When I first joined social media to connect with other writers, I thought it was the best thing ever. I loved talking to other writers, gaining insights, learning, and feeling part of something bigger than myself. But I slowly realised that it was also creating a lot of uncomfortable feelings in me. I would often feel worse after engaging in social media. Seeing other people's successes sometimes inspired me, but it sometimes alienated me and created feelings of 'What's wrong with me? Why am I not achieving success?' It also opened my eyes to the political and moral complexities of social media interaction, where simple manners and respect don't always exist. I find that immensely stressful, and I can get quite nervous before I write anything on social media, in case my words are misinterpreted, attract criticism, or accidentally offend someone.

   However, I have met many autistic people for whom online

communities have been wonderful, and they have found friendship, fun, and connection through online gaming, music, social media, and more. Social sites run by communities, and not by companies, can be less likely to encourage harmful forms of communication, provided the community is healthy. It is worth exploring, but always check in with yourself and ask whether the activity is causing you to feel comfortable rather than uncomfortable feelings, and whether you can manage the uncomfortable feelings.

- *Sensory soothing strategies*: Loneliness feels like a hollowness to me, so making myself more aware of the feelings in my body can really help counteract the hollow feeling. Working on my interoception senses is the key here. Doing exercise to get my heart beating, moving and strengthening the muscles around my ribs, and increasing my breathing rate in a controlled manner all bring feeling back into my chest and gut. Warmth also helps, such as a hot water bottle around my heart. Thick drinks like smoothies or soup, or food you can strongly feel going down the throat, can also help to reduce the hollow feeling. Proprioceptive grounding can really help me with loneliness too, because it helps my body feel more connected within itself, and connection is the opposite of loneliness. So I might ask for a hug, lift weights, use a weighted blanket, or lean into a wall.

What to Do When I Feel: Shame?

- *Connection*: Because shame can feel like unworthiness, it can help me to connect with someone who loves me, and remind myself that that person sees me as a worthy companion and human.

- *Talk about it*: Talking about how I feel can help me see the emotion more clearly, and see that it's not warranted logically.

- *Get physical*: I physically feel shame around my heart, and so getting my heart beating helps me feel as though my heart is thumping away that shame. More vigorous or intense exercise helps with this.

- *Sensory soothing strategies*: Proprioception is my best sensory activity for shame, to bring calm into my body. I also find that activating my vestibular system in a strong way can help, almost as if it re-jiggles the feelings in my body and mixes them up, and therefore the shame isn't as strong. Standing on my head or doing balance exercises can achieve this for me. I used to roll head-over-heels a lot as a child when I felt shame, but I can't do this properly any more.

- *Do something I'm good at*: Whether it's engaging in a special interest, or a hobby like cooking, or making extra effort in my 'mum' role by doing something with my kids that I know they will love, doing something I'm good at helps me to reduce the feeling of shame by allowing me to feel worthy of something.

What to Do When I Feel: Anxiety?

- *Use a Quick Calm Plan (see Chapter 3)*: When I feel anxiety surfacing, I immediately think 'What's my Quick Calm Plan for this anxiety?' I often text my plan to someone, such as a friend (she also texts me hers, which is a lovely comfort, and we get ideas from each other) or my husband. Texting it to someone makes me feel accountable to the plan, and means I'm more likely to do it.

- *Sensory soothing strategies*: I need two types of sensory soothing strategies for anxiety. Firstly, I need to soothe the knot in my gut. I do this by holding a hot water bottle against my tummy. The heat soothes the knotted feeling, and helps me to release tension in my ribs and muscles. If I'm not at home, I try to get a warm drink as the warmth helps ease the knot.

  Secondly, I need to create a sense of safety using sensory tools. Examples include warm drinks, lying down if I'm dizzy with anxiety (lying down will change the vestibular sense input and make me feel safer), heavy blankets (to ground the proprioceptive sense), listening to music, and watching a TV programme that brings me visual joy. I might pick some flowers in the garden and put them in a vase next to me, as I find flowers so uplifting visually. If I find my body tense and doing repetitive movements, I might get a fidget like a clicker, or twirl a piece of silky fabric through my fingers, as this stops my body getting sore from anxious tension.

- *I drink a warm non-caffeinated drink*: It has to be caffeine-free or decaffeinated as caffeine makes my anxiety spiral – it speeds up my heart and makes me light-headed, which makes me feel more anxious. The warmth is soothing, the drink brings feeling back to my throat and helps ensure I don't get dehydrated (I am prone to under-eating and under-drinking when anxious).

- *Nature*: If I'm able to, I take a walk alone. Time alone in nature really soothes my anxiety.

- *Pros and cons*: If I'm anxious over a decision or a choice, I write out a pros and cons list. Choices are a huge source of anxiety for me, and this is a tactic I've used since I was a child, as I process my thoughts much better on paper than in my head.

- *Think up ridiculous worst-case scenarios*: If I'm anxious about something specific, I use my imagination to make myself laugh by imagining hilarious and ridiculous worst-case scenarios. This might end up with 'and then aliens invade the earth' or 'and then I die and become a ghost and haunt someone awful in a hilarious manner' etc. It is supposed to be silly and ridiculous, and doesn't always work, but often helps me to break an obsessive thought pattern.

- *Watch comedy*: I have a really immature sense of humour, and whilst I often don't get jokes in conversations, I crack my sides laughing at the type of comedy where people slip on banana skins. As a teenager, one of my brothers used to walk into doors and trip over his own foot, just to make me laugh. I am able to recall these moments and they still make me laugh. I also watch movies or funny TV shows to help get rid of anxious thoughts.

- *Get into a creative flow*: When I feel anxious, it really helps to get out of my head, and make my mind focus on something completely different. Writing is the best thing for me to feel in a state of creative flow, and so I always have a number of different writing projects on the go, so I can dip into different projects depending on what I feel like in the moment.

- *Breathing techniques*: Breathing deep into my belly or repeating 'Breathe in, breathe out, pause' are techniques I use to control my breathing. See Chapter 3 for recommendations on how to avoid hyperventilating during acute anxiety.

- *Special interests*: Engaging in one of my special interests gives my brain a break from the obsessive or intrusive anxious thoughts that often come with my anxiety.

What to Do When I Feel: Disappointment?

- *Think of my gratitudes*: When I first tried the practice of naming my gratitudes, I thought it was a useless task. I did not feel better after writing out three things I was grateful for in my day. But I made a habit of it despite my doubt, and even joined a gratitude group with three family members. We text each other the things that we are grateful for in our days. Slowly, I started to not only list the gratitudes, but to really feel them.

  My physical disabilities have meant I had to give up my nursing career, and many other ambitions and hobbies, which brings me frequent waves of disappointment. But naming what I am grateful for has a powerful impact on me, and really does make me feel less disappointed. It helps me to see what I do have, and what I do achieve, rather than what I don't.

- *Sensory soothing strategies*: When I feel disappointed, I seek the feeling of comfort, and so I indulge my senses in comfort. I eat wholesome, comforting food for my taste sense (often my favourite foods that my step-mother made me as a child). I put on comfortable clothes and use soft blankets for my touch sense. I sit on my rocking chair to comfort my vestibular sense. I ask my husband or one of my children for a hug for my proprioceptive sense.

- *Seek comfort*: I watch comforting movies, or listen to comforting music, or read a book that I love that gives me a feeling of comfort.

- *Talk about it*: I often need to talk out my disappointment with my family or friends. Talking helps me to put things into perspective and release the disappointment.

- *Remind myself of the facts*: I am regularly disappointed by my inability to do activities due to my rheumatology disabilities, and some days I am unable to walk even with crutches, as the pain is too severe. This means I often have to cancel all my plans, and can end up spending a day in bed with such bad brain fog that I can't read, write, or do anything that feels worthwhile. I feel so disappointed by the end of the day.

  My autistic sensitivities can also cause me to feel disappointed, such as when I can't socialise as I much as I would like, or if I feel too overwhelmed to do something I want to do.

  Rather than feeling disappointed in myself for having to turn down opportunities or invitations, I try to identify the things which are actually restricting me, for example 'My day is too full to add in another social engagement' or 'I'm not going because I have to work in the morning, which means I won't have time to rest and reset after the event'. Focusing on the facts prevents me blaming myself, which make a huge difference to my self-esteem.

- *Cry it out*: I often feel better after a good cry. If tears aren't coming naturally, I might watch a sad movie to get the tears flowing. I often feel as though I can physically feel the disappointment pouring out of me with the tears.

What to Do When I Feel: Excitement or Extreme Happiness?

These feelings are typically considered a desirable emotional state, but I often find them very dysregulating. I can get almost manically giddy and excited at times, and this will often end in a meltdown, so I need to calm myself from extended periods of these emotions. This was very common when I was a teenager, but happens rarely nowadays.

- *Dance*: Dancing gets the excited energy out of my body. I start with giddy songs, but slowly work towards calmer songs.

- *Exercise*: This focuses the energy and lets it out, so it doesn't build up like electricity trying to escape.

- *Sensory soothing strategies*: Cold water is a big help when I feel overly excited, as it helps to shock me back down to earth. Putting cold water on my neck or inner wrists can help shock my system back to calmness, and takes the physical heat out of my skin that tends to build up when I feel unnaturally excited or happy.

  Feeling fresh air on different body parts really helps too, and I often go outside and focus on feeling the air or wind on different parts of my body to help calm me down. I usually start with feeling wind on my eyes and eyelashes, and work my way down my body. These are both strategies to calm the touch sense, which is the sense that feels the most jittery to me when I'm giddy or excited.

- *Be alone*: I can calm down from giddiness better when I am alone, and I have often had to excuse myself from people to go calm down from laughter or overwhelming excitement or giddiness to prevent a meltdown.

- *Jaw massage*: My jaw can get really tense when my face is stuck in a smile or a laugh. Extreme laughter gives me a jaw ache and headache. Massaging my jaw and cheeks can ease this, and provide a deep calm to my face (this not only releases tension, but also works on calming the tactile sense).

- *Get creative*: The energy that extreme excitement brings can be very helpful in creativity, and channelling the excited energy into a creative project can be very calming and productive. However, I can easily get carried away with creative projects, and can realise that I've spent hours on a project, and that suddenly it's very late at night. I can't sleep when I've just finished working on something exciting and creative, as my brain will keep coming up with new ideas. It's important that I set boundaries around my creativity, and make sure I give myself time to unwind from excited creativity before bedtime. I therefore set an alarm to stop, and plan to watch a short TV programme and drink herbal tea after the creative project, to reset my mind for bedtime.

- *Special interest*: Engaging in one of my special interests can be very calming and help bring my excited energy back down.

What to Do When I Feel: Embarrassment?

- *Say it out loud*: I often find that simply saying that I'm embarrassed to whomever I'm embarrassed in front of can immediately reduce the feeling of embarrassment, especially if I add a bit of humour into it. Stating it and acknowledging it seems to shrink it.

- *Laugh about it*: My step-mother is remarkable at helping me laugh at my embarrassment rather than wallow in it, so I often phone her if I've been embarrassed and she helps me turn it into something funny.

- *Change the subject*: If I'm embarrassed in a social situation (this happens a lot), I try to change the subject and put the moment behind me. This can be hard as I can't always think of what to say, so it doesn't always work.

- *Take a moment alone*: I have often excused myself to go the bathroom if I feel embarrassed. Time alone allows me to name the feeling, i.e. acknowledge that I feel embarrassed, but it also helps me think outside of the embarrassment. This allows me to come up with an embarrassment recovery plan such as thinking of something funny to say about it, or a subject change. I have even phoned people from the bathroom to explain what happened and asked for help coming up with a subject change or something funny to say about the embarrassing thing that happened.

- *Sensory soothing strategies*: Embarrassment feels like a flush of deep heat in my body, and causes my heart to race, so I focus my soothing strategies on those areas. I splash cold water on my face, inner wrists and back of the neck, which helps cool me down, and can shock me out of the numbness that embarrassment can bring. I drink a very cold drink, or hold a cold drink to my chest. If I'm with my husband I ask him for a tight hug.

- *Special interest*: If it's a more prolonged embarrassment rather than just a flash of embarrassment in a social moment, I use my special interest to distract me and calm me. Engaging in my special interest, especially if using creativity, is my strongest tool to distract and calm me from recurring thoughts that bring embarrassed feelings.

Using Creativity to Support Your Emotions

I know a lot of autistic people, and people with no diagnosis but strong autistic traits. A common theme I've noticed about them all is that they all feel better in themselves when they are being creative. I believe that creativity can be remarkably helpful to improve any baseline state of emotion.

It's important here to address the outdated view that autistic people lack creativity. It is simply not true. In fact, researchers that looked at studies of autism and creativity found that autistic people were found to have a higher level of originality within creative work, and their work had a significantly higher level of detail than that of non-autistic participants (Pennisi et al. 2021). There are many autistic people that excel in their creative field, and I believe there would be many more if autistic people were encouraged to explore their creativity. The notion that autistic people lack imagination and creativity needs to be abandoned.

I stopped being creative for a few years when I was in the throes of babies and work, and I couldn't figure out why I had a strong sense of missing something about myself. I eventually discovered that I missed having a creative outlet. While people may typically think of creativity as making art, I see creativity as creating something that brings you joy, creative thinking, creative expression, or something that allows you to enter a creative flow. This can be making Lego, doing DIY creative projects, creative computer coding, art etc.

When I began with creative writing, I soon found myself craving more creative outlets, and began painting and drawing. Being creative gives me a sense of satisfaction, and a sense of joy. It stops my thoughts for a while and gives my brain a break from ruminating, and seems to put a pause on my emotional fluctuations. It has also given me a social outlet as I began going to creative writing workshops and conferences, where I met like-minded people who were happy to talk about my special interests of reading and writing all day long. I also enjoyed the subtle socialising I did at the painting classes; I could chat if I wanted to, or just focus on the art if I didn't feel like talking that evening. It can be a lot easier for me to socialise when there's no expectation of constant conversation, or when there's a specific topic like painting or books to talk about.

I am not particularly good at painting or drawing, but that doesn't matter. What matters is switching off my thinking brain and allowing myself to get lost in the creative endeavour.

IDEAS FOR CREATIVITY
(This list could be endless, so I'm just including some ideas.)

- Creative writing.
- Visual art: painting, drawing, clay, sculpture.
- Drama.
- Building models, Lego, construction kits.
- Gardening.
- Creative or expressive computer programming.
- Design.
- Gaming that involves elements of design or creativity.
- Music – singing, playing instruments, creating sound.
- Fashion creativity or design.
- House design, decoration.

- Flower arranging.

- Jewellery making.

- Carpentry.

- Metal work.

- Graphic design.

- Knitting.

- Sewing, quilting.

- Invention.

- DIY projects.

Long-Term Uncomfortable Emotions

Sometimes an emotion is not ready to go away, and we need to allow ourselves to sit with it, be patient with it, and make a plan for managing it. An example of an emotion that can be around for a long time is grief. Through my experience of bereavement, I discovered that grief is not an emotion that leaves quickly, and even when it does ease off, it tends to return unexpectedly.

One of the hardest emotional times I ever went through was after a long-term romantic relationship break-up. It was a horrendous emotional roller-coaster of sadness, guilt, fear, doubt, relief, anxiety, and more. I felt free one minute and trapped the next minute. I later learnt that new loss can drag up grief and loss from the past, so when I was trying to cope with the break-up of the relationship, I was also dealing with the loss and grief of both my father and step-brother dying when I was a child. I honestly thought I would never get through that amalgamation of pain, but time worked its magic, and I did get over it.

Long-term uncomfortable emotions need long-term plans. My step-mother has taught me a lot about dealing with long-term uncomfortable emotions. Despite a number of bereavements in her life, she is the most energetic person I know. She insists on not allowing an uncomfortable emotion to drag on indefinitely. She acknowledges it, and then does something about it. She jumps into the ocean, even in winter, if she needs to get rid of grief. She walks, and paints, and tries new creative endeavours when she feels emotional pain. Whenever I say to her that I'm feeling down, she says 'What are you going to do about it?' This really helps me to get pro-active about my emotions, rather than just allowing them to stay through acceptance.

Long-term uncomfortable emotions may indicate a mental illness, and it's important to consider whether your long-term or reoccurring uncomfortable emotions are acceptable to you in your life, or if you need to question whether it's something that you need to get help for. When sadness or emptiness won't lift no matter what you do, it might be depression. When anxiety affects your ability to function, then you may have an anxiety disorder that would benefit from professional help. There are mental health professionals for a reason, and looking after your mental health is just as important as looking after your body, so I do recommend professional support when uncomfortable emotions are reducing your quality of life. Chapter 15 will look at mental illnesses a bit more closely.

KEY POINTS

◇ Having an Emotional Regulation Plan for individual uncomfortable emotions can help reduce emotional overwhelm.

◇ Having a visual plan prepared for each uncomfortable emotion eliminates the need to think flexibly or problem solve when you are feeling distress from an emotion.

◇ It's important to include sensory soothing strategies in each Emotional Regulation Plan, as soothing the body helps to reduce the chances of feeling overwhelmed by an emotion.

◇ Using your creativity can be a useful way to regulate your baseline emotions. There are many ways to be creative, and it's worth exploring what creativity works for you.

◇ Some emotions last for a long time. Grief is an example of an emotion that is expected to last for prolonged periods, and can come and go. However, if you experience recurring and continuous uncomfortable emotions, it may suggest you need professional help managing your emotions. It may also indicate a mental health illness, for which help is available.

References

Pennisi, P., Giallongo, L., Milintenda, G., and Cannarozzo, M. (2021) 'Autism, Autistic Traits and Creativity: A Systematic Review and Meta-Analysis'. *Cognitive Processes* 22, 1–36. https://doi.org/10.1007/s10339-021-01047-0

Chapter 15

Therapy for Emotional Regulation

CHAPTER AIMS

> To introduce some therapies that can be used with autistic adults, both talk-based and alternatives to talk-based therapies.
> To discuss what kind of adaptations therapists can make to ensure their practice is accessible to autistic people.

Introduction

There are many types of therapies and interventions that can help autistic adults with emotional regulation challenges, alexithymia, and anxiety. It is definitely worth trying out different therapies, and therapists, until you find one that really works for you. I suggest asking around for recommendations, or contacting an autism organisation and asking them for recommendations. Try to have an open mind if one attempt at therapy doesn't work for you, because perhaps the same therapy with a different therapist will work brilliantly. Equally if one type of therapy doesn't work for you, maybe another type of therapy will.

The therapy that really worked for me (after two attempts at counselling that made little to no improvement in my mood or my anxiety), was psychotherapy.

My first therapist was excellent at teaching me to recognise and name my emotions. He also helped me to understand how a number of significant traumas I had experienced in my childhood still affected my emotional regulation in adulthood.

After three years with that therapist, I wanted to move to someone with more understanding of autism, and someone who was more strategy-based. It was emotionally hard to move therapist, but I knew it needed to be done, as the first therapist was resistant to my increasing suspicions that I was autistic, and this became a stumbling block between us. Moving therapists was absolutely the right choice. I am still with the psychotherapist I moved to, and she is a huge support in my life. She has a particular strength in helping me find solutions to challenges, and many of my daily strategies come directly from working with her. She is a kind and non-judgemental person, and has a gift for coming up with simple and achievable solutions for both daily problems and more unusual or bigger problems.

It's important to be aware that your therapist isn't there to take on your problems for you, and they aren't a family member or a friend that you can call whenever you have a problem (unless it's to organise an actual session). They are professionals who will work with you during your allocated session to help you find solutions to challenges in your life, and to teach you skills to support yourself, in particular with emotional regulation.

This chapter will name some therapies than can help with emotional regulation, but please note I haven't tried them all myself. What works for one person may not work for another, and what type of therapy you choose to do is a very personal choice. It's important to ensure that the therapist you pick is registered with the appropriate professional accreditation body for your country.

Talk Therapies

Therapies based around talking are called talk therapies. Talk therapies include:

- *Psychotherapy*: This is the use of psychological methods to support a person to understand their emotions, to change unhelpful behaviours, improve coping skills, increase well-being, and find solutions to problems. The therapist involved is called a psychotherapist, and will have trained in psychotherapy.

There are many different techniques that a psychotherapist might use, and different therapists will have trained in different approaches. For example, EMDR (eye movement desensitisation and reprocessing) is a treatment to help people deal with traumatic memories. Another example of a treatment that a psychotherapist may use is CBT (cognitive behavioural therapy). CBT focuses on changing unhelpful thought patterns, and improving behaviours in order to improve mental well-being and quality of life. Research has shown that CBT can help with alexithymia (Poquereusse et al. 2018).

- *Clinical psychology*: This involves the diagnosis of psychological, emotional, or behaviour disorders, and the creation of treatment plans to support clients to meet goals, and to improve their coping skills. Psychologists help clients to find solutions for emotional or behavioural disorders. The therapist involved will have trained in psychology, and then done further study to qualify as a clinical psychologist.

  Like psychotherapists, clinical psychologists also use different treatments and approaches such as EMDR or CBT to help you manage your individual challenges.

- *Counselling*: Counselling gives you the space to talk about your problems and challenges, to express your feelings, and to explore your thoughts. Counsellors listen to your problems and may suggest ways to tackle these problems, improve your coping skills, and help you learn how to change how you react to things to reduce anxiety and stress. Counsellors train in counselling, and may specialise in specific areas such as bereavement or depression.

Please note: Psychotherapists and clinical psychologists are not usually medically qualified doctors or psychiatrists, and thus cannot prescribe medications. A psychiatrist is a type of doctor who specialises in mental health problems, and can prescribe medications to support mental health. Some psychiatrists or psychologists will also have training in psychotherapy, and so it's important to find out exactly what qualification your therapist has, to make sure they are qualified in the type of support you are seeking.

Talk Therapy and Verbal Communication Challenges

I acknowledge that talk therapy won't suit all autistic adults, for example those who are unable to speak, or have difficulties with speaking verbally. If you wish to engage in talk therapy, but have challenges with verbal communication, I suggest exploring what alternative ways of communication might work for you in a therapy session, but you yourself are the best person to know what will work for you.

If you are able to speak, but experience difficulty talking in certain situations, you could try sessions on the phone or on the computer. While I prefer in-person therapy sessions, I occasionally do therapy sessions over the phone when my rheumatology conditions flare up. The benefit of this is that the therapist can't see me, and I can lie down, pace back and forth, or stim all I like throughout the session without feeling someone watching me (please note: I am not suggesting there's anything wrong with stimming in front of a therapist, it's just not something I'm comfortable doing personally). I can lie in a hammock at home or lie under a weighted blanket to ground myself, which naturally aids thought processing and my verbal communication skills.

If you cannot communicate verbally, you could explore using a computer, writing, or having online sessions where the therapist talks and you type back etc. This may be challenging if you have any challenges with writing or typing, such as dyslexia or visual language processing difficulties. I would hope that a good therapist would be open to trying alternative communication methods, and be flexible about trying new methods. It is definitely worth researching and approaching therapists to find out what will work for you.

Working with a speech and language therapist could help you to find new ways to communicate, and you can work with them on improving your verbal or non-verbal communication skills.

Alternatives to Talk-Based Therapies

If talk-based therapy is not for you, either as it is not suitable or due to personal preference, then there are a range of other therapies that might work better.

These include:

- *Mindfulness-based therapies*: These involve teaching you to be fully present within yourself, aware of your feelings, what you are doing and where you are, and to reduce thought patterns that cause you to react or over-react to emotional changes. Mindfulness-based therapies that focus on interoception have been found to help with alexithymia (Poquereusse et al. 2018).

- *Occupational therapy*: This can help with the interoception sense. Learning to recognise and regulate what you feel in your body can help you notice physical clues that you are experiencing an emotion. Occupational therapy can also help you regulate your sensory system, which will in turn help your emotional regulation.

- *Animal therapy*: Animal-assisted therapy has been found to reduce stress, improve emotion, and increase social interaction in autistic people (O'Haire 2017). The most common forms of animal-assisted therapy are horse therapy (also known as equine therapy or hippotherapy) and dog therapy. Therapy dogs and pets are also popular for autistic people for helping with emotional regulation.

  Even having a pet with no therapy attached can be beneficial in helping you feel calm and emotionally regulated.

- *Art therapy*: Art therapy involves psychotherapy through creative art rather than through talking. The therapist interprets the art produced by the client, and helps the client to explore and manage their emotions. You don't need any experience of art to try this therapy.

- *Drama therapy*: Drama therapy involves psychotherapy through the medium of drama.

- *Music therapy*: Music therapy involves psychotherapy through the medium of music.

Group Therapy

Some people prefer group therapy, which means you are not the only client working with the therapist at one time. This means that not all the focus is on you individually, and you can learn from other people's experiences. I tried group therapy for anxiety, but it was not with other autistic people, so I felt little or no connection to the other people. Their anxiety issues were not the same as mine, and so I couldn't gain from their insights in a way that helped me. It would have benefitted me a lot more had I known I was autistic at the time, and found a group for autistic people.

Adapting Therapy for Autistic Clients

Whatever therapy you decide to try, it's important that the therapist is willing to make adaptations for your autistic needs and strengths. According to the NICE (National Institute for Health and Care Excellence) guidelines (2021), there are a number of adaptations that can be made to improve the effectiveness of psychosocial interventions for autistic adults. If you think any of these guidelines would help you during therapy, it's well worth asking your therapist to incorporate them into your session. These NICE guidelines for the therapist include:

- *Setting out explicit rules*, and explaining the rules.

- *Use simple language and avoiding extensive use of metaphor* (for the very literal thinkers).

- *Work more on changing behaviour rather than over-emphasising cognition and understanding* (I don't think this is always appropriate, as I like the cognitive explanations. However, I do understand where this guideline is coming from. I remember asking my driving teacher to please stop explaining how the car worked, and just tell me how to drive it. After 20 previous teeth-chattering driving lessons, this finally allowed me to 'get it' and I quickly learnt to drive once I stopped trying to figure out what was happening. My driving instructor couldn't understand this at all. I can therefore see how some autistics will benefit from less explanation and more emphasis on behavioural change).

- *Use of visual and written information*, as many autistic people are visual thinkers, and can process information better when it is in visual form.

- *Include a family member, carer, or support person if the autistic client agrees or wishes* (I have never needed to bring another person with me, but I understand that it would benefit some people).

- *Provide regular breaks to maintain attention.*

- *Use of special interests* (by chance, I share an interest with my therapist, in that we both love reading and writing, and I really enjoy when this comes up in a session).

To these NICE guidelines, I would also add my own suggestions for therapists working with autistic clients. These include:

- *Avoid scented candles, perfume, or air fresheners*: These are highly distracting, and can shift the focus away from working on one's emotions. An autistic person might smell the scent as intensely strong, and if they don't like it, the environment can feel unbearable. I recommend asking before using these, to ensure the scent is agreeable to the client.

- *Avoid overly bright lights*: Lamps or natural light are much more gentle and calming. The environment needs to feel safe for the autistic person to be comfortable engaging in therapy, and bright lights can be stressful.

- *Angle the chairs so that the autistic person is not expected to be in very close proximity to the therapist*, and in a way that the autistic person can lay their eyes on things other than the therapist. Being able to naturally avoid eye contact without having to make a huge effort to do so can be very helpful.

- *In the first session, explain what the autistic person can expect* from the therapy. This should include how often sessions will occur, what you expect from the client and what they can expect from you, when and how they will pay (unless the therapy is free through the public health system), how long the sessions will last, and how they are structured. Also explain what happens if the autistic client sees you in public; are they to say hello or pretend you don't know each other for confidentiality?

- *Have ready-prepared visuals* to allow the autistic person to take information home to process it in their own time.

- *Ask the autistic person what their preferred means of contact is*, whether phone call, text, or email. Talking on the phone may be anxiety inducing, so alternative methods can help. I also suggest giving a warning text or email if you are going to phone saying why, for example a text saying 'I'll call you later to rearrange an appointment, as I need to cancel today's appointment'. One thing I hate is missed calls as I imagine all sorts of worst-case possibilities for why the person is calling me. However, I often don't answer the phone when someone unexpectedly calls; I can literally stand there looking at the phone, unable to answer it because I don't know what the call is going to be about and therefore it's unpredictable, and unpredictable things bring anxiety.

- *Avoid a cluttered environment, but don't have an empty environment either*: In my experience of counselling and psychotherapy, I find that when I'm trying to avoid eye contact, I like having things I can rest my eyes on in the room, like a painting or a pretty curtain. However, cluttered objects can make me preoccupied with their lack of symmetry, or I can get stuck on counting and comparing if anything is missing from previous sessions. Missing books from bookshelves is particularly bothersome to me, as I form an association of what is constant in the room, and if something is gone in my next session, it can throw me.

  The worst environment I attended counselling in was a very clinical setting, almost hospital like, and the environment made it hard to feel safe and comfortable. It also made the session feel medicalised, rather than just a normal part of looking after my mental health.

- *Write out, or allow the autistic person to write out, any strategies or plans* that you have agreed they will try after the sessions. I often find it hard to remember what I hoped to work on after a session, so having it written down reminds me to do it.

- *Consider having a weighted lap blanket to provide proprioceptive calming feedback* during the session, which may help the autistic person to feel grounded during emotionally challenging parts of the session. Perhaps cover it in a pillowcase that gets changed between clients for hygiene. I would dislike the thought of using a blanket other people used before me, even if it's just on my lap.

- *Allow the autistic person time to process questions and concepts*, and consider asking them to tell you if they need something rephrased. If they don't answer a question immediately, give them time to answer. Sometimes we take a bit longer to process questions and come up with an answer.

- *Don't presume the autistic person will remember everything you have said* in previous sessions. When we are emotionally challenged, our thinking ability goes down. It can be so difficult to feel intense emotions and we might have no mental energy left to remember explanations and instructions.

- *Be very clear when you are asking questions*: Vagueness can make me get lost in my head, if I'm trying to work out what the therapist is asking. I therefore ask my therapist to rephrase what she's said, but it might help if you give the client permission to do this, or even give them a phrase or hand gesture that they can use.

- *State clearly that the autistic person is allowed to question your techniques and insights*, and that you won't be offended. Autistic people are literal, but we can be terrified of offending people accidentally (from past experience). Giving us permission to question allows us to get a literal understanding, and to make sure we comprehend what you've said. It also allows us to say if we don't think something will work for us.

KEY POINTS

◊ There are many types of therapies that can help you learn to recognise your emotions, and regulate your emotions.

◊ Seeing a therapist can help you learn to support yourself with challenges in life.

◊ There are many adaptations that therapists can make so that their service is more accessible to autistic adults. It can be helpful to discuss any adaptations you would need or like with your therapist, to see if they can help with this.

References

NICE (2021) 'Autism Spectrum Disorder in Adults: Diagnosis and Management'. Clinical Guideline (CG142). Accessed 13 January 2022 at: www.nice.org.uk/guidance/cg142/chapter/Recommendations#organisation-and-delivery-of-care-2

O'Haire, M. (2017) 'Research on Animal-Assisted Intervention and Autistic Spectrum Disorder 2012–2015'. *Applied Developmental Science* 21 (3), 200–216. https://dx.doi.org/10.1080/10888691.2016.1243988

Poquereusse, L., Pastore, L., Dellantonio, S., and Esposito, G. (2018) 'Alexithymia and Autism Spectrum Disorder: A Complex Relationship'. *Frontiers in Psychology* 9, 1196. https://dx.doi.org/10.3389/fpsyg.2018.01196

Chapter 16

Mental Health and Mental Illness in Autism

CHAPTER BREAKDOWN

CHAPTER AIMS

›   To highlight the high prevalence of mental illness and mental health challenges in autistic people.
›   To briefly introduce a number of mental illnesses.
›   To explain what you can do if you think you are experiencing a mental illness, or if you think you are struggling to manage your mental health.
›   To discuss some medications that are commonly used to support the mental health of autistic people, as well as medication used for mental illnesses.

DISCLAIMER

Before I begin this chapter, I wish to remind the reader that although I am a registered general nurse, I am not a trained mental health professional. It is beyond the scope of this book to treat or diagnose any mental illness, and I advise you to speak with your doctor if you have, or suspect you have, a mental illness.

Mental Health and Mental Illness

There is a significant difference between mental health and mental illness.

Your mental health refers to your emotional, psychological, and social well-being, and it affects what you do, how you think, how you act, and how you relate to other people. Mental health, just like physical health, can fluctuate; sometimes being very good, sometimes being mildly under par, or sometimes being hugely challenged. A mental illness is a condition, or mental health disorder, that affects your mood, thinking, and behaviour.

Having good mental health does not simply mean you do not have a mental illness. *You can have a mental illness, but have good mental health, because you have the mental illness under control and well treated.* Equally, you can have no mental illness but have poor mental health, for example if you repeatedly have poor sleep and are too exhausted to do the things that bring meaning to your life.

It is a normal part of life to experience challenges to your mental health, but it is how we react to those challenges that determines our state of mental health. Having good mental health means being able to maintain a state of well-being and good level of function, despite daily life stresses and challenges.

Causes of Mental Illness

Mental illnesses affect a large proportion of people around the world, but the rate of mental illness jumps significantly in autistic people. There are many causes of mental illness, but the exact cause of each individual case of mental illness is often unknown. Some mental illnesses are genetic, and so tend to run in families, such as schizophrenia. This doesn't mean you will develop schizophrenia just because it's in your family, but it might mean you have a genetic predisposition to develop it.

Some mental health illnesses can be caused by one or more triggers, such as environmental factors, trauma, abuse, extreme stress, grief, chronic physical illness etc. To give an example, someone might develop an eating disorder due to a combination of puberty onset, a high level of baseline anxiety, a culture of dieting, developing a poor or distorted self-image due to exposure to social media or mass media, stress, trauma etc.

Severe and prolonged challenges to your mental health can also trigger some mental illnesses, such as depression or anxiety.

In my opinion, there are many aspects of being autistic that can have a direct impact on your mental health, and can increase the likelihood of developing certain mental illnesses. These include, but are not limited to:

- *Living with sensory processing differences.* For example, if you feel fear when you hear unexpected loud noises, you could develop anxiety about going out and about in a world full of loud noises. Anxiety can go hand in hand with an unregulated sensory system.

- *Social differences can create mental health challenges.* If you find it hard to fit in socially, it's easy to see how you can become full of shame and loneliness. Having a lack of connection with other people could increase your risk of depression, as can trying really hard to fit in.

- *Masking,* which means hiding your autistic traits to appear non-autistic, has been linked to difficulty sustaining relationships, autistic burnout, and suicidality (Pearson and Rose 2021).

- *Difficulty sleeping,* which is common in autistic people, can make it harder to have the energy to look after your mental health. Sleep deprivation and insomnia act in a vicious circle on mental health; they are often a symptom of mental illness, but a symptom that makes the mental illness worse.

- *In Ireland, 85% of autistic adults are under- or unemployed* (AsIAm 2019). In the UK, less than 22% of autistic adults are in any form of employment (Office for National Statistics 2020). A lack of employment can cause financial difficulty, a lack of purpose or meaning, isolation, a lack of connection with society etc., which can all lead to mental health challenges. This could contribute to the development of a mental illness such as depression.

Autism and the Prevalence of Mental Illness

Research has found significantly higher rates of some types of mental illness amongst autistic people compared to non-autistic people. Different research studies have found slightly different rates of each mental illness in autistic people, but all the research literature I could find agreed that the rates are considerably higher in the autistic population.

One large American study that looked at over 1000 autistic adults found that 54% of the autistic adults had at least one 'psychiatric disorder', with diagnosis rates at:

- 29% for anxiety disorder

- 26% for depression

- 11% with bipolar

- 8% with obsessive compulsive disorder

- 8% with schizophrenia.

(Croen et al. 2015)

In 2019, *The Lancet Psychiatry* published a large review of 96 research studies that looked at the prevalence of mental illnesses amongst autistic people, and found similarly high rates of mental illnesses amongst autistic people, with diagnosis rates at:

- 17–23% for anxiety disorder

- 9–17% for sleep disorder

- 9–13% for depressive mood disorder

- 7–10% for obsessive compulsive disorder

- 3–6% for bipolar disorder

- 3–5% for schizophrenia.

(Lai et al. 2019)

Autistic Burnout

Autistic burnout can be described as 'chronic exhaustion, loss of skills, and reduced tolerance to stimulus' that lasts for an extended period of time (Raymaker et al. 2020, p. 141). Autistic burnout can not only reduce your quality of life, but can also reduce your ability to perform and manage daily tasks. This can make daily living very difficult, ranging from difficulty with looking after yourself, to sustaining employment, to maintaining relationships.

One study found that autistic burnout can happen when expectations placed on the autistic adult outweigh their abilities. This is caused by an increase in life stressors that add to the cumulative load (i.e. the pressures and demands) on the autistic adult. The inability to get relief from this load, mainly through barriers to support, tipped the adults into autistic burnout (Raymaker et al. 2020). The most common life stressor identified in this study was masking, which means suppressing your autistic traits in order to appear more non-autistic.

Masking can be both conscious and unconscious, and can involve concealing your true self in order to reduce the effects of stigma you experience simply from being autistic. But by reducing external consequences (such as bullying, or stigma, or not fitting in), masking increases internal consequences (such as exhaustion and sensory overload), which increases the risk of autistic burnout (Pearson and Rose 2021). Examples of masking include forcing yourself to not stim in public, forcing yourself to experience sensory stressors because you feel obliged to (e.g. having to wear work clothes that aggravate your tactile sense), or spending huge amounts of energy acting how you think you are expected to act in a social situation, rather than just 'being yourself'.

I was unable to find research that identified ways to prevent and treat autistic burnout, but as burnout can look similar to depression, I believe it's important to be aware that if you have all the signs of depression but you don't feel sad or empty, it's possible you have burnout rather than depression. It's therefore important to speak to your health professional about this, and educate them about it if they are not familiar with autistic burnout.

I often laugh with my husband about how in old books or movies (especially Agatha Christie books), if someone has a nervous complaint, the doctors prescribe them 'a week by the seaside'. If someone went to a doctor nowadays and described the signs of autistic burnout, it's possible they'd be prescribed an anti-depressant. My husband and I have a joke that when I'm feeling close to burnout, we say 'Time for the seaside'. We are extremely lucky to live in a coastal county in Ireland, and are only a 25-minute drive from the nearest beach. Not only that, but my in-laws have a seaside holiday cottage that we can stay in a few times a year.

A week by the seaside has a truly a remarkable effect on me; not only because going away reduces the demands on me, but because the seaside is my favourite sensory environment to be in; I love the noise of the waves, the sight of the sea, the smell of salt, I love spinning and spinning on the beach. A week of restorative stimming, sensory pleasure, reduced demands, no socialising, and a change of scenery is the best thing I can do to prevent or treat my autistic burnout.

The seaside isn't an option for everyone, and sometimes work and school demands prevent me from going to the coast. When this happens, I simply do my best to reduce the demands on myself: I cancel appointments, I postpone socialising, I increase sensory self-care, I increase the time I spend on my special interests, and I am extremely kind and caring to myself.

Depression

Approximately 322 million people worldwide live with depression (World Health Organization 2017). Many research studies have looked at how many autistic people have depression, and while they have all found slightly different rates, they have unanimously found that the rates of depression are much higher for autistic than non-autistic people. For example, one large US study published in 2015 found that 25% of autistic adults had depression, compared to 9% of non-autistic adults (Croen et al. 2015). Another review of many research studies found that autistic people are approximately four times more likely to experience depression at some point in their lifetime than non-autistic people (Hudson et al. 2019).

Signs of depression, as per the World Health Organization (2019), include:

- sadness

- loss of motivation

- loss of pleasure

- guilt

- poor self-worth

- poor sleep

- concentration challenges
- physical complaints with no identified cause
- difficulty functioning and coping with daily life
- severe cases may include suicidal thoughts.

I myself have experienced bouts of depression since I was a late teenager, but thankfully I no longer get these bouts for more than a few days at a time, due to a huge improvement in my mental health care and self-understanding.

Depression for me feels much worse than sadness: it feels like I'm being dragged down by despair, and am consumed by a deep and terrible bleakness. In a bout of depression, I find it hard to get joy from anything, even the things I usually love. I feel crushingly alone, and as if I will never feel joy or calm again. In my earlier bouts of depression, I used to become convinced that I'd always felt this low, and experienced distorted thoughts that tried to convince me I would never not feel so bleak again. It took me a long time to first go to my GP about depression, but the relief was enormous when I finally did. I was not prescribed medication on that visit, but simply talking to a professional and having my depression named and acknowledged lifted an enormous weight off my shoulders.

Anxiety Disorders

Heightened anxiety is common amongst autistic people. I often think of the quote 'For… twenty years I tried to find psychological reasons for the panic attacks. I now realise that because of my autism, my nervous system was in a state of hypervigilance' by Temple Grandin, in her well-known book on her life with autism, *Thinking in Pictures* (Grandin 1995, p. 123).

Anxiety is a normal and natural emotion, whose purpose is to protect us. But if anxiety starts to play a starring role in your life, or if anxious thoughts are recurring or intrusive, or affect your ability to function, then it may be more than just normal anxiety; it may be an anxiety disorder.

Anxiety disorders are much more common in autistic people than non-autistic people. One large European study found that over 20% of autistic adults have an anxiety disorder, compared to 8.7% of non-autistic adults (Nimmo-Smith et al. 2020). This study found that autistic adults without intellectual disability were found to have higher rates of anxiety disorders, and the most common anxiety disorders found in autistic adults were obsessive compulsive disorder (OCD) and phobia-related anxiety disorder.

What Is an Anxiety Disorder?

Approximately 264 million people in the world live with an anxiety disorder (World Health Organization 2019). There are a number of disorders characterised by excessive and long-lasting anxiety. These include, but are not limited to, the following disorders:

- generalised anxiety disorder (GAD)
- panic disorder
- phobias
- social anxiety disorder
- post-traumatic stress disorder (PTSD)
- OCD.

Generalised Anxiety Disorder

GAD involves persistent anxiety or worrying in a way that interferes with daily life, and can include physical symptoms such as sleep difficulty, muscle tension, concentration challenges, and restlessness (American Psychiatric Association 2021, section 'Generalised Anxiety Disorder'). Whilst the worrying is usually focused on everyday things such as health, job responsibilities, chores etc., the worrying reaches excessive levels.

Panic Disorder

A panic disorder involves repeated attacks of intense anxiety and fear, which manifest physically in your body, as well as mentally in your thoughts. A panic attack can include a combination of these symptoms:

- palpitations
- increased heart rate
- shaking or trembling
- feeling you can't catch your breath or breathe properly
- dizziness
- pains in the chest

- light-headedness
- feeling chilled or very hot
- nausea
- feeling of doom
- feeling detached
- fear of dying
- fear that you are having a heart attack.

This list is based upon the American Psychiatric Association (2021) section 'Panic Disorder', you are advised to seek exact wording for any references made to DSM-5 criteria. If you have a panic disorder, the panic attacks can come on suddenly and typically last 5–30 minutes (NHS 2020).

Over-breathing, i.e. hyperventilation, is common during panic attacks (see Chapter 3 for more on hyperventilation). This can make the symptoms of panic attacks worse, as it can increase dizziness, light-headedness, and breathlessness, which in turn increase panic and anxiety.

Phobias

A phobia is an excessive fear of a thing, situation, or activity. The fear can be persistent and debilitating. The person with the phobia tends to know their fear is excessive, but they are unable to stop feeling the fear despite this knowledge (American Psychiatric Association 2021, section 'Phobias, Specific Phobia').

Agoraphobia

Agoraphobia is an intense fear of certain situations or places – usually where escape will be difficult or embarrassing. This may include:

- open spaces
- enclosed spaces
- leaving home
- queues
- crowds
- public transport

- elevators.

The phobia is out of proportion to the situation, and exposure to the place or situation almost always triggers anxiety. The phobia might develop after a previous panic attack in that situation or place, and usually lasts more than six months to be classified as agoraphobia (Mayo Clinic 2017). Agoraphobia can be debilitating to daily life functioning, such as being unable to leave the house without a companion, or unable to leave the house at all.

Social Anxiety Disorder

Social anxiety disorder is an intense fear of social situations, mainly about how you will be perceived, or how you will perform, in a social situation. This might include anxiety about conversations, fear of criticism, fear of how you will react including blushing or sweating, or fear of being judged (NHS 2020).

Post-Traumatic Stress Disorder

PTSD is an anxiety disorder that can develop after a traumatic or extremely distressing event, or after a prolonged experience of trauma.

Obsessive Compulsive Disorder

OCD has many overlaps with autistic traits, but there are distinct differences that set them apart.

The symptoms of OCD include two main parts:

1. *Obsessions*: The obsessions in OCD include repetitive worries, doubts, actions, or thoughts.

2. *Compulsions*: The obsessive thoughts or worries cause compulsive behaviour or rituals.

Examples include repeatedly checking if the door is locked, even though you know you checked it already, because you think something terrible will happen if you don't. Another example is having a specific ritual before you do an activity, because you fear you will be unsafe if you don't do it, even if there is no logical reason for doing it.

In my experience, a lot of people can have moments of this sort of obsessive behaviour. But OCD is more than a few moments here and there.

The level of obsessive compulsions in OCD can have a serious impact on the quality of your life, and can be exhausting and very upsetting.

Difference between Autistic Repetitive Behaviour and OCD

Autistic people often engage in repetitive behaviour, have repetitive thoughts, and form rituals around their activities. But there are significant differences between OCD and autistic repetition.

Autistic people use their repetitions and rituals as a self-soothing technique, and these are often a source of enjoyment or comfort. With OCD, the obsessive and compulsive behaviours are upsetting, intrusive, and unwelcome (National Autistic Society 2020). In short, the repetitive behaviours in autism reduce anxiety, whereas the repetitive behaviours in OCD increase anxiety (National Autistic Society 2020). But it is possible to be both autistic and have OCD at the same time.

Bipolar Disorder

Bipolar disorder affects approximately 45 million people worldwide (World Health Organization 2019). Bipolar disorder can consist of both manic periods and depressive periods, separated by times when the mood returns to normal. It can also occur without depressive periods, moving from normal mood to manic episodes.

Symptoms of manic episodes, as per the World Health Organization (2019), may include:

- irritability

- over-activity

- rapid speech

- over-elevated self-esteem

- elevated mood (mania)

- decreased need for sleep.

Eating Disorders

Eating disorders are a severe disturbance in a person's relationship with food, and their eating behaviours. Research suggests that 20–30% of people with an eating disorder are autistic or have autistic traits (Solmni et al. 2020).

One large UK study found that adolescents with an eating disorder had a 20% increase in the autistic traits of social and communication disorders in childhood (Solmni et al. 2020).

Eating disorders are not a lifestyle choice; they are a mental illness, and can be very serious. They can have a very damaging effect on the body, and can cause a loss of body functions. There are a number of different types of eating disorders, as follows:

Anorexia

A person with anorexia will restrict their diet, or avoid eating, to the point of damaging their body through starvation. Some people with anorexia also have binge–purge episodes, when they eat large quantities of food, and then vomit that food to avoid putting on weight. They may engage in compulsive behaviours to avoid putting on weight, such as excessive exercising.

People with anorexia have body dysphoria: they see themselves as needing to lose weight, despite being underweight. They will have an intense fear of gaining weight. Anorexia can lead to death through starvation, or suicide.

Bulimia Nervosa

Bulimia nervosa involves frequent episodes of binge-eating large quantities of food, and then taking excessive steps to avoid weight gain through forced vomiting, using laxatives or diuretics, excessive exercise or fasting. A person with bulimia may have a normal body weight, but will have a preoccupation with their weight and avoiding weight gain.

Binge-Eating Disorder

Binge-eating disorder involves frequent episodes of binge-eating large amounts of food, and not having control over this. Unlike bulimia nervosa, this binge-eating is not followed by excessive means to rid the body of the food afterwards. This can lead to being overweight or obese.

Avoidant Restrictive Food Intake Disorder

A person with avoidant restrictive food intake disorder (ARFID) will limit and restrict the amount or type of food they eat to the point that their body cannot function properly. People with ARFID do not have a distorted body image or fear of weight gain, like in anorexia. The problem lies with the actual eating of food. It can stem from a number of difficulties around food, including (Bodywhys 2022):

- Sensory aversion to food, including intolerance of textures, tastes, or smells. This can also cause a fear of trying new foods, and thus limit one's diet so much that it causes nutrient deficiency.

- Phobia of eating, for example due to a fear of choking.

- Reduced interest in eating. This can occur for reasons such as not feeling hungry, or feeling full too quickly after eating small portions.

In children, the limited diet in ARFID restricts the child's growth and development. In adults, ARFID can prevent the body functioning through a lack of calories.

Suicidality

Suicidal thoughts can be particularly high in the autistic population. One review of multiple studies found that there can be varying rates of suicidal thoughts in an autistic population, from 10–66% (Hossain et al. 2020).

A large study published in 2016 found that autistic adults without intellectual disability had a significantly higher risk of suicide than non-autistic adults or autistic adults with intellectual disability. Autistic women were found to be ten times more likely to die by suicide than non-autistic women, and autistic men were six times more likely to die by suicide than non-autistic men (Hirvikoski et al. 2016). The researchers suggested that reasons for this may include increased rates of depression, social isolation, reduced coping skills, and reduced life satisfaction.

Warning signs of suicide:

- Having thoughts of ending your life.

- Gathering or organising the means to end your life, for example stockpiling drugs to prepare for overdose.

- Becoming preoccupied with death and thoughts of dying.

- Reckless behaviour such as driving dangerously, or engaging in risky and dangerous activities.

- Feeling trapped and without hope.

- Feeling like life is not worth living.

- Self-destructive behaviour such as increased alcohol or drug intake.

- Getting your affairs in order to prepare for after your death, or saying goodbye to people as if you will not see them again.

(Mayo Clinic 2018)

If you are suicidal, it's important to recognise that this is a mental illness. Suicidal thoughts are nothing to be ashamed of, and there is help and treatment available. The right treatment can help you to stop feeling suicidal, help you manage your challenges, help you find hope again, and help you to manage suicidal thoughts. The quicker you get help, the better. It's important to avoid alcohol, drugs, or behaviours that could reduce your ability to keep yourself safe and in control of your actions.

If you are having suicidal thoughts despite knowing that you don't want to end your life, it is still important to get help to manage these thoughts and to help you to feel safe with your thoughts.

If you are having thoughts of suicide, self-harm, or harming others, it's important that your first step is going to get professional help from your medical doctor or psychiatrist. You can also present yourself to an acute hospital accident and emergency department, as thinking you might end your life is an emergency, and should be treated like one. There are also out-of-hours helplines available if you need to talk to someone or seek support.

I also advise that you talk to people you are close to about this. Getting help as early as possible can really help with these thoughts, and can have a hugely beneficial effect in preventing suicide, and helping you move away from suicidal thoughts. Many people have self-harm thoughts, suicidal thoughts, or thoughts of harming others, and the thoughts can be extremely frightening. But you don't have to go through it alone, as there is help available.

Steps to Take if You Think You Are Experiencing Mental Illness

1. *Firstly, be proud of yourself for recognising a mental illness, or a potential mental illness, in yourself*: Recognising this is an important step, and is

nothing to be ashamed of. You just have to look at the huge statistics of people who have mental illness to know that you are not alone; you are simply one of many people who are having, or have had, a period of challenged mental health.

2. *Get professional help*: Go to your GP (or family doctor) and explain that you are experiencing a change in your mental health. A GP can advise you about what therapies might help you, and whether trying prescribed medication is an appropriate step to take. They can also refer you to an appropriate therapist, or services that are available that might help you. When I went to my GP about my mental health, I felt like a weight had been lifted off my shoulders. I was listened to, supported and reassured, and a plan of supportive action was put in place; the first step being psychotherapy, followed by checking back in with the GP to see if further steps were needed.

3. *Talk about it*: Telling people you are close to (in an emotional sense) about how you feel is a good step when you are concerned about your mental health. It is important that you feel safe with the person that you choose to talk to. If you don't get a helpful reaction from one person, don't let that put you off telling another person. Some people have negative or outdated opinions on mental illnesses, and may tell you unhelpful things like 'you just need to stop worrying' or 'you just need to do more exercise'. But mental illness can be a deep and complex issue, and it can't always be cured by going for a jog. And unfortunately, someone with severe anxiety can't just 'stop worrying'.

4. It can help to tell someone that you don't want them to tell you how to fix your mental illness, you simply want to talk about it, and feel that someone is empathising with you. *Talking about it can take some of the weight out of mental illness*, as in the proverbial saying 'A problem shared is a problem halved'.

5. *Consider if any changes to your lifestyle (even small changes) might improve your mental health*: Increasing your exercise, connecting with friends, eating a healthier diet, cutting out sugar, reducing or cutting out alcohol (alcohol is a depressant), taking a break, and having a holiday are all things that may improve your mental health.

6. *Consider joining a reputable support group*: This can allow you to share

your experiences with others who are also living with the mental illness that you are experiencing. Support groups can also be a source of information, support, reassurance, and strategy sharing. I specify 'reputable' support groups as I have come across groups online that call themselves 'support groups', but actually consist of a lot of false information and negativity. I therefore recommend asking your health professional if there is a support group run by your local or national health service. Many of these will be run by health professionals who can ensure the information being shared is fact and not fiction.

Medications Widely Used for Mental Health

There are many types of medication that a doctor may prescribe to improve your mental health. It is important that you always speak with your doctor before trying any medicine, especially ones for mental health. This is because medicines can have serious and harmful side-effects for some people.

For example, I have a heart arrhythmia called long QT syndrome (which can cause sudden death), and taking certain medications is very dangerous for me. I am therefore very limited in what medications I can take, including being unable to take many anti-anxiety medicines and many anti-depressants.

If you have a history of any medical illness, it is important to discuss this with your doctor before beginning any medication for your mental health. In particular, anti-depressants and anxiolytics (anti-anxiety medicines) can have some serious side-effects, and they should only be taken if prescribed for you, and monitored by a doctor.

In this section, I will briefly discuss a number of common medicines that may be prescribed by your doctor to support your mental health. Please note: I am only introducing the more common medicines and supplements. It is beyond the scope of this book to delve into all types of psychiatric medicines used to treat mental illness.

Anti-Depressants

There are many different types of anti-depressants that your GP can prescribe for you, if you both deem them necessary to significantly improve your quality of life, or to reduce the challenging effects of a mental illness.

Despite the name, anti-depressants are not only used for depression; they can also be prescribed for anxiety disorders, OCD, panic disorder,

PTSD, eating disorders, and severe phobias. Anti-depressants can also be prescribed for chronic pain, including chronic nerve pain (NHS 2021). They are not recommended as the first line of treatment in adolescents, or in cases of milder depression (World Health Organization 2019).

Anti-depressants are often used as a long-term mental health strategy, but can also be prescribed for short-term treatment, for example during a time of grief, after a trauma, or during a particularly challenging time in your life. Another reason people may take short-term anti-depressants is to help them feel more emotionally able to try out therapy, such as psychotherapy (see Chapter 14). Many research studies have found that psychotherapy along with anti-depressants for people with depression, anxiety disorder, or OCD has a significantly higher success rate than anti-depressants alone (Cujipers et al. 2014).

It is really important to watch for any side-effects if you start anti-depressants, and report any deterioration in mental health, including suicidal thoughts, to your doctor. If the anti-depressants your GP prescribes do not improve your symptoms, your GP may switch you to a different anti-depressant, or refer you to a medical professional who specialises in mental health medicine, such as a psychiatrist. It is extremely important that you work with your GP, or prescribing doctor, if you are reducing, changing, or coming off anti-depressants to avoid serious side-effects or harm.

Medication for Anxiety

There is a huge range of medicines that can be used to manage the physical symptoms of anxiety. These can range from nutritional supplements, to drugs that inhibit the heart speeding up, to strong sedatives.

Here are some examples of medicines that can be used for reducing the symptoms of anxiety:

Beta-Blockers

Beta-blockers, which are usually used for heart conditions, are sometimes prescribed for anxiety, as they reduce the body's response to adrenaline. This means they can reduce the 'fight, flight, or freeze' response you experience during an acute attack of anxiety. For this reason, they are sometimes used for stage fright or public speaking. They are not habit-forming or addictive, but can have side-effects such as lowering blood pressure, which may cause dizziness.

Cannabidiol (CBD Oil)

Cannabidiol, or CBD oil, is an increasingly popular treatment for anxiety. Although the research is currently limited, studies looking at the use of CBD oil for anxiety, PTSD, and seasonal affective disorder have shown very positive results for its effectiveness in reducing acute anxiety (Blessing et al. 2015). CBD oil comes from the cannabis plant, but does not contain the psychoactive ingredient THC (tetrahydrocannabinol), and so does not give you the 'high' sensation that's associated with cannabis.

A number of studies have found CBD oil to safely reduce anxiety, insomnia, and chronic pain. Although CBD has been found to be safe, it is thought it may alter the effectiveness of some medicines including blood-thinning medicines (Harvard Health Publishing 2021).

The availability of CBD oil varies in different parts of the world. In Ireland and the UK it can be sold without prescription as a health supplement. CBD oil is sold widely in some parts of the US without prescription, but it is not yet legal in every state. In Australia, CBD oil became legal in 2021, but there are currently delays in the regulation of products containing CBD oil, making it widely unavailable (*The Guardian* 2021).

Anxiolytics

Anxiolytics are a group of medicines that reduce the symptoms of anxiety. There are a number of different types of anxiolytics, from mild relaxants to strong sedatives. Probably the most common anti-anxiolytics prescribed are benzodiazepines. Benzodiazepines are used medically as a sedative, a muscle relaxant (e.g. to relieve muscle spasms), as a relaxant before surgery, and for acute anxiety. However, benzodiazepines are habit-forming and can be addictive. They should be used carefully, and under the instructions of a doctor. They can cause side-effects such as sleepiness or drowsiness, and thus may affect your ability to drive or carry out daily functions safely.

Hormone Therapy

Our bodies rely on hormones for a range of basic body functions, from falling asleep to digesting the food we eat, from how we grow to mood management. Hormonal imbalances can have a huge impact on our mood, energy levels, and mental health. If you notice a change in your mood, energy levels, or your general health and well-being, it is well worth getting your bloods checked to ensure there have been no changes in your general health and hormones.

There are many hormonal therapies that can be prescribed to ensure your body is working to the best of its abilities, and to support your mental health. For example, if your thyroid hormones are low, you might be extremely tired and have low energy, which can mimic depression. If your thyroid hormones are high, you may be agitated, hyper, or experience a spike in anxiety.

Not all hormones can be routinely measured by your GP, but there are still supplements or medicines that can be trialled to see if they improve your symptoms.

Here are some examples of hormone therapies that can support mental health:

Melatonin: The Sleep Hormone

Difficulties with sleep are very common amongst autistic people. This can range from having difficulty falling asleep to waking in the night and being unable to get back to sleep. One study of 288 adults in the UK found that 90% of the autistic participants reported significantly poor sleep quality (Halstead et al. 2021).

Melatonin is a hormone with a daily cycle: at night time, shortly before sleep, our bodies' levels of melatonin are supposed to peak, and decline through the night until reaching their lowest point as we wake. However, research has found that autistic people can have lower levels of melatonin than non-autistic people, and taking melatonin supplements has been found to improve falling asleep and sleep quality for autistic people (Lalanne et al. 2021).

Melatonin supplementation shouldn't be the first action to improve sleep. Good sleep hygiene includes having a strong bedtime routine, using no screens or blue light in the bedroom, eating a healthy diet but avoiding big meals right before bed, going to bed at the same time every night, exercising and seeing natural light during the day (something to be mindful of if you frequently use sunglasses or tinted lenses to protect your vision sense from overwhelm), and having darkness at night. If good sleep hygiene isn't enough to give you a good night's sleep, it is well worth speaking to your health professional about whether to add melatonin into your bedtime routine.

Improving your sleep can really improve mental health. Having a good night's sleep is one of the most important things for me to prevent autistic burnout.

Serotonin: The Happy Hormone

Serotonin is a hormone and a neurotransmitter that sends messages between nerve cells in the body. It plays an important role in our mood, our digestion, sleep, and more. If your brain doesn't have enough serotonin available to use, it can cause mood disturbance, poor sleep, and depression.

One of the most common groups of anti-depressants is the SSRIs (selective serotonin re-uptake inhibitors). It is thought that they improve depression by increasing the amount of serotonin available to the brain.

Female Menstrual Hormones

Fluctuations in female body hormones can affect mood and mental health. There are even some mental illnesses directly related to female body hormones, such as premenstrual dysphoric disorder (a severe form of premenstrual syndrome) and post-natal depression (after having a baby). If you experience cyclical changes in your mental health, it might be worth exploring if these are related to hormonal changes. Keeping a record of your mood and mental health over the course of a few menstrual cycles can help you to spot if hormonal changes are contributing to mood or mental health disturbances. Your GP can discuss hormonal therapies or support systems to help you manage this.

The peri-menopausal years are also associated with significant mental health challenges, with the highest rate of suicide amongst women in Ireland occurring between the ages of 45–54 (National Office for Suicide Prevention 2019), which coincides with the age of peri-menopause. While peri-menopause symptoms can be mild for some women, they can be severe for others. The rates of depression doubles in peri-menopausal women, and women with a history of anxiety often have a reoccurrence of anxiety at this time (Harvard Health Publishing 2020). Hormone replacement therapy can be used to reduce the challenging symptoms of the peri-menopause, and support mental health.

Nutritional Supplements

Deficiencies or imbalances in nutrition can have a direct impact on mental health. If you have mental health challenges, it is well worth asking your doctor for a blood test to ensure you are not deficient in any of the nutrients that your body needs to run at its optimum ability. Nutritional deficiencies or imbalances can cause symptoms of mental illness, and it will be hard to manage a mental illness if you do not address nutritional deficiencies.

To give some common examples:

- If you are low in iron, you might feel tired, exhausted, and lack energy or motivation. These are all symptoms of depression, and thus may be mistaken for depression.

- Having low levels of B vitamins can reduce energy levels and cognitive function, including memory.

- Vitamin B12 and folate work together to enhance the production of serotonin and dopamine, which allow us to feel happiness and pleasure. If you are deficient in vitamin B12 and folate, your brain will not be able to access enough serotonin or dopamine, and thus you may experience symptoms of depression.

- Vitamin D, the sunshine vitamin, plays an important role in mood management, and low vitamin D can produce symptoms of depression.

- Omega 3 oils (commonly known as fish oils, but Omega-3 can also be extracted from certain types of algae) are thought to improve mood management and cognitive function.

KEY POINTS

◊ Mental health difficulties are common in autistic people, and are nothing to be ashamed of.

◊ If you think you have a mental health illness, or feel you need support for your mental health, you can speak with your medical professional. They can help you access support services.

◊ The earlier you go to your doctor or health professional if you suspect a mental illness, the better.

◊ There are many medications that can be used to support your mental illness. It's important to speak with your doctor before trying out any medicine for your mental health.

◊ It's a good idea to get your hormone levels and nutritional status checked with a blood test if you experience mental health challenges, to ensure you are not experiencing deficiencies or imbalances.

References

American Psychiatric Association (2021) 'What Are Anxiety Disorders?' Accessed 10 December 2021 at: https://psychiatry.org/patients-families/anxiety-disorders/what-are-anxiety-disorders

AslAm (2019) 'Majority of Irish Support Autistic People in Jobs, Schools, and the Community, But Don't Understand Autism Well, Survey Finds'. Accessed 23 February 2022 at: https://asiam.ie/autism-public-perceptions-survey

Blessing, E.M., Steenkamp, M.M., Manzananes, J., and Marmar, C.R. (2015) 'Cannabidiol as a Potential Treatment for Anxiety Disorders'. *Neurotherapeutics: The Journal of American Society for Experimental Neurotherapeutics* 12 (4), 825–836. https://dx.doi.org/10.1007/s13311-015-0387-1

Bodywhys (The Eating Disorders Association of Ireland) (2022) 'ARFID'. Accessed 29 July 2022 at: www.bodywhys.ie/understanding-eating-disorders/arfid/

Croen, L.A., Zerbo, O., Qian, Y., Massolo, M.L., Rich, S., Sidney, S., and Kripke, C. (2015) 'The Health Status of Adults on the Autism Spectrum'. *Autism* 19 (7), 814–823. https://doi.org/10.1177/1362361315577517

Cujipers, P., Sijbrandij, M., Koole, S.L., Andersson, G., Beekman, A.T., and Reynolds, C.F. (2014) 'Adding Psychotherapy to Antidepressant Medication in Depression and Anxiety Disorders: A Meta-Analysis'. *World Psychiatry: Official Journal of the World Psychiatric Association (WPA)* 13 (1), 56–67. https://dx.doi.org/10.1002/wps.20089

Grandin, T. (2006) *Thinking in Pictures: My Life with Autism*, 2nd edition. New York: Vintage Books.

The Guardian (2021) 'CBD Will Go on Sale in Australia, But First Manufacturers Will Have to Prove It Works'. Accessed 9 July 2022 at: www.theguardian.com/australia-news/2021/feb/07/cbd-will-go-on-sale-in-australia-but-first-manufacturers-will-have-to-prove-it-works

Halstead, E., Sullivan, E., Zambelli, Z., Ellis, J.G., and Dimitrou, D. (2021) 'The Treatment of Sleep Problems in Autistic Adults in the United Kingdom'. *Autism* 25 (8), 2412–2417. https://doi.org/10.1016/j.smrv.2011.02.001

Harvard Health Publishing (2020) 'Menopause and Mental Health'. Accessed 13 March 2022 at: www.health.harvard.edu/womens-health/menopause-and-mental-health

Harvard Health Publishing (2021) 'Cannabidiol (CBD) – What We Know and What We Don't'. Accessed 14 March 2022 at: www.health.harvard.edu/blog/cannabidiol-cbd-what-we-know-and-what-we-dont-2018082414476

Hirvikoski, T., Mittendorfer-Rutz, E., Boman, M., Larsson, H., Lichtenstein, P., and Bolte, S. (2016) 'Premature Mortality in Autism Spectrum Disorder'. *British Journal of Psychiatry* 208 (3), 232–238. https://doi.org/10.1192/bjp.bp.114.160192

Hossain, M.M., Khan, N., Sultanta, A., Ma, P., McKyer, E.L.J., Ahmed, H.U., and Purohit, N. (2020) 'Prevalence of Comorbid Psychiatric Disorders among People with Autism Spectrum Disorder: An Umbrella Review of Systematic Reviews and Meta-Analyses'. *Psychiatry Research* 282, 112922. https://doi.org/10.1016/j.psychres.2020.112922

Hudson, C.C., Hall, L., and Harkness, K.L. (2019) 'Prevalence of Depressive Disorders in Individuals with Autism Spectrum Disorder: A Meta-Analysis'. *Journal of Abnormal Child Psychology* 47 (1), 165–175. https://doi.org/10.1007/s10802-018-0402-1

Lai, M.C., Kassee, C., Besney, R., Bonato, S., Hull, L., Mandy, W., and Ameis, S.H. (2019) 'Prevalence of Co-Occuring Mental Health Diagnoses in the Autism Population: A Systematic Review and Meta-Analysis'. *The Lancet Psychiatry* 6 (10), 819–829. https://doi.org/10.1016/S2215-0366(19)30289-5

Lalanne, S., Fougerou-Leurent, C., Anderson, G.M., Schroder, C.M., Nir, T., Chokron, S., and Tordjman, S. (2021) 'Melatonin: From Pharmacokinetics to Clinical Use in Autism Spectrum Disorder'. *International Journal of Molecular Sciences* 22 (3), 1490. https://doi.org/10.3390/ijms22031490

Mayo Clinic (2017) 'Agoraphobia'. Accessed 8 March 2022 at: www.mayoclinic.org/diseases-conditions/agoraphobia/symptoms-causes/syc-20355987

Mayo Clinic (2018) 'Suicide and Suicidal Thoughts'. Accessed 6 March 2022 at: www.mayoclinic.org/diseases-conditions/suicide/symptoms-causes/syc-20378048

National Autistic Society (2020) 'OCD: A Guide for Professionals'. Accessed 21 January 2022 at: www.autism.org.uk/advice-and-guidance/topics/mental-health/ocd/professionals

National Office for Suicide Prevention (2019) 'Briefing on CSO Suicide Figures 6th November 2019'. Accessed 9 July 2022 at: www.hse.ie/eng/services/list/4/mental-health-services/connecting-for-life/publications/nosp-briefing-cso-data-nov-2019.pdf

NHS (2020) 'Social Anxiety (Social Phobia)'. Accessed 8 March 2022 at: www.nhs.uk/mental-health/conditions/social-anxiety/

NHS (2021) 'Uses of Antidepressants'. Accessed 13 February 2022 at: www.nhs.uk/mental-health/talking-therapies-medicine-treatments/medicines-and-psychiatry/antidepressants/uses/

Nimmo-Smith, V., Heuvelman, H., Dalman, C., Lundberg, M., Idring, S., Carpenter, P., Magnusson, C., and Rai, D. (2020) 'Anxiety Disorders in Adults with Autism Spectrum Disorder: A Population-Based Study'. *Journal of Autism and Developmental Disorders* 50 (1), 308–318. https://dx.doi.org/10.1007%2Fs10803-019-04234-3

Office for National Statistics (2020) 'Outcomes for Disabled People in the UK: 2020'. Accessed 23 February 2022 at: www.ons.gov.uk/peoplepopulationandcommunity/healthandsocialcare/disability/articles/outcomesfordisabledpeopleintheuk/2020

Pearson, A. and Rose, K. (2021) 'A Conceptual Analysis of Autistic Masking: Understanding the Narrative of Stigma and the Illusion of Choice'. *Autism in Adulthood* 3 (1), 52–60. https://doi.org/10.1089/aut.2020.0043

Raymaker, D.M., Teo, A.R., Steckler, N.A., Lentz, B., Scharere, M., Delos Santos, A., Kapp, S.K., Hunter, M., Joyce, A., and Nicolaidid, C. (2020) '"Having All of Your Internal Resources Exhausted Beyond Measure and Being Left with No Clean-Up Crew": Defining Autistic Burnout'. *Autism in Adulthood: Challenges and Management* 2 (2), 132–143. https://dx.doi.org/10.1089/aut.2019.0079

Solmni, F., Bentivegna, F., Bould, H., Mandy, W., Kothari, R., Raj, D., Skuse, D., and Lewis, G. (2020) 'Trajectories of Autistic Social Traits in Childhood and Adolescence and Disordered Eating Behaviours at Age 14: A UK General Population Cohort Study'. *The Journal of Child Psychology and Psychiatry* 62 (1), 75–85. https://doi.org/10.1111/jcpp.13255

World Health Organization (2017) 'Depression and Other Common Mental Disorders: Global Health Estimates'. Accessed 25 January 2022 at: https://apps.who.int/iris/bitstream/handle/10665/254610/WHO-MSD-MER-2017.2-eng.pdf

World Health Organization (2019) 'Mental Disorders'. Accessed 21 January 2022 at www.who.int/news-room/fact-sheets/detail/mental-disorders

Abbreviations (Abbr) and Glossary

ADHD (Abbr) Attention Deficit Hyperactivity Disorder ADHD also incorporates the previous diagnosis of ADD (attention deficit disorder).

People with ADHD might experience many symptoms, including but not restricted to: difficulty maintaining focus or paying attention, distractibility, intense energy or hyperactivity, tendency to be always moving or fidgeting, impulsivity, difficulty with organisation and getting things done, tendency to creatively think outside the box, ability to hyper-focus when very interested in the topic/task.

Alexithymia Alexithymia means having a difficulty or inability to recognise and name your emotions. See Chapter 12.

Anchor Senses This is my own term for the proprioception and vestibular senses. See Chapter 7.

ASC (Abbr) Autistic Spectrum Condition ASC is a term increasingly used by professionals diagnosing autism to replace the word 'disorder' in the diagnostic label ASD (autism spectrum disorder) with the word 'condition'. This is to move away from seeing autism as a disorder, and towards seeing it as a natural part of human neurodiversity.

ASD (Abbr) Autism Spectrum Disorder ASD is the diagnostic term often used by professionals to diagnose someone as autistic.

Autistic Burnout This is when an autistic person hits a period of intense fatigue and stress, due to the demands of life as an autistic person. It might include increased sensitivity to sensory stimuli, and sometimes includes the temporary loss of skills such as talking. See Chapter 16.

Basic Need Sense This is my own term for the interoception sense. See Chapter 8.

CBT (Abbr) Cognitive Behavioural Therapy CBT is a form of talk therapy that aims to help the client to change the way they think and behave in order to manage problems or improve their mental health. See Chapter 14.

Cognition/Cognitive Cognition is the mental process (the cognitive process) of thinking, remembering, understanding, reasoning etc.

DSM-5 (Abbr) *Diagnostic and Statistical Manual of Mental Disorders*, **5th edition** The DSM is the American Psychiatric Association's guide to mental illness and disorders. It outlines criteria, signs, and symptoms of different mental illness and mental disorders. Neurodiverse conditions such as autism and ADHD are included in this guide, with criteria for diagnosis set out. The 5th edition was the 2013 updated version of the manual.

EMDR (Abbr) Eye Movement Desensitisation and Reprocessing EMDR is a form of psychotherapy used to process trauma or distressing experiences, aiming to train the brain to manage and heal from the trauma or experience. See Chapter 14.

Emotional Regulation Emotional regulation involves a state of emotional balance, or being able to regulate and manage your emotions. See Chapter 14.

EF (Abbr) Executive Function Executive function is the ability to get things done, from the initial stage of recognising something needs to be done, to planning to do it, carrying it out, problem solving (using flexible thinking), completion of the task, and evaluation after the task.

Famous Five Senses This is my own term for the five senses that collect information from outside our bodies:

- sight (visual)
- sound (auditory)
- taste (gustatory)
- smell (olfactory)
- touch (tactile).

See Chapter 9.

Flexible Thinking This is the cognitive ability to think of a new way to do something in order to solve a problem or to improve functioning. Flexible thinking is one of the skills in executive function. See Chapter 2.

GP (Abbr) General Practitioner A family doctor.

Hypermobility/Joint Hypermobility Syndrome (JHS) Hypermobility means your joints have a greater range of motion than 'normal' joints, causing increased physical flexibility. It is sometimes called being double jointed.

If hypermobile joints cause significant discomfort or pain, it might suggest a genetic condition called 'joint hypermobility syndrome', which can be assessed and diagnosed by a rheumatologist. JHS can have other symptoms including digestive issues, joint dislocations, dizziness, fatigue, or recurrent injuries. More extreme cases or symptoms of JHS might suggest a form of Ehlers Danlos syndrome. See Chapter 7.

Hypermobile Ehlers Danlos Syndrome (hEDS) There are 13 types of the connective tissue condition called EDS, but hypermobile EDS is the most common type. In hEDS, the body's connective tissue is loose and thus doesn't do a good job 'connecting' the body's tissues including the skin, muscles, and ligaments. Symptoms can include over-extending joints, chronic pain, skin issues including increased stretchiness or slow or difficult wound healing, and digestive issues including constipation, blood pressure drops, dizziness, faintness, extreme fatigue, headaches etc. Some people with hEDS also have POTS (postural orthostatic tachycardia syndrome), which involves postural changes to blood pressure and a racing heart rate. hEDS is assessed and diagnosed by a rheumatologist. See Chapter 7.

Hyperventilation Hyperventilation means breathing out too much carbon dioxide due to over-breathing or breathing too fast. See Chapters 3 and 16.

HSE (Abbr) Health Service Executive The National Health Service of Ireland.

ICD-11 (Abbr) *International Classification of Diseases*, 11th edition This is the World Health Organization's guide on disease classification, with coded health information and causes of death. It includes criteria, signs, and symptoms of neurodiverse conditions including autism. This is the diagnostic tool often used outside America for autism diagnosis, but the DSM-5 is also used outside America by some diagnostic clinicians. The 11th edition replaced the 10th edition, the ICD-10, in 2022.

Interoception The sense that tells us what we feel inside our body, and how we feel. This includes pain, hunger, thirst, heart rate, the need to go to the toilet, what emotion we are feeling etc. Sometimes known as the 'eighth sense', and referred to as the Basic Need Sense in this book. See Chapter 8.

Masking Autistic masking is a complex strategy used by some autistic people to hide their autism, or to appear non-autistic. It can include conscious and unconscious behaviours. It can include hiding your natural autistic behaviours, such as stimming, in order to avoid stigma, bullying, trauma, or negative attention. See Chapter 16.

Meltdown A meltdown is an intense response to becoming overwhelmed from sensory over-stimulation, emotional dysregulation, or cognitive demands. A meltdown can be described as an explosive loss of control of yourself and your actions. It is sometimes compared to a volcano erupting; if the overwhelm builds up inside (like lava in a volcano) it will eventually explode. See Chapter 11.

Nervous System The nervous system includes the brain, spinal cord, and nerves. The purpose of the nervous system is to analyse the information collected by our senses, and to decide what to do with that information. Our nervous system then tells our body how to react to sensory information. See Chapter 5.

Neurodivergent A person is neurodivergent if they have any of the following (but not limited to) neurodiverse conditions or differences:

- autism
- ADHD (attention deficit hyperactivity disorder)
- bipolar
- dyscalculia
- dyslexia
- dyspraxia

- OCD (obsessive compulsive disorder)

- ODD (oppositional defiance disorder)

- tourettes.

(Note: There is often confusion about which terms to use around neurodiversity. Neurodiversity is the concept that there are many kinds of human brains: autistic brains, non-autistic brains, ADHD brains, bipolar brains etc. Thus, 'neuro' for brain and 'diversity' for difference and variation. When we talk about celebrating neurodiversity, we are celebrating the variety and differences in all human brains.

If speaking about an individual, the current correct term to use is: he/she/they are neurodivergent.

If you are talking about an environment or a group, they are neurodiverse.

So, a group of autistic people are neurodiverse, and an environment can be neurodiverse. But one autistic person is not neurodiverse, they are neurodivergent.)

NHS (Abbr) National Health Service The National Health Service of the UK.

OCD (Abbr) Obsessive Compulsive Disorder OCD is a mental health disorder that causes obsessive and intrusive thoughts and fears, which tends to lead to compulsive behaviours that interfere with daily life. It can have varying degrees of severity, and generally gets worse during times of stress. See Chapter 16.

OT (Abbr) Occupational Therapist An occupational therapist is a trained professional who focuses on improving a person's ability to engage in their 'occupations', which means their daily life activities or tasks. The aim of occupational therapy is to improve a person's independence through teaching skills, adapting the environment, or introducing tools to improve the quality of life. There are many types of occupational therapists, but when I refer to OTs in this book, I'm referring to OTs who are trained in sensory integration, which is a specialisation within occupational therapy.

PDD-NOS (Abbr) Pervasive Developmental Disorder Not Otherwise Specified An earlier individual diagnosis of one form of autism, now grouped together with other individual labels of autism, under the diagnostic label ASD, autistic spectrum disorder.

PERMA (Abbr) The PERMA model of well-being. PERMA stands for Positive emotion, Engagement, Relationships, Meaning, and Achievements. See Chapter 4.

Proprioception Proprioception is the body's self-awareness sense. It is what tells us where our body is in space, where it is in relation to things in the environment, what position we are in etc. See Chapter 7.

Sensory Avoidance This means avoiding a sensory input because you over-respond to it, and thus experience the input too intensely and it causes an uncomfortable reaction. See Chapter 5.

Sensory System The sensory system is how the body collects information from inside our bodies and from the world around us. See Chapter 5.

Sensory Overload Sensory overload refers to your senses being overwhelmed due to either too much sensory information, a build-up of sensory stress, or as a direct response to one sensory trigger. Your sensory system might feel 'overloaded', bombarded, or overwhelmed. See Chapter 11.

Sensory Processing This is the process of (firstly) collecting information through your senses about the world around you and what's going on inside your body, and (secondly) interpreting and responding to that information through behaviour and motor responses (a motor response is the passing of information from the nervous system to a muscle to get the muscle to move or take action). See Chapter 5.

Sensory Regulation This is the regulation of the sensory system. It includes managing and responding appropriately to sensory input and information. A regulated sensory system is less likely to become overwhelmed or overloaded.

Sensory Seeking This means seeking out a sensory stimulation. This can be because you under-respond to the sense and thus your body seeks more input to that sense, or because you simply enjoy that sensory input. See Chapter 5.

Sensory Soothing Strategy This is a strategy that can be used to soothe the sensory system, or a specific sense. See Chapter 6.

Sensory Stimulus A sensory stimulus is anything that stimulates one of your senses. See Chapter 5.

Shutdown A shutdown is a response to overwhelm (emotional, sensory, or cognitive) that causes the individual to disconnect or disengage from the environment. In a shutdown, an individual might feel detached from other people, and be unable to manage complex thoughts or tasks. It can feel like a 'freezing' of the brain, or an internal explosion (as opposed to the external explosion in a meltdown). See Chapter 10.

SPD (Abbr) Sensory Processing Disorder or Sensory Processing Difference. This is a difference in how a person collects information through their senses, analyses the information in the nervous system, and responds to the information. See Chapter 5.

Special Interests An autistic special interest is an interest in a topic or activity that an autistic person has an extremely enhanced interest in, and can intensely focus on. Engaging in one's special interest is often used as a calming strategy by autistic people. An autistic person can have one, none, or many special interests at any one time in their life. The intense focus and interest can last for a short period of time, or might last years. See Chapter 4.

Stim/Stimming A stim is a repetitive self-soothing behaviour, for example moving a part of your body in a repetitive fashion such as flapping your hands, clicking a pen, or making repetitive noises such as humming, in order to soothe yourself. When someone is doing a stim, it's said they are 'stimming'. Stimming is common in autistic people. See Chapter 3.

Trigger A trigger is something that sets off your stress response. There are different types of triggers. A sensory trigger is something that stresses your sensory system and can cause overwhelm. A trauma trigger is something makes you re-experience the emotional distress from a trauma. An anxiety trigger is something that makes you feel acute anxiety. See Chapter 2.

WHO (Abbr) World Health Organization The World Health Organization is the United Nations health agency. Its aim is to promote and improve public health across the whole world, for everyone in the world. They have a significant role in responding to global health emergencies, epidemics, and pandemics, offering guidance and direction based on scientific research and observation.